THE POLITICS OF TRANSATLANTIC TRADE NEGOTIATIONS

TTIP promises to generate significant yet still uncertain implications for transatlantic relations, global governance and the international rules-based order. This volume breaks new ground by helping readers understand the theoretical aspects of TTIP, its meaning for the United States and Europe, and its impact on third countries and multilateral institutions.
> Daniel S. Hamilton, Director of the Center for Transatlantic Relations,
> Johns Hopkins University SAIS, USA

This volume addresses a crucial issue of global and interregional trade governance by including an international team of leading scholars from a variety of disciplines and viewpoints. Collectively the authors identify the major stakes and provide a comprehensive and highly competent overview of the main political implications of the 'Transatlantic Trade and Investment Partnership' negotiations from both sides (North America and Europe), while keeping in mind the controversial interplay with global governance and emergent economies. Highly recommended for students, scholars, practitioners and informed citizens looking for critical and solid orientation in a very sensitive and uncertain matter.
> Pascal Lamy, former Director-General of the World Trade Organization and
> Honorary President of the Paris-based think tank Notre Europe, France

A timely, multi-disciplinary collection on an important subject, this volume will serve as a great starting point for students and scholars trying to make sense of the controversies surrounding the Trans-Atlantic Trade and Investment Partnership.
> Amrita Narlikar, Director of the GIGA German Institute of Global and Area
> Studies, Germany and University of Cambridge, UK

Globalisation, Europe, Multilateralism

Institutionally supported by the Institute for European Studies at the
Université libre de Bruxelles

Mario TELÒ, Series Editor

As a leading research institution and a Jean Monnet Centre of Excellence in European Studies, the Institut d'Études Européennes of the Université Libre de Bruxelles (IEE-ULB) supported the launch of this global series with a view to bringing together multidisciplinary research in global governance and EU studies. The series can draw on a wide and global network of partner universities across five continents. Among its numerous resources special mention is to be made of the Erasmus Mundus GEM PhD School on 'Globalisation, Europe, Multilateralism' and the GR:EEN European research project on 'Global Reordering: Evolving European Networks'.

Volumes included in the series share innovative research objectives centred on: globalisation, the EU's changing position therein, resulting forms of multilateral cooperation, and the role of transnational networks as well as multipolarity in the contemporary international order. A wide array of possible approaches to these shared themes are welcomed, including among others: comparative regionalism, public and foreign policy analysis, EU governance and Europeanisation studies, discourse analysis, area studies, and various institutional perspectives.

With a shared aim to contribute to innovations in the study of both European Integration and International Relations, the series includes: collaborative volumes, research based monographs and textbooks. Each publication undergoes an international refereeing process, and enjoys the advice and feedback of an international editorial board.

The Politics of Transatlantic Trade Negotiations
TTIP in a Globalized World

Edited by

JEAN-FRÉDÉRIC MORIN
Laval University, Canada

TEREZA NOVOTNÁ
Université libre de Bruxelles, Belgium

FREDERIC PONJAERT
Université libre de Bruxelles, Belgium

MARIO TELÒ
*Université libre de Bruxelles, Belgium and
University LUISS-Guido Carli, Italy*

Routledge
Taylor & Francis Group

LONDON AND NEW YORK

First published 2015 by Ashgate Publishing

Published 2016 by Routledge
2 Park Square, Milton Park, Abingdon, Oxon OX14 4RN
711 Third Avenue, New York, NY 10017, USA

Routledge is an imprint of the Taylor & Francis Group, an informa business

Copyright © Jean-Frédéric Morin, Tereza Novotná, Frederik Ponjaert and Mario Telò 2015

British Library Cataloguing in Publication Data
A catalogue record for this book is available from the British Library

The Library of Congress has cataloged the printed edition as follows:
The politics of transatlantic trade negotiations : TTIP in a globalized world / editors, Jean-Frédéric Morin, Tereza Novotná, Frederik Ponjaert and Mario Telò.
    pages cm. -- (Globalisation, Europe, multilateralism series)
  Includes bibliographical references and index.
  ISBN 978-1-4724-4361-8 (hardback) -- ISBN 978-1-4724-4364-9 (pbk) --
  1. United States--Foreign economic relations--European Union countries. 2. European Union countries--Foreign economic relations--United States. 3. United States--Commercial policy. 4. European Union countries--Commercial policy. 5. United States--Commercial treaties. 6. European Union countries--Commercial treaties. I. Morin, Jean-Frédéric, editor.

  HF1456.5.E8P627 2015
  332.67'3091821--dc23

                                                                                    2014043021
ISBN 9781472443618 (hbk)
ISBN 9781472443649 (pbk)

Contents

List of Figures and Tables

List of Contributors

Vinod K. Aggarwal is Professor at the University of California, Berkeley, with appointments in the Travers Department of Political Science and the Haas School of Business. He serves as Director of the Berkeley Asia Pacific Economic Cooperation Study Center, Editor-in-Chief of the journal *Business and Politics*, and Global Scholar at Chung-Ang University. He is the author or editor of 21 books and over 100 articles and book chapters. His most recent book is *Responding to China's Rise: US and EU Strategies* (edited with Sara Newland). He received his BA from the University of Michigan and his MA and PhD from Stanford University.

Erick Duchesne is Full Professor of Political Science, member of the Québec School of Advanced International Studies (HEI-Laval) and Director of the joint undergraduate programme in Economics, Law and Political Science (BIAPRI) at Laval University. His main field of specialization is International Political Economy with a focus on international trade negotiations, World Bank reforms and economic sanctions. He is also the former editor (2006–08) of *Politique et sociétés*.

Andreas Dür is Professor of International Politics at the University of Salzburg. He holds a PhD from the European University Institute in Florence, Italy (2004). In his doctoral thesis, he studied 80 years of transatlantic trade liberalization. Ever since, his research has focused on interest groups and trade policy. Among his publications is *Protection for Exporters: Discrimination and Power in Transatlantic Trade Relations, 1930–2010* (2010). He is also a co-editor of *Trade Cooperation: The Purpose, Design and Effects of Preferential Trade Agreements* (2014).

Simon J. Evenett is Professor of International Trade and Economic Development at the University of St. Gallen. His research and professional interests include how businesses manage relations with governments and regulators, international trade negotiations and disputes, protectionism and the World Trade Organization. He obtained his PhD in Economics from Yale University and a BA (Hons) in Economics from the University of Cambridge. He has taught at the University of Oxford, the Ross School of Business at the University of Michigan and Rutgers University. In addition, he has served as a World Bank official twice, was a Non-Resident Senior Fellow in the Economics Studies programme of the Brookings Institution and is co-director of the most established group of international trade economists in Europe.

Andrew Gamble is Professor of Politics and a Fellow of Queens' College in the University of Cambridge. He is a Fellow of the British Academy and the UK Academy of Social Sciences. In 2005 he received the Isaiah Berlin Prize from the UK Political Studies Association for lifetime contribution to political studies. His most recent book is *Crisis without End: The Unravelling of Western Prosperity*.

Robert O. Keohane is Professor of Public and International Affairs in the Woodrow Wilson School at Princeton University. He has served as Editor of International Organization and as President of the International Studies Association and the American Political Science Association. He is a member of the American Academy of Arts and Sciences, the American Academy of Political and Social Science, the American Philosophical Society and the National Academy of Sciences; and he is a Corresponding Fellow of the British Academy. His publications include *Power and Interdependence* (with Joseph S. Nye, Jr, originally published in 1977), *After Hegemony: Cooperation and Discord in the World Political Economy* (1984), *Designing Social Inquiry* (with Gary King and Sidney Verba, 1994) and *Power and Governance in a Partially Globalized World* (2002). His recent work focuses on a variety of related topics, including multilateralism, climate change and anti-Americanism.

Lisa Lechner is a PhD Fellow and Researcher in International Politics at the University of Salzburg. Between 2005 and 2013 she studied International Economics and Political Science at the Leopold Franzens University of Innsbruck and the Audencia Nantes (École de Management) in France. In her doctoral thesis, she examines human rights provisions in trade agreements and their impact on human rights compliance.

Petros C. Mavroidis is Edwin B. Parker Professor of Law at Columbia Law School (New York City) and Professor at the University of Neuchatel (Switzerland). He is currently on leave at the Robert Schuman Centre at the European University Institute, Florence.

Hartmut Mayer has been Official Fellow and Tutor in Politics (International Relations) at St Peter's College, University of Oxford and a member of Oxford University's Department of Politics and International Relations since 1998. He is also Adjunct Professor of European and Eurasian Studies at Johns Hopkins University's Paul H. Nitze School of Advanced International Studies (SAIS) in Bologna, Italy. He holds a BA from the Free University of Berlin, an MALD from the Fletcher School of Law and Diplomacy at Tufts University, an MPhil from Cambridge University (Gonville and Caius College) and a DPhil from Oxford University (St Antony's College). He has held Visiting Professorships at Hitotsubashi University in Tokyo, the University of Hamburg and the GIGA German Institute of Global and Area Studies. Most recently, he has visited at the Université libre de Bruxelles (ULB) and at SciencesPo in Paris. He has also been a visiting researcher at the European University Institute (EUI) in Florence, the Finnish Institute for International Relations (UPI) in Helsinki, at the Siftung Wissenschaft und Politik (SWP) in Berlin and a JSPS Fellow at Waseda University in Tokyo.

Sophie Meunier is Research Scholar in the Woodrow Wilson School of Public and International Affairs at Princeton University and Co-Director of the EU Program at Princeton. She is the author of *Trading Voices: The European Union in International Commercial Negotiations* (2005) and *The French Challenge: Adapting to Globalization* (with Philip Gordon, 2001), winner of the 2002 *France-Amériques* book award. She is also the editor of several books on Europe and globalization, most recently *The Politics of Representation in the Global Age* (2014). Her current work deals with the politics of foreign direct investment in Europe. Meunier contributes regularly to the French and American media. She is Chevalier des Palmes Académiques.

Jean-Frédéric Morin is Associate Professor at Laval University and Canada Research Chair in International Political Economy and Transnational Interaction. Before joining Laval University, he was professor at Université libre de Bruxelles in Belgium (2008–14) and post-doctoral researcher at McGill University in Canada (2006–08) His most recent research projects look at global regime complexes, transnational expert networks and international policy transfers in the fields of trade, intellectual property and the environment. Some of his recent publications appeared in leading journals such as *International Studies Quarterly*, *European Journal of International Relations* and *Review of International Political Economy*.

Julia Morse is a PhD candidate in the Woodrow Wilson School for Public and International Affairs at Princeton University. Her research focuses on international institutions and security cooperation, with particular attention on the global regime complex on combating the financing of terrorism. Prior to Princeton, she worked at the US State Department and the Federal Bureau of Investigation.

Jens L. Mortensen is Associate Professor at the Department of Political Science, University of Copenhagen, and GR:EEN Associate Professor at Department of Business and Politics, CBS. He works on trade-related issues on IPE, governance and EU external relations. He is currently working on the GR:EEN project 'Revitalising the WTO? The New EU Trade Agreements' (forthcoming). Latest publications include 'Seeing Like the WTO: Numbers, Frames and Trade Law' (*New Political Economy*).

Tereza Novotná is a GR:EEN and FNRS Post-Doctoral Researcher at the Institute for European Studies, Université libre de Bruxelles. Tereza received her PhD in Politics and European Studies from Boston University in 2012 and other degrees from Charles University Prague. She has held various visiting fellowships at, among others, SAIS Center for Transatlantic Relations, Harvard's Center for European Studies, University of Birmingham (IGS), SWP Brussels, DGAP (supported by a DAAD grant), IWM in Vienna and the Max-Planck Institute in Cologne. Although her current work focuses primarily on TTIP, EEAS and EU foreign policy, her broader research interests include EU enlargement, democratization and integration processes, the politics of Central and Eastern Europe as well as Germany. Her research has been published in *German Politics and Society*, *West European Politics*, *Studies in Ethnicities and Nationalism*, *Perspectives*, *Journal for Contemporary European Research* and *E-Sharp* as well as in numerous policy and media outlets.

Richard Ouellet is a Full Professor of International Economic Law, member of the Québec School of Advanced International Studies (HEI-Laval) and Deputy Director of *Revue* études *internationales* at Laval University. His main field of specialization is WTO law with a focus on trade disputes related to the application of the SPS and TBT agreements and Article XX of the GATT. He is also the former director (2009–12) of the masters and doctoral programmes of HEI-Laval.

Joost Pauwelyn is Professor of International Law at the Graduate Institute of International and Development Studies (IHEID) in Geneva, Switzerland and Co-Director of the Institute's Centre for Trade and Economic Integration (CTEI). He is also a Visiting Professor at Georgetown Law Center in Washington DC. He specializes in international economic law, in particular the law of the WTO and foreign investment law. He also advises governments and non-state actors in WTO dispute settlement and investor-state arbitration. In the autumn of 2012 he was Visiting Professor at Stanford Law School and in the spring of 2013 Visiting Professor at Harvard Law School. Before joining the Graduate Institute in 2007, he was a tenured professor at Duke Law School. He also taught at Neuchâtel, Columbia University and New York University. He served as legal officer at the WTO from 1996 to 2002 and practised law at a major Brussels law firm. Joost received degrees from the universities of Namur and Leuven, Belgium as well as Oxford University and holds a doctorate from the University of Neuchâtel. He was appointed on the roster of WTO panellists and as arbitrator under Free Trade Agreements and the Energy Charter Treaty.

Frederik Ponjaert is Researcher and Lecturer at the Institute for European Studies at Université libre de Bruxelles and the KULeuven and Associate Lecturer in Comparative Regionalism at SciencesPo, Paris. His research focuses on comparative regionalism, with an emphasis on European and Asian realities, the foreign policies of Germany and Japan, and regional policy processes. He is also the scientific coordinator of the Erasmus Mundus GEM-PhD School and the manager of the GEM Ashgate book series *Globalisation, Europe, Multilateralism*. Recent publications include: 'The Political and Institutional Significance of an EU-Japan Trade and Partnership Agreement' in *The European Union and Japan:*

A New Chapter in Civilian Power Cooperation? (2014); 'Public Research Projects in Europe and East Asia: Cooperation or Competition? A Comparative Analysis of the ITER and Galileo Experiences' (*East Asia*, 2010); 'The EU and its Far-abroad: Interregional Relations with Other Continents', in *The European Union and Global Governance* (2009) and 'Japan in East Asia: The Dynamics of Regional Cooperation from a European Perspective' (*Studia Diplomatica*, 2007).

Michael Strange is Senior Lecturer in global political studies at the Department of Global Political Studies, Malmö University. His research covers various aspects of the global political economy with particular focus on the role of institutions and civil society within the politics of international trade law. He has authored the research monograph *Writing Global Trade Governance: Discourse and the WTO*, and has been published in highly-ranked journals such as *Geopolitics*, *Alternatives*, *Journal of Civil Society* and *Media, Culture & Society*.

Mario Telò is Emeritus President of the Institute for European Studies, Université libre de Bruxelles and Professor of European Institutions and International Relations at ULB and LUISS University, Rome. Jean Monnet Chair ad honorem, he was elected in 2006 a Member of the Royal Academy of Sciences, Belgium. He served as an advisor to all EU institutions for many years. Among his 30 books, the most recent are *EU and New Regionalism* (third edition, 2014), *Globalization, Europe, Multilateralism* (2014), *The EU Foreign Policy* (2013) and *International Relations: A European Perspective* (2009; in French in 2007, 2010 and 2013 and in Mandarin in 2009). For 40 years, he has taken part on a regular basis in the media debate on the future of the European Union.

Zhang Xiaotong is Executive Director of Wuhan University Research Centre for Economic Diplomacy, Executive Director of Wuhan University-University of the West Indies Centre for Caribbean Studies, and Associate Professor of the School of Political Science and Public Administration, Wuhan University. He worked at the US Desk of the Chinese Ministry of Commerce between 2011 and 2012, and served as Trade Attaché at the Chinese Mission to the European Union between 2004 and 2010. He obtained a PhD in political science at Université libre de Bruxelles, Belgium. His major research interests include economic diplomacy, European studies and US-China relations. He recently published *Brussels Diary*, a biography about his work experiences as a trade diplomat, and is working on an English book: *China's Economic Diplomacy in the 21st Century*. He is also a founder of a peer-reviewed electronic journal: *Journal of Economic Diplomacy*. He is a frequent speaker at the OECD, European Parliament, Chatham House and an invited lecturer at London School of Economics.

Foreword

by Karel De Gucht,
European Commissioner for Trade (2010–2014)

President Kennedy once said, 'neither we nor the members of the European Common Market are so affluent that we can long afford to shelter high cost farms or factories from the winds of foreign competition'. Today, this is still true. We live in a global economy in which no single country has access to every input it needs for its economy to function. We need to rely on each other, especially during this economic crisis. Opening up markets through trade agreements is, therefore, an essential part of this realization. The Transatlantic Trade and Investment Partnership (TTIP) is a valuable player in adjusting to the economic crisis, reducing the reliance on protectionism and measuring up to the impact of emerging economies like China, India and Brazil.

This first-rate edited volume rightfully asserts that the 'TTIP has always been more than a trade agreement'. It certainly has been for me. The TTIP is a complex negotiation. It is the largest bilateral trade initiative ever negotiated. Not only because it involves the world's two largest economies, the European Union (EU) and the United States, but also because of its potential global reach in setting an example for future partners and agreements. It covers trade in large volumes, different goods and services, touching upon a variety of government policies and innovatively includes investment. However, for all its complexity, the practical reality of this negotiation is simple: either we reach a deal that creates real new opportunities for both sides, while staying true to our values, or we will fail.

So why do we aim so high? TTIP can stimulate a lot of growth and create jobs. It can improve the choice for consumers and lower the prices for products or services. It can help both the EU and the US maintain their positions in a changing world. However, it can only accomplish these goals if the agreement and negotiations are ambitious – in market access, rules and regulatory cooperation. This book categorically addresses TTIP's ambitious character from all the possible angles.

The 'easiest' part of negotiations is possibly the removal of duties on goods. Arguably, the average tariff barriers are already low but do remain high for certain products and exporters, like German ceramic and ice cream makers. There is no reason why they should not go to zero. The other issues are harder to address. For instance public procurement. I cannot see TTIP coming about without the US doing away with 'Buy America and Buy American'. Despite the success of T-Mobile in the US, improved market access for services is difficult, experienced by sectors like aviation or dredging. Services are intangible and often heavily regulated. It is, therefore, imperative to establish a level playing field through regulatory convergence.

We also need strong and innovative rules on energy, raw materials, sustainable development and investment protection. The EU and US already agree on this principle, confirmed by their joint World Trade Organization (WTO) action against China on the export restrictions of raw materials. Also particularly in light of today's energy crisis, with falling oil prices and threats of closing the gas tap, TTIP is a strategic asset. If the US can guarantee unrestricted oil and gas exports to the EU, it can lessen its dependence on Russia and promote the search for own (alternative) energy possibilities. Sustainable development is an integral part of the TTIP implementation, where both sides retain the right to protect labour rights or the environment, provided they do not weaken these rules for commercial advantage or as a form of protectionism.

The WTO already provides for many of the rules needed, but regarding regulatory issues, gaps remain. For example, pharmaceutical factories in France producing for the American market are inspected twice by both parties for compliance on the same agreed set of rules. In the end, we aim for the same result: to make it easier, thus more cost effective, for companies, particularly smaller ones, to conduct business across the Atlantic in compliance with both European and American regulations, and most importantly without losing the high level of regulatory protection enjoyed by the public. We therefore have to be pragmatic, creative and realistic in finding ways to enhance cooperation, bring about more coherence and remain firm on our protection standards. One should not have the illusion that mutual recognition will do the job.

While promoting free trade is obvious from an economic point of view, it is politically less straightforward. The relationship between the US and the EU is based on a balance of partnership and competition. We share the same values and are the closest of all the regions in the world but EU and US companies are also global players vying for the same market share. Strong interests and opinions from protected sectors and relevant stakeholders continue to play an influencing role. Furthermore, any difficulties in finding the right balance are further exacerbated by for example the NSA spying scandal or leaks of confidential, largely incomplete, information. Therefore, transparency on the negotiations, one-on-one consultations with stakeholders and close cooperation with Parliament is paramount. To strengthen this, I launched an unprecedented public consultation on one of the most sensitive issues – investment protection.

The debate on investment protection is the most controversial part of the TTIP. There exist many misunderstandings, particularly on the Investor-State Dispute Settlement (ISDS). Provocative are the claims that this agreement encourages multinationals to test or even bully governments, by means of suing or blocking regulations, and thereby minimizing the space for governments to regulate in the public's interest. This is just not the case. The aim is to tighten up the existing system of the numerous bilateral investment treaties into one strong investment agreement providing both guarantees to governments in maintaining their sovereignty in policy-making and to protect investment against discrimination. We need to find a proper balance.

Even if the objective of the TTIP is simple, achieving it is a work in progress involving a wide range of actors in both Europe and the US. TTIP is a 'living agreement' and the benefits, both economically and strategically, protecting and strengthening our values, are in all of our interests. No matter what the view of the reader on TTIP is, however, this collective volume brings an original contribution to the transatlantic debate about TTIP negotiations.

Acknowledgements

When negotiations on the Transatlantic Trade and Investment Partnership (TTIP) were launched in July 2013, an idea sprang to our minds to bring together scholars and policy-makers who could examine the prospects and challenges that the TTIP talks may face from their specific perspectives. Moreover, given the fact that TTIP is a new and theoretically challenging phenomenon, we decided to place it within the context of our ongoing multiannual research project about the impact of regional and interregional cooperation on evolving global governance. As a result, we organized a large 'AGORA© forum' on the 'Evolutions in the Transatlantic Relationship within a Multipolar World: Defensive Move or Constructive Engagement?' that took place at the Institute for European Studies at Université libre de Bruxelles (ULB) in Brussels in October 2013 and that was made into a documentary film which is available at http://www.youtube.com/watch?v=Q8A9KhunfyA. The AGORA© event also provided us with direct impetus for putting together this edited volume.

We would therefore like to warmly thank all the participants at our AGORA© forum, particularly our keynote speakers Robert O. Keohane and Pascal Lamy, but also those who eventually became the authors of our book chapters such as Andrew Gamble, Hartmut Mayer, Jens L. Mortensen and Xiaotong Zhang and those who expressed their views during our lively discussions: Roderick Abott, Anthony Allen, Thierry Aerts, Tomas Garcia Azcarate, Nelli Babayan, Bertrand Badie, Louis Belanger, Juliette Bird, Robert Boyer, Sandy Boyle, Joseph T. Burke, Hilbren I. Buys, Caterina Carta, Tom Casier, Inge Ceuppens, Megan Dee, Jean-Christophe Defraigne, Barbara Delcourt, Pasquale De Micco, Cecile Despringre, Maurizio Di Lullo, Nicola Forster, Andreas Galanakis, Ettore Greco, Christian Hoehn, Alexandra Homolar, Shada Islam, Angela Liberatore, Pascal Kerneis, Johannes Kleis, Joachim Koops, Justine Korwek, Amrita Narlikar, Christian Olsson, Uwe Optenhoegel, Fernando Perreau de Pinninck, Reinhard Quick, Denis Redonnet, Jean Arthur Regibeau, Maria Joao Rodrigues, Kyoko Sakuma-Keck, Ana Isabel Sanchez Ruiz, Simon Schunz, Rene Schwock, Ulrich Speck, Stuart Summer, Jiro Takamoto, Jean Paul Thuillier, Dan Van Raemdonck, Enrique Velazquez, Antonio Villafranca, Eleni Xiarchogiannopoulou and Jonathan Zeitlin, as well as all our GEM PhD students who served as shadow rapporteurs but cannot all be named here. For further details, please consult the event website at: http://agora-forum.eu.

In addition, during the summer 2014, a number of our book authors and other experts kindly accepted our invitation to teach our doctoral students about international trade and TTIP in particular during the 2014 GEM-GR:EEN Summer

School. We would also like to extend our thanks to all of our lecturers for doing so. Moreover, during both occasions, TTIP negotiators and other senior practitioners such as Damien Levie (European Commission's DG TRADE Deputy Negotiator) and Elena Bryan (Office of the US Trade Representative) shared with us their invaluable insights into how the TTIP talks work in practice. Since such a dialogue between academia, policy circles and civil society is of a crucial importance particularly given the salience of TTIP among the wider public, and it is also one of the goal of our GR:EEN programme to engage with these three groups, we are very happy that such discussions could have taken place and thank all our non-academic guests for sharing their views and experiences.

Neither the book nor the research could have taken place without generous support from the European Commission, DG Culture and Education and DG Research and Innovation. They contributed through the multidisciplinary Erasmus Mundus GEM PhD School and the GR:EEN FP7-funded integrated research project (project number 266809). For further information on both projects, please go to www.erasmusmundus-gem.eu and www.greenfp7.eu.

Although an edited volume is a collective endeavour, a few individuals deserve particular mention and our thanks for their special roles: Johan Robberecht for coordinating the two events and film preceding this book; Thibaut L'Ortye for his unthankful task of compiling and formatting the chapters, annexes and additional proofreading; the Institute for European Studies at ULB for financing Thibaut's work; Brenda Sharp and her colleagues at Ashgate for an efficient and quick production of this book and, last but certainly not least, all the anonymous referees as well as other collaborators who read, reviewed and helped improve the content and structure of the chapters and the book. We are very grateful for your support, yet any errors remain solely ours.

The Editors
Brussels, January 2015

List of Abbreviations

AB	Appellate Body
ACP	African, Caribbean and Pacific Group of States
ACTA	Anti-Counterfeiting Trade Agreement
ACTPN	Advisory Committee for Trade Policy and Negotiations
APEC	Asia-Pacific Economic Cooperation
ASEAN	Association of Southeast Asian Nations
ASEM	Asia-Europe Meeting
BDI	Bundesverband der Deutschen Industrie (Federation of German Industries)
BIT	Bilateral investment treaty
BND	Bundesnachrichtendienst (German Federal Intelligence Service)
BRICs	Brazil, Russia, India and China
BRICS	Brazil, Russia, India, China and South Africa
CAN	Andean Community of Nations
CAP	Common Agricultural Policy
CARICOM	Caribbean Community
CARRIFORUM	Caribbean Forum
CCM	Convention on Cluster Munitions (Oslo Convention)
CCW	Convention on Certain Conventional Weapons
CDU	Christlich Demokratische Union Deutschlands (Christian Democratic Union of Germany)
CEO	Corporate Europe Observatory
CETA	Comprehensive Economic and Trade Agreement
CFSP	Common Foreign and Security Policy
CI	Consumers International
CMO	Crisis-management operations
CRTA	Committee on Regional Trade Agreements
CSU	Christlich-Soziale Union in Bayern (Christian Social Union in Bavaria)
CU	Customs Union
CUSFTA	Canada-United States Free Trade Agreement
CVI	Children's Vaccine Initiative
DDA	Doha Development Agenda
DG	Directorate-General
DG ENTR	Directorate-General for Enterprise and Industry
DG MARKT	Directorate-General for Internal Market and Services
DG SANCO	Directorate-General for Health and Consumers

DG TRADE	Directorate-General for Trade
DGB	Deutscher Gewerkschaftsbund (Confederation of German Trade Unions)
DPJ	Democratic Party of Japan
DSB	Dispute Settlement Body
DSU	Dispute Settlement Understanding
EC	European Communities
ECI	European Citizens' Initiative
ECJ	European Court of Justice
ECOWAS	Economic Community of West African States
ECSC	European Coal and Steel Community
EEAS	European External Action Service
EEC	European Economic Community
EFTA	European Free Trade Association
EP	European Parliament
EPA	Economic Partnership Agreement
ESDP	European Security and Defence Policy
ESI	Export similarity index
EU	European Union
FDI	Foreign direct investment
FDP	Freie Demokratische Partei (Free Democratic Party)
FISA	Foreign Intelligence Surveillance Act
FoEE	Friends of the Earth Europe
FTA	Free trade agreement
FTAA-ALCA	Free Trade Area of the Americas – Área de Libre Comercio de las Américas
GATS	General Agreement on Trade in Services
GATT	General Agreement on Tariffs and Trade
GAVI	Global Alliance for Vaccines and Immunization
GMO	Genetically modified organism
GPA	WTO Government Procurement Agreement
HLWG	High-level working group
HRVP	High Representative of the Union for Foreign Affairs and Security Policy/Vice-President of the European Commission
HS 2	Two-digit harmonized system tariff code
IAP	Individual action plan
IATP	Institute for Agriculture and Trade Policy
IEA	International Energy Agency
IGO	Intergovernmental organization
ILO	International Labour Organization
IMF	International Monetary Fund
IP	Intellectual property
IRENA	International Renewable Energy Association
ISDS	Investor-to-state dispute settlement

ITC	International Trade Centre
JEUFTA	Japan-EU Free Trade Agreement
LDP	Liberal Democratic Party
LOS	Law of the Sea Treaty
LTA	Long-Term Agreement on Cotton Textiles
MAI	Multilateral Agreement on Investment
MEP	Member of the European Parliament
MERCOSUR	Southern Common Market
METI	Ministry of Economy, Trade and Industry (Japan)
MFN	Most-favoured nation
MINTs	Mexico, Indonesia, Nigeria and Turkey
NAFTA	North American Free Trade Agreement
NAMA	Non-agricultural market access
NATO	North Atlantic Treaty Organization
NGO	Non-governmental organization
NPT	Nuclear Non-Proliferation Treaty
NSA	National Security Agency
NTA	New Transatlantic Agenda
NTB	Non-tariff barrier
OECD	Organization for Economic Cooperation and Development
OSCE	Organization for Security and Cooperation in Europe
OWINFS	Our World Is Not For Sale
PSI	Proliferation Security Initiative
PTA	Preferential trade agreement
RCEP	Regional Comprehensive Economic Partnership
RIO	Review of International Organizations
RTA	Regional trade agreement
S2B	Seattle to Brussels network
SAARC	South Asian Association for Regional Cooperation
SADEC	Southern African Development Community
SME	Small and medium enterprise
SOE	State-owned enterprise
SPD	Sozialdemokratische Partei Deutschlands (Social Democratic Party of Germany)
SPS	Sanitary and phytosanitary
TABD	Transatlantic Business Dialogue
TACD	Transatlantic Consumer Dialogue
TBT	Technical barriers to trade
TEC	Transatlantic Economic Council
TFEU	Treaty on the Functioning of the European Union
TISA	Trade in Services Agreement
TM	Transparency Mechanism
TPA	Trade Promotion Authority
TPP	Trans-Pacific Partnership

TPRM	Trade Policy Review Mechanism
TRIPS	Agreement on Trade-Related Aspects of Intellectual Property
TTIP	Transatlantic Trade and Investment Partnership
TWN	Third World Network
UK	United Kingdom
UN	United Nations
UNAIDS	Joint United Nations Programme on HIV and AIDS
UNCTAD	United Nations Conference on Trade and Development
UNDP	United Nations Development Programme
UNICEF	United Nations Children's Fund
UNSC	United Nations Security Council
US	United States
USITC	United States International Trade Commission
USTR	United States Trade Representative
WEU	Western European Union
WHO	World Health Organization
WIPO	World Intellectual Property Organization
WTO	World Trade Organization

Introduction

Tereza Novotná, Jean-Frédéric Morin, Frederik Ponjaert and Mario Telò

Despite being intended primarily as an economic agreement creating a transatlantic common market, the launch of the talks on the Transatlantic Trade and Investment Partnership (TTIP) has put transatlantic relations back at the forefront of the political agenda on both sides of the Atlantic. After the transatlantic rift under the George W. Bush administrations (2000–2008) and the Obama administration's 'pivot to Asia', the start of the TTIP negotiations has reaffirmed the strategic importance of the transatlantic partnership for both the United States (the US) and Europe. Indeed, TTIP promises not only to boost jobs and growth, but also to create closer cooperation between the US and the European Union (EU) in policy areas which were not traditionally at the heart of interactions between politicians across the Atlantic: investment and trade.

In addition, the form which TTIP will eventually take, the rules that it will set and its openness for other parties to join or emulate the deal may in the end influence other free-trade agreements and multilateral institutions around the world and the future system of international collaboration at the global level. Yet, perhaps most importantly, TTIP can play a key role in determining what type of global governance will be here with us for the remainder of the twenty-first century, whether creating a 'transatlantic pole' or leading to a more open 'multilateral' arrangement. Last but not least, since particularly on the European side there are new actors who are emerging on the political scene that can shape and be shaped by the process and outcomes of the TTIP negotiations, any changes in transatlantic cooperation may have knock-on effects for the EU's dealing with transparency issues and civil society groups, EU diplomacy and the balance of powers between EU institutions and EU Member States. This edited volume therefore contributes to the academic scholarship on transatlantic relations, global and EU governance both by providing rich empirical findings and by discussing wider theoretical implications of TTIP.

By focusing on the first year and a half of TTIP negotiations, without making any specific predictions regarding the final outcome and timing of these talks, the book is the first volume on TTIP which has been published on either side of the Atlantic that systematically analyses theoretical aspects of TTIP, the beginnings of the TTIP talks and the role of individual actors, possible impacts on third parties as well as on multilateral institutions and regimes complexes. The book grew out of an 'Agora Forum' event which was organized in October 2013 by the Institute for European Studies at Université libre de Bruxelles where many of the authors presented, including Robert O. Keohane and Pascal Lamy as two keynote speakers. Meanwhile, the pool of the authors has expanded and the volume currently includes scholars from various academic institutions around Europe and North America, but also from outside the transatlantic basin. Some of the authors also have an outstanding practitioner experience, thereby adding a policy spin to their scholarly chapters.

In order to structure better the authors' contributions and make the book accessible for academics, students and policy-makers as well as a wider audience, the edited volume has been divided into four parts, with each concentrating around a broader theme and including three or four chapters:

- Part I: Theoretical and Historical Context
- Part II: Negotiations, Actors and Agencies
- Part III: Knock-on Effects and Unintended Consequences for Third Parties
- Part IV: Impact on Multilateral Institutions and Regime Complexes

Part I provides multifaceted analyses of the theoretical and historical context of the TTIP negotiations with a particular emphasis on economic and political global issues. It explores the key question: what impact will TTIP have on the future of multilateral cooperation within an emerging multipolar and globalized world?

While Andrew Gamble focuses on the dramatic changes in the post-Cold War international system which have led to an unprecedented multipolar structure, Robert O. Keohane and Julia Morse draw attention to the various forms of cooperation/competition between multilateral regimes and Mario Telò analyses the interactions between the economic and political dimensions of the transatlantic relationship and their interplay with global governance. The four authors concur on the thesis that the current post-hegemonic era does not stop multilateral cooperation but rather seriously challenges its various preceding forms due to several reasons that are both economic and political.

For Andrew Gamble, the global power relations started dramatically changing after the decades of the 'liberal peace' (in the 1990s), the 'liberal wars' (after 9/11) and financial and economic crises (since 2007). The emergence of the BRICS (Brazil, Russia, India, China and South Africa) and the MINT (Mexico, Indonesia, Nigeria and Turkey) countries as well as six years of crisis affecting the Western economies, and those of Eurozone members in particular, have had an uneven impact on the global economy, provoking power shifts and making the perspective of any sustainable recovery very patchy. Gamble's prognosis for TTIP is uncertain: TTIP (as well as the Trans-Pacific Partnership, or TPP) seems to be an expression of the US's efforts to find a new way of affirming its centrality and primacy and, simultaneously, can create new 'medieval tendencies' of fragmentation.

According to Robert O. Keohane and Julia Morse, countering the legacy of the Bretton-Woods multilateral system takes two main forms: regime-shifting and competitive regime-creation. Both tendencies can be observed across issue areas, including trade. Among others, Keohane and Morse examine the following questions: will some institutions (such as those originating from TTIP or TPP) become the winners of the process of contested multilateralism, while other institutions (such as WTO) may lose their authority or status? Is the Bretton-Woods legacy of global and comprehensive organizations condemned to a gradual demise? Throughout the last decade, Keohane provides a twofold answer to the issues of a changing multilateralism: firstly, he outlines the emergence of counter-multilateral regimes and more contingent forms of cooperation (as discussed in the chapter by Keohane and Morse in this book) and, secondly, he focuses on the key challenge of a less contingent legitimacy in his other studies on the twenty-first-century multilateralism.

Notwithstanding whether we agree or disagree with the normative perspectives on this kind of regionalism and inter-regionalism, Mario Telò in his chapter argues that both these territorial trade regimes will increasingly matter within the post-hegemonic global context. In fact, they are an inevitable consequence of the WTO quasi-deadlock. Telò therefore asks: will Europeanism as a result increasingly overlap with Atlanticism and will the concepts of Europe and the West increasingly coincide? Such questions are relevant both for theoretical and political reasons and, consequently, for the European public opinion in particular. However, the answer is not necessarily an affirmative one since a deeper transatlantic trade and investment partnership does not automatically produce the EU's subordination to the US. On the contrary, in the international context of a post-hegemonic and multipolar world and in the internal context of complex foreign policy-making on both sides of the Atlantic, the EU can demonstrate its relative autonomy in several policy fields, as we could observe in the case of Germany, one of the leading EU Member States, and its debates on internal (private data protection) as well as international (foreign policy) security.

Without a process of negotiations, there is no deal between two and more partners: negotiations are thus central to any (trade) agreement. Part II therefore focuses on TTIP negotiations and, primarily, the role of various actors that can have an impact on them and thus shape the final TTIP agreement, i.e. from actors and agencies at the political level (EU Member States, the Commission and US Trade Representative, or USTR) through individual politicians up to different business lobbies, civil society groups and the publics. The authors agree that despite the fact that the Commission and USTR lead the TTIP talks, it may in the end be the pressure by the other actors involved which can strike down (or support) any deal.

In her chapter, Tereza Novotná argues that thanks to the way in which TTIP negotiations are conducted on the EU side, the balance of powers between the European Commission, EU Member States and other new EU-level bodies, such as the European diplomatic service (EEAS) that is led by an EU foreign policy chief may be shifted in favour of the EU-level institutions and to the detriment of EU Member States. However, since trade is not yet fully coordinated with the EU's foreign policy structures through a 'comprehensive approach', it is unlikely that EEAS and the incoming HR/VP will eventually hold the upper hand and win the contest over who is setting the strategic direction of TTIP and, consequently, of transatlantic relations in the near future.

Since Germany is one of the key EU Member States, both politically and economically, as well as the country with the tradition of an effective protest mobilization through various grassroots groups (since the 1960s), Hartmut Mayer's chapter focuses on the TTIP debate in Germany and the decline in German public support for TTIP and the US policies in general. After discussing substantive issues that appear in TTIP debates in other EU Member States (such as fears of introducing the investor-state dispute settlement, or ISDS and downgrading the environmental, health and consumer protection standards), Mayer explores a specific 'German' concern: spill-over effects of the NSA spying scandal and Chancellor Merkel's phone tapping by the US intelligence agencies on the German perceptions towards TTIP and the US. According to Mayer, civil society mobilization around the data privacy protection which led to an effective 'Stop TTIP' campaign has already dampened the initial enthusiasm for TTIP among the German political class and, although unlikely that the German government would strike down any TTIP deal, it may have a hard time persuading the German public that its green light is a desirable course for German policy.

The influence of other types of civil society groups on TTIP negotiations is also discussed in the two other chapters by Dür and Lechner and by Strange in Part II of this book. Andreas Dür and Lisa Lechner look at the business interests lobbying on TTIP on both sides of the Atlantic. By providing extensive empirical data, Dür and Lechner argue that businesses have good access to key decision-makers both in the EU and in the US and, contrary to some criticisms about the lack of influence over the TTIP process, the US and EU businesses make good use of it.

On the other hand, the chapter by Michael Strange explores the increasing possibilities of social movements to create transatlantic coalitions to contest TTIP. Although social movements complain about lacking transparency and access to draft negotiation positions, they manage to mobilize and join forces across the Atlantic in communicating their demands. As a result, and perhaps rather paradoxically, particularly if a TTIP agreement is reached, the contestation experience may help the public spheres both in the EU and across the Atlantic converge.

Part III of the book looks in greater detail at the impact that TTIP might have beyond the EU and the US. Given economic weight and the magnitude of the transatlantic trade relations of these two players, it goes without saying that TTIP will resonate deeply in the global trade system. Any specific and more detailed impact of TTIP, however, remains uncertain. While some third countries could benefit from a transatlantic regulatory harmonization, others could suffer from trade deviations. In fact, TTIP might have mixed effects, partly positive and partly negative, in several countries.

Contributors to Part III make clear that TTIP's impact on third countries will be legal, political and economic. In their chapter, Vinod Aggarwal and Simon Evenett discuss the likelihood that norms crafted by TTIP negotiators will diffuse and spread to other regions in the world. Similarly, Erick Duchesne and Richard Ouellet consider if a transatlantic agreement will influence the geography of the WTO dispute settlement mechanism, while Zhang Xiaotong focuses on the various ways in which TTIP could affect the strategic and geopolitical thinking of Chinese officials who are concerned by China's potential loss of its power and role in setting the rules. Finally, Frederik Ponjaert examines the intricate interconnectedness of three simultaneously launched mega-free trade deals negotiations, i.e. TTIP, TPP and the Japan-EU Free Trade Agreement (JEUFTA).

Aggarwal and Evenett reflect on the possibility that third countries might try to join TTIP which is nonetheless a scenario they deem unlikely after careful consideration. A more probable reaction by third countries is, as discussed in Duchesne and Ouellet's chapter, a renewed interest in multilateral negotiations, including for partial or sectorial agreements. Some countries, however, as Zhang Xiaotong argues, could also respond to TTIP by accelerating their regional or bilateral negotiations. A fourth possibility is, as suggested by Ponjaert, that negotiations surrounding the various mega-deals will mostly run in parallel to one another without much of a mutual reinforcement because they are all motivated by different sets of endogenous imperatives and exist within distinct institutional environments. They will remain correlated, but not internally linked negotiation processes with a very high chance for an increasingly greater complexity because of different regulatory and other outcomes.

Given the fact that TTIP is not negotiated in a vacuum that is detached from other multilateral organizations and negotiations, the WTO in particular but, if successful, will have a great effect on setting the standards and negotiations within these multilateral institutions and regime complexes, Part IV discusses TTIP's potential impact on the WTO and other potential multilateral agreements.

By examining the systemic drivers which have recently propelled the multiplication of preferential trade agreements (PTAs), Petros Mavroidis focuses on the search for deeper integration within a smaller group of countries. Since the principle of non-discrimination prevents any rapid progress on non-tariff barriers (NTBs) within the WTO, creation of smaller clubs seems inevitable. TTIP is therefore part of a broader trend. In his chapter, Mavroidis therefore suggests a new pragmatic way forward for a WTO 2.0 which would be more in tune with the reality of the PTAs proliferation.

Echoing the cautionary principle and the enduring concerns of global trade experts such as Bhagwati, in his chapter Jens Mortensen explores the possible negative consequences that TTIP may have on the global multilateral system and analyses how the WTO oversight process can be reformed to ensure that TTIP does not become a stumbling block for the global trade system. Despite successive reforms, the WTO verification mechanism of PTAs that were signed between developed countries remains fragmented without any single oversight forum. The chapter therefore calls for a further reform since the future position of the WTO at the centre of the global trade system hinges on its ability to oversee, scrutinize and approve the formation and operation of PTAs, particularly those leading to deeper liberalization such as TTIP. If the global multilateral system will not be able to take on new roles, the greatest challenge to the WTO system will not be any ambitious PTAs such as TTIP, but the ossification of the WTO-system as such.

Sophie Meunier and Jean-Frédéric Morin explore wider environmental factors that are associated with both the origin and impact of TTIP. The authors stress and describe the existing trade and investment regime complexes within which TTIP is negotiated. The rich ecology that TTIP must consider implies both constraints and uncertainties. On the one hand, TTIP cannot exclusively focus on transatlantic needs but must also take into account the decades of global multilateral liberalization and the multiple existing bilateral agreements. Therefore, any possible impact of TTIP as a stepping-stone or stumbling-block remains uncertain and will depend on the exact provisions that TTIP negotiators may ultimately agree on. On the other hand, the key role of NTBs further increases the unpredictability of what kind of agreement may in the end be concluded, thus increasing uncertainties of TTIP's long-term impact even further. Ultimately, the learning dynamics and evolving nature of TTIP will be the two fundamental factors.

In his chapter, Joost Pauwelyn describes various ways in which deep PTAs such as TTIP can provide public goods and reshape the global trade regime. The chapter identifies five mechanisms through which TTIP could provide benefits also for third parties. Mega-regional deals such as TTIP are considered to be potential providers of concessions that are 'non-rivalrous' and 'non-excludable' by necessity, volition, circumvention, emulation or through most-favoured nation (MFN) clauses. As a result, the central concern for TTIP negotiators must be to distinguish clearly between what they can offer exclusively and what will be extended also to third parties and hence will inevitably fall within the sphere of public goods. If PTAs are, indeed, less discriminatory, this should lead us to rethink WTO rules on PTAs and the complementarity (rather than conflict) between the WTO and PTAs.

Notwithstanding whether an eventual TTIP deal comes to pass, a thorough examination of an ongoing process of TTIP negotiations, as presented by this volume, allows the book authors to highlight dynamics which underline the relationship between the US and the EU and to show what possible consequences a TTIP agreement may lead to. The reaction of politicians, businesses, social movements and other civil society groups all demonstrate that they may disagree on whether or not TTIP is a good thing, but they all tend to agree that it will have a lasting impact. If TTIP is successfully concluded, it will probably encourage emergence of more large-scale trade deals, while if TTIP negotiations fail, we may experience a reverse trend. Either way, TTIP promises to have vast implications not just for economics but for global governance and the international system for years to come.

PART I
Theoretical and Historical Context

Chapter 1

Multipolarity and the Transatlantic Trade and Investment Partnership

Andrew Gamble

The Global Context: An Unprecedented Multipolarity and Economic Crisis

The proposal for a Transatlantic Trade and Investment Partnership (TTIP) between the United States and the EU has arisen at a time when the international order is undergoing substantial change. The drivers of this change are firstly the global shift in the international economy from a unipolar to a multipolar order and, secondly, the aftermath of the 2008 financial crash and the complex set of policy responses to it. Each of these will be analysed in turn.

The international order which was established after the Second World War was bipolar, defined by the confrontation between the United States and the Soviet Union. The two superpowers created spheres of interest around themselves which reflected both geopolitics and political economy. With the end of the Cold War in 1989–91 and the breakup of the Soviet Union, the international order became unipolar because the United States was the only remaining superpower, and had an unrivalled ascendancy – economic, military and ideological. It prompted speculation about a new world order, the end of history, a return to 'One World', for the first time since before 1914. The US enjoyed an unprecedented military predominance, and the disappearance of the barriers which the Soviet Union had erected around itself and its satellites allowed the consolidation and extension of the multilateral international market order which had been fashioned under US leadership since 1945. This now became a universal framework and the disappearance of any alternative to it was a powerful incentive for all states to engage with the liberal international market order and accept its framework of rules and standards for international trade and investment, which the United States had done so much to shape.

This new international order was a great success. The political and economic restructuring of the 1970s had created an order based around freely floating currencies and liberal rules on trade and capital flows. These had encouraged strong trends toward globalization and liberalization, an increase in the interconnectedness of the international economy, which was particularly marked in the growing complexity of production chains, the expansion of financial and trade flows as well as cultural and information exchanges. The most significant achievement of this period was the emergence of a new group of rising powers.

There had been other states which had broken through into fast growth, such as Singapore, Taiwan and South Korea. What was key about the new group in the 1990s was that it included some of the largest and most populous countries on the planet – China, India and Brazil. Their ability to maintain rapid rates of growth was of major significance because if it could be sustained it raised the possibility of a major shift in the balance of the international economy and the international state system taking place, from West to East and from North to South.

This sudden spurt in the industrialization and modernization, in particular of China and India, has changed all calculations. It was quickly realized that the unipolar moment would not last very long. The rapid growth of countries outside the traditional West meant that the world looked to be heading for multipolarity, many centres of power rather than just one. This had implications for the governance of the international order and how the interests of all the rising powers as well as the established ones could be accommodated. In addition, Russia began to revive at the end of the 1990s, boosted by the increased demand from an expanding international economy for its vast reserves of energy and other natural resources. The Soviet Union had broken up but it had not been defeated militarily or occupied, and although some attempts were made to westernize and liberalize the new Russia, they had only partial success. Under Boris Yeltsin's successor, Vladimir Putin, Russia began to assert an identity and interests which were distinct, signalling its intention that it would not be incorporated into the West and would continue to form a pole on its own.

By the beginning of the twenty-first century the trend towards multipolarity and away from unipolarity was captured in the acronym of the BRICs. Coined by Jim O'Neill at Goldman Sachs, this acronym brought together Brazil, China and India with Russia, characterizing these four as rising powers which because of the size of their territories and their populations constituted a counterweight to the established Western powers (O'Neill 2001). Although there were some attempts during WTO negotiations to get the BRIC countries to co-operate and co-ordinate their negotiating strategy, in general their interests were too divergent. They did not form a bloc. However, each one was potentially so large that they did not need to do so. Each one was potentially a pole of a new multipolar international order. The rapid development after 2000 of another group of countries with substantial territory and population showed how variegated the international economy was likely to become. This group included Nigeria, Mexico, Indonesia and Turkey, and was labelled by O'Neill the MINTs (O'Neill 2013).

The sign that something profound was taking place was the estimate by the UN in 2001 that for the first time in human history the number of people living in cities now exceeded the number living on the land. It still meant that there were huge numbers engaged in subsistence agriculture, but it signalled that a very different international order was now arising, one which would eventually no longer be dominated by the Western powers. The West in the form of first Europe and then the United States had created the international market order of the modern world and dominated it for the past 250 years. The leading powers in 2000 were the same as they had been in 1900, with the exception of Japan. This is very unlikely to be the case in 2100, or even in 2050. In the period before 1914 the world was multipolar, but the poles were mostly within Europe, which dominated much of the rest of the world through its colonial empires. There was nevertheless after 1815 a degree of co-operation between the European powers and a common framework of rules and standards established through the economic and financial hegemony of Britain. This all broke down after 1914 and three decades of multipolarity without co-operation ensued, resulting in two world wars and the collapse of the liberal international order of the nineteenth century.

Stability was restored after the Second World War through the reconstruction of a liberal international order under American leadership which included Western Europe and important parts of East Asia. The bipolar security relationship was at first extremely tense but over time grew more stable and predictable. The advent of unipolarity seemed to presage a new era of harmony and stability, but this was quickly dispelled, first by a new phase of wars and interventions, particularly after 9/11 (and the war on terror), and secondly by the way the forces unleashed by globalization themselves undermined unipolarity. The world is now in transition between a unipolar and a multipolar world. In certain respects the world is still unipolar, particularly in terms of military capacity. The US continues to outspend all other countries by a large margin, still has its network of 700 military bases around the world and enjoys a marked superiority both in weaponry and in its capacity to project its power. Despite the difficulties the United States has faced in winning small wars and making occupations successful, it still faces no major geopolitical threat from any other power. The main driver for multipolarity comes in the economic and social spheres. This poses a major challenge for US leadership, raising the question of how the rising powers can be incorporated in a stable system of multilateral governance. As the example of the first half of the twentieth century shows, there is no automatic link between multipolarity and multilateralism. It is possible for multipolarity to be associated with conflict and fragmentation. In this case, economic blocs also tend to become military blocs.

The multilateral framework is still holding but it has become subject to great pressure. One of the main reasons for this is the 2008 financial crash and its aftermath. It is often described as a global financial crisis, but at first it was much more regionally specific. It primarily affected the financial systems and economies of North America and Europe and, in particular, those of the United States and the United Kingdom. The eurozone appeared at first relatively shielded from the financial meltdown which was regarded as primarily a phenomenon of Anglo-Saxon capitalism. The rising powers appeared even less affected. While output plunged in North America and Europe by up to 9 per cent in 2009, the worst recession since 1945, the rising powers continued to grow, despite the large reduction in demand for their exports. It seemed to be a turning point. The rising powers appeared to have achieved a level of development which made them independent of what happened in the rest of the international economy. If this were true it would have meant a dramatic acceleration towards multipolarity.

At first the international community behaved as though it were true. The crisis brought home the new reality in the international economy. The G8 was marginalized and instead the G20 was used as the forum for discussing the crisis and what should be done about it. The G20 included all the members of the G8 – USA, Japan, Germany, France, UK, Italy, Canada and Russia – but also China, India, Brazil, Mexico, Indonesia, Turkey, South Africa, Saudi Arabia, South Korea, Australia and Argentina, as well as separate representation for the EU. Although this body still excluded almost 90 per cent of the member states of the United Nations (Payne 2010, Wade and Vestergaard 2012), it accounted for 85 per cent of global GDP and was much more representative than previous bodies. The summits established a new permanent secretariat located in Geneva rather than Washington, and embarked on some significant discussions about the future of financial regulation. The new focus on the G20 seemed to signal a move towards a more representative form of governance for the international economy.

The aftermath of the 2008 crash has been complex. Instead of a normal V shaped recovery common after previous recessions, the recovery proved fitful and subject to setbacks. A second wave of the crisis affected the eurozone in 2010–12 with a sovereign debt crisis which seriously impacted the performance of the rest of the EU as well as the US (Lapavitsas 2012). It highlighted the way in which almost all the Western economies were entering a long period of slow and painful restructuring. The strength of the forces pushing the Western economies into deflation was shown by the low level of interest rates in the US and the UK, still only just above zero, five years after the crash, as well as by the scale of the quantitative easing which the central banks employed to keep their banks afloat and asset prices high (Gamble 2014). Governments adopted austerity and retrenchment packages (Blyth 2013), but debt levels at the end of five years were still very high. The risk of some economies slipping into a deflationary trap like Japan in the 1990s remained real (Koo 2009). Although the US and the UK economies began recovering strongly in 2013/14, the prospects for a sustained recovery remained clouded. One reason for this was that from 2013 a third phase of the crisis seemed to be gathering force, with problems now occurring in the rising powers, with marked slowdowns in growth in Brazil, India and even China. In 2008/9 China had avoided any adverse effect upon its own economy from the downturn in Western economies by launching a major fiscal stimulus. This succeeded in maintaining high rates of growth but at the expense of creating a major credit bubble and over-investment in infrastructure projects and housing where there was no identifiable income stream. A major correction appeared inevitable. How much of a shock it would provide to the rest of the international economy depended on whether China could successfully manage to remove the excess credit avoiding an uncontrolled collapse. It was clear, however, that by 2014 all parts of the international economy had been affected by the 2008 crash, although in very different ways, and the path to sustainable recovery, and the regaining of the levels of growth experienced before the crash was going to be much harder than originally anticipated.

The Uncertainties about TTIP: Between a New US primacy and a Fragmented New Medieval System

This is the context in which the options for the transatlantic partnership are being discussed and in which the specific proposal for a free trade agreement between the United States and the EU has been made. In the past few years many of the assumptions of the post-Cold War period have been called into question, and the nature of the transatlantic partnership has been one of them. The end of the Soviet Union and the enlargement of the European Union removed the security issues which had made NATO such an important alliance, the bedrock of European security. In the new era of liberal peace in the 1990s, many European countries saw little need to maintain defence spending at its previous levels and this is a trend which has continued. In the phase of liberal war (the war on terror) which succeeded liberal peace the United States became increasingly irritated and frustrated with many of its European allies, accusing them of free-riding on the US security guarantee and not being prepared to make the hard choices to defend themselves and the West. These recriminations came to a head at the time of the Iraq War (Kagan 2004).

Such divisions in the alliance prompted speculation that the US and Europe would increasingly diverge. The need for security co-operation was lessening and European publics gave little support to the foreign policy stances which the US was taking, particularly once neo-conservatives were in the ascendancy in Washington after 9/11. Similarly, US and European interests in economic policy seemed to be diverging as well. The European social model was regarded by many in Europe as a better model than the Anglo-American free market model, and they thought themselves vindicated by the events of the 2008 crash. There were suggestions before the crash that the EU might increasingly form its own economic pole in the new multipolar world, offering a different model of political economy and a different model of governance to the rest of the world (Telò 2006, Rifkin 2005). There was never any intention to break with the United States; the two economies had become increasingly intertwined and the role of the US in providing public goods was still acknowledged. Nevertheless the euro project itself was in part conceived as the means by which the 'exorbitant privileges' which the United States enjoyed from possession of the dollar could gradually be reined in (Eichengreen 2012). The euro, once established, was seen as having the capacity to be an alternative reserve currency which other countries might come to prefer to the dollar. Although many argued that the EU remained subordinate to the US and worked within limits established by it (Cafruny and Ryner 2007), there were signs of an increasing European autonomy, noticeable for example at the Doha Round negotiations in the WTO. The Europeans in trade matters at least reached a common negotiating position and acted as a bloc. The potential for doing so in other fields was evident to many observers. It seemed to spell a gradual loosening of ties with the US and a more antagonistic relationship.

The 2008 crash has changed many of these calculations. In its aftermath, the eurozone plunged into a deep crisis from which it is only now emerging and many European economies remain very fragile. Several have still not regained the level of output they had in 2007. The crisis has drawn attention to how much the world has shrunk and how large other parts of it have grown. The Eurocentrism of the past is rapidly fading and the world is being rebalanced. Yet Europe and the US still command close to 50 per cent of global GDP, and although this will steadily decline, they still possess all the advantages of their accumulated wealth, infrastructure and human capital. The rules have been set in ways which benefit the established powers and their interests. Faced with the rise of India, China and the other new powers, the response from the European Union has been twofold. On the one hand, there is the desire to exploit the opportunities which a multipolar world provides for increasing trade and investment, if necessary forming new bilateral links with the rising powers in case multilateral links are not possible. The huge opportunities which the new growing markets of the East and the South represent are seen as essential for future growth prospects. On the other hand, the emergence of a multipolar world in which Europe is no longer the centre of the world but only one pole within it is an alarming prospect, since there is no guarantee that in the new world order as it develops there will be the same priority given to Western rules, procedures and interests. Such considerations make Europeans feel more kindly disposed towards the United States. As Hilaire Belloc advised about the boy who ran away from his nurse and was eaten by a lion: 'Always keep a-hold of nurse, for fear of finding something worse' (Belloc 1987).

One of the key factors in shaping whatever new order now emerges is the response of the United States to the emergence of a multipolar world. If multipolarity becomes established, it will mean a significant diminution in the power of the United States. Although formally the world only became unipolar after the end of the Soviet Union, the two rival spheres of interest which made up the bipolar Cold War system were both organized along unipolar lines with one dominant hegemon at the centre of each. The United States has enjoyed this status now for 70 years and its political class shows no inclination to abandon it. This will make the transition to a new order with a multilateral system of governance difficult to accomplish since that would require substantial concessions from the United States to create a system of collective governance (Ikenberry 2012, Kupchan 2013). The US would clearly prefer to remain the global leader, shaping the rules of the international order and being their ultimate guarantor. Other states including the rising powers would be encouraged to participate fully in the existing international order. As the deadlock in the Doha Round at the WTO shows, this is unlikely to be acceptable to many of the new players. The rising powers proved strong enough to block the kind of agreement which the US and the EU sought. A way through the deadlock has so far not been found.

Yet the US has been prepared, as noted earlier, to acknowledge the need for new systems of governance. It agreed to the enhanced profile for the G20, and encouraged a new system of financial regulation, and a new regulatory institution, the Financial Stability Board, to be established after 2008. Similarly it proposed increases in the voting shares of key rising powers including China and India on the IMF, mainly at the expense of the Europeans. But the US retained its own 15 per cent share and the right that gives it to a veto over any decisions the Fund reaches. The real test of US intentions will come when the rising powers' stake in the international economy means that one or more of them become entitled to shares equal to that of the US itself (Wade 2011). The EU could claim such a share now, but the wish of its largest members to retain individual representation on bodies like the IMF prevents that. The same is true of the UN and the G20. The failure of member states to allow the EU to represent them on all international bodies is a significant weakness, since it means that there is often confusion as to what the EU position is. It also has the effect of reinforcing the subordination of the EU to the US in the transatlantic relationship because the US is able to retain bilateral links with many European states. Unable among themselves to agree a common position on some issues, the Europeans look to the United States to provide leadership for the Western interest.

The US clearly senses this, and after the G20 lost momentum and the WTO remained deadlocked, the US has decided to move ahead with negotiations on the TTIP with the EU and the TPP with its main allies in East Asia. The US is seeking to strengthen its alliance with the Europeans and with key states in East Asia. The first excludes Russia and the second excludes China. Indeed, apart from Mexico, none of the BRICs or the MINTs is involved. If the negotiations are successful, the US will have re-invigorated two of its key regional networks. The negotiations take on new significance because of the increased security tensions with Russia over the Ukraine and with China over the East China Sea. The attempt to link once again the security and the political economy interests of states in these two regions is reminiscent of the strategy employed with such success by the US during the Cold War.

From the EU perspective, the strengthening of the transatlantic partnership through a successful conclusion of the TTIP would mean acknowledging the continuing global leadership role of the United States and the abandoning or at least the postponement of any idea that the EU might form an independent pole in a multipolar order. Instead, the new architecture would see the creation of two linked poles both tied to the United States and the possible establishment of other poles around Russia, China and India. This would imply a fragmented international order in which the US would be seeking to strengthen its position against those states not willing to participate fully in the rule-based order which it favours. Yet the position would be a confused one because of many overlapping jurisdictions and memberships. Because of events in Ukraine, the G8 has been suspended and the G7 has been reconstituted. However, Russia and China are both members of the G20 and are also members of the Security Council. Serious economic sanctions against Russia will be very painful for the Western economies, and particularly for many European economies, but they are thinkable. Serious economic sanctions against China are more difficult to contemplate because of the importance of China to the international economy and particularly to the United States.

The emerging multipolar world has clear features of the new medievalism which was first discussed in the 1970s (Bull 1977). The EU is a primary locus of this new medievalism because of the variety of arrangements, overlapping authorities and jurisdictions which it has institutionalized. In a new medieval world, there will be times when a stronger transatlantic relationship appears desirable. This period of heightened uncertainty for the EU following the 2008 crash and the eurozone crisis has increased the attractions of strengthening links with the US. The TTIP is aimed at harmonizing standards particularly in non-tariff areas. There is considerable opposition in the EU to the proposals because of the fear that the EU will agree to a lowering of the higher standards of the European social model to the lower standards in the US. The proposed ability of companies to sue governments if they feel that local regulations harm their business is also the subject of controversy, mainly because decisions will not go through national courts but through a special council composed of experts who will have the authority to interpret the terms of the agreement. It will be a sign of how far the EU collectively sees the strengthening of ties with the US as a priority at the present time because of fears about the stagnation of the European economies and the obstacles to returning to growth. Any trade deal negotiated has to be approved by the US Congress which is likely to refuse to ratify if too many concessions are made to the Europeans. In the EU, any deal has to be approved by the European Parliament and some member states may also demand the right to ratify it.

These political obstacles make a successful conclusion to the negotiations far from certain, but the fact that they are happening at all shows that as the world becomes more multipolar, so there is a tendency for states to cling to the pole they know. The advantages of the transatlantic relationship which were played down in the period before the crash have been played up in the period since the crash. The EU appears willing to make substantial concessions to the US to make a deal possible and this, in turn, signals the importance the EU still places on the US continuing to play a global role.

Chapter 2

Counter-multilateralism

Robert O. Keohane and Julia C. Morse[1]

The concept of *counter-multilateralism* developed in this chapter emphasizes that contemporary multilateralism is characterized by competing coalitions and shifting institutional arrangements, informal as well as formal. Multilateralism is not necessarily cooperative and characterized by integrated rules. Nor is the alternative to established multilateralism, simply unilateralism or bilateralism. Frequently, multilateral institutions are challenged through the use of other multilateral institutions, either without resort to unilateralism or bilateralism or in conjunction with those strategies. Although states and non-state actors are often committed to multilateral strategies, they may disagree about the policies that multilateral institutions should pursue.

Counter-multilateralism is an umbrella term to describe a set of strategies pursued by states, multilateral institutions, and non-state actors. These strategies—using formal and informal multilateral practices to challenge established multilateral institutions—provide ways to promote policy and institutional change that are quite distinct from unilateral or bilateral policies designed to challenge and change the *status quo*. The purpose of this chapter is to demonstrate the value of the concept of counter-multilateralism as a way of describing this set of clearly multilateral but disruptive phenomena.

Counter-multilateralism involves the use of different multilateral institutions to challenge the rules, practices, or missions of existing multilateral institutions. *More precisely, the phenomenon of counter-multilateralism occurs when states and/or non-state actors either shift their focus from one existing institution to another or create an alternative multilateral institution to compete with existing ones.* Such challenges may or may not entail the creation of new multilateral institutions, but they always involve conflict between the rules, institutionalized practices, or missions of two different institutions. When these challenges to dominant institutions are successful, they typically increase the complexity of an international regime by adding elements to it or strengthening formerly weaker institutions with it. These challenges may constitute reactions to actions of

---

1   This chapter is a shortened version of Julia C. Morse and Robert O. Keohane, "Contested Multilateralism," which appeared in the *Review of International Organizations (RIO)*, published on-line (open access) 23 March 2014. Much of the text in this shortened version is almost identical to the version published in *RIO*, except that here we use the term, "counter-multilateralism" instead of "contested multilateralism."

multilateral institutions, but they may also stem from *anticipation* that established institutions will not respond in ways that the challenging actors view as satisfactory. In this chapter we discuss a variety of instances of counter-multilateralism and refer to others discussed at greater length in Morse and Keohane (2014).

Counter-multilateralism can be observed across many different issue areas in international relations, including counter-terrorism and non-proliferation that are central to state security. Counter-multilateralism is so common in contemporary world politics that the strategies of dissatisfied powerful states on core issues of national security often run through multilateralism rather than in stark opposition to it. We argue that even powerful states may be stymied by established institutional practices, yet when this situation arises, they often resort to multilateral rather than unilateral or bilateral practices.

The concept of "counter-multilateralism" puts into a broader conceptual context the significance of the Transatlantic Trade and Investment Partnership (TTIP), which clearly has implications for other forms of multilateralism, including the WTO.

In the first section we define counter-multilateralism more precisely; lay out essential conditions for counter-multilateralism to exist; describe the pathways through which we expect it to appear; and distinguish two basic types, *regime shifting* and *competitive regime creation*. The second section then provides some examples, both of regime shifting and competitive regime creation. Our cases are drawn from issue-areas that range from intellectual property, energy, and health to security issues involving conventional weapons, counter-terrorism, and nuclear non-proliferation. Our framework is intended to show what these processes have in common, and suggest that they may be analyzed collectively through the lens of counter-multilateralism.

Counter-multilateralism Defined

This section begins by elaborating our definitions. It then continues by specifying some key baseline conditions for counter-multilateralism, describing pathways for its emergence, and distinguishing two basic types of counter-multilateralism. Finally, it concludes by highlighting how strategies of counter-multilateralism can expand regime complexes.

Three criteria define a situation as involving counter-multilateralism:

1. A multilateral institution exists within a defined issue-area and with a mission and a set of established rules and institutionalized practices.
2. Dissatisfied with the *status quo* institution, a coalition of actors—whether members of the existing institution or not—shifts the focus of its activity to a challenging institution with different rules and practices. This challenging institution can be either pre-existing or new.

3. The rules and institutionalized practices of the challenging institution conflict with or significantly modify the rules and institutionalized practices of the *status quo* institution.

Dissatisfied intergovernmental organizations (IGOs), civil society actors, and weak states are likely only to be able to act effectively to counter the policies of established multilateral institutions with the aid of powerful states, so for them, multilateralism is often the only way to contest effectively such policies. Powerful states, however, may have bilateral or unilateral options. But even they often have incentives to act multilaterally, both to mobilize support and attendant resources, and to gain legitimacy for their contestation of established multilateral policy.

Although counter-multilateralism always involves the use of either an established or new multilateral institution to challenge a *status quo* institution, the outcome of such a challenge is open-ended. Challenges can collapse without long-term impact, leaving a regime complex effectively unchanged. Often, however, these challenges create or expand a regime complex in a way that leads to fundamental changes in institutional practices or changes the distribution of power between institutions. Some challenges may have an impact only over a long time horizon. A dissatisfied coalition composed primarily of weak states, for example, may only be able to mount a symbolic challenge, critiquing an existing institutional practice but being unable to force immediate change. Over time, however, such a challenge may change actor preferences, ideas, and values in a way that delegitimizes an institution, forcing concomitant change or institutional exit.

Counter-multilateralism refers to conflict *between*, not *within*, multilateral institutions. Conflicting resolutions by the UN Security Council and the UN General Assembly do not constitute counter-multilateralism, nor do conflicting actions by the European Parliament and the European Council, or adverse judgments on the legitimacy of such actions by the European Court of Justice. Conflicting actions by these bodies represent internal disagreements, not counter-multilateralism, and do not change the nature of regime complexes. Nor does counter-multilateralism describe situations in which one multilateral institution has already granted authority in a particular domain to another such institution, which then makes decisions invalidating the first institution's actions. For instance, if the WTO Appellate Body rules against the EU in a trade case, this is not counter-multilateralism. Counter-multilateralism occurs when states, and sometimes also non-state actors, are dissatisfied with an existing institution, find pathways to intra-institutional reform blocked, and decide to shift their focus to other institutions or to create a new one.

Our case studies illustrate that counter-multilateralism is common in world politics and that this concept provides a new way to interpret key events and describe more coherently the processes leading to more fragmented regime complexes. The concept of counter-multilateralism emphasizes that the central strategic question for states is rarely "multilateralism vs. unilateralism," but rather *what kind of multilateralism* will best achieve long-term objectives.

Pathways to Counter-multilateralism

When dissatisfied actors are unable to change the *status quo* there is a possibility of counter-multilateralism. Whether the dissatisfied coalition opts for a strategy that generates counter-multilateralism will depend on the availability of an outside option, the degree to which communication is impeded by lack of credibility, and the existence of institutional or domestic constraints. The possible pathways to counter-multilateralism are illustrated in Figure 2.1 and discussed below.

When a dissatisfied coalition—composed of states or a combination of states and non-state actors—seeks to change a blocked institution, the coalition's ability to pursue outside options is a necessary condition for successful counter-multilateralism. Outside options include switching to an already-existing alternative multilateral institution or creating a new institution more in line with the coalition's preferences, with respect either to substantive policy or institutional form—formal or informal, hierarchical or networked, integrated or loosely coupled. The key is that the challenging coalition must have an alternative to the existing institution that would serve its interests, and the coalition must be able to threaten, credibly, to use this alternative organization or practice. State power is a major determinant of whether coalitions have outside options. A group of dissatisfied actors that includes states with significant resources and institutional leverage will have an easier time identifying credible outside options than a coalition of weaker actors.

If dissatisfied actors have an outside option, we should normally expect adaptation by the existing institution, since its authority and the scope of its impact will be adversely affected by the establishment of alternative organizations or practices. However, existing institutions may fail to adapt. We posit that such failure to adapt occurs through one of two pathways.

First, since dissatisfied actors have incentives to claim that they have outside options even when they do not, their incentives to misrepresent can generate problems of credibility. If the dissatisfied coalition is unable to make credible threats and promises about either its willingness or ability to leverage outside options to force change, it may take actions that result in counter-multilateralism. This is one of the pathways in Figure 2.1.

Even in situations where the dissatisfied coalition is credible, policy adjustment may not occur if there are diverging state interests, or ideational or institutional constraints. Veto players—states, organizational bureaucracies, or other crucial actors—may block changes desired by the challenging coalition because they see their interests—on substantive policy or with respect to institutional authority—threatened by change. Established conceptions of institutional roles and purpose are often persistent. This situation, in which power comes to the fore, is represented by the other pathway to counter-multilateralism in Figure 2.1.

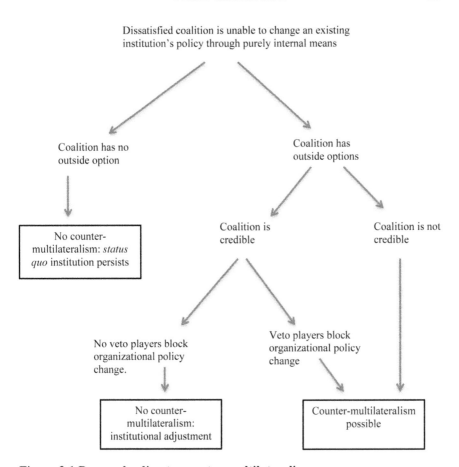

Dissatisfied coalition is unable to change an existing institution's policy through purely internal means

Coalition has no outside option

Coalition has outside options

No counter-multilateralism: *status quo* institution persists

Coalition is credible

Coalition is not credible

No veto players block organizational policy change.

Veto players block organizational policy change

No counter-multilateralism: institutional adjustment

Counter-multilateralism possible

Figure 2.1 Process leading to counter-multilateralism

Regime Shifting and Competitive Regime Creation

The most familiar form of counter-multilateralism is *regime shifting*, which occurs when challengers to a set of rules and practices shift to an alternative multilateral forum with a more favorable mandate and decision rules, and then use this new forum to challenge standards in the original institution or reduce the authority of that institution (Helfer 2009). Regime shifting can be led by states or international institutions.

Developed countries' efforts to shift authority from the World Intellectual Property Organization (WIPO) to the GATT/WTO negotiating forum provide a clear example of regime shifting. Developed countries grew dissatisfied with WIPO as a negotiating forum for intellectual property after a series of events in the 1970s and 1980s. In the late 1970s, US companies became concerned about the lack of intellectual property protection in developing countries, and began to push for new international standards. When US companies went to WIPO, however, to advocate updates to the Paris Convention on patent protection, they encountered significant resistance from developing countries (Santoro 1995). By the early 1980s, US companies had convinced the US government and leaders of other developed countries of the need for more stringent patent protection, but they were unable to bring about significant change within the WIPO forum. With countries pushing in opposite directions and a one-country, one-vote forum in WIPO, developed countries concluded that they needed a different venue to strengthen the intellectual property regime.

Developing countries did not anticipate the full effects of the shift to the GATT/WTO forum for intellectual property negotiations, assuming that they would be able to limit the scope of negotiations primarily to trade in counterfeit goods (Watal 2001). Instead, the United States was able to convince countries through a combination of multilateral and unilateral actions (such as the threat of trade sanctions) to support broad-based intellectual property negotiations within the GATT/WTO. Developing countries were so concerned about being excluded from the new free trade system that they acceded to the shift of venue (Watal 2001).

The Agreement on Trade-Related Aspects of Intellectual Property Rights (TRIPS) was adopted in 1994. The final agreement was almost identical to a draft put forward by the GATT Secretariat, which had prepared a "take it or leave it" document. In effect, the developed countries that had negotiated the WTO forced developing countries to accept this draft or be excluded from the benefits of tariff reductions (Steinberg 2002, Yu 2005). TRIPS sets minimum standards for intellectual property to be implemented by all WTO members and allows enforcement through the WTO dispute settlement mechanism. Since the establishment of TRIPS, WIPO has struggled to remain relevant (May and Sell 2006, May 2010). In this case, the developed countries' challenge to WIPO occurred due to a strong outside option—the WTO negotiations—and an informational gap: developing countries did not accurately understand the motivations and intentions of developed countries.

Other examples of regime shifting include the effort by developing countries and UN agencies to challenge the TRIPS agreement on intellectual property; the creation of the Basel Committee and other innovations in global financial regulation; the World Bank's entry into global health governance; and the challenge by the European Court of Justice to the UN Security Council sanctions regime regulating terrorist financing.

The second form of counter-multilateralism is *competitive regime creation*, which occurs when the coalition of dissatisfied actors creates a new institution or establishes a new informal form of multilateral cooperation to challenge the existing institutional *status quo*. To ensure that the new forum has a more favorable policy orientation, the coalition may opt for direct control strategies, such as limiting membership to like-minded states (Downs et al. 1998), establishing informal channels of control (Stone 2011), or structuring voting in a favorable manner. Alternatively, the coalition may create an institution with a mandate more consistent with the interests of its members. By challenging the institutional *status quo*, the dissatisfied coalition creates additional bargaining leverage *vis-à-vis* the *status quo* institution. Examples of competitive regime creation discussed in Morse and Keohane (2014) include the Proliferation Security Initiative (PSI), the International Renewable Energy Association (IRENA), and decisions by donor countries, IGOs, and private foundations to challenge the World Health Organization's (WHO) monopoly of authority over health issues by creating the Global Alliance for Vaccines and Immunization (GAVI), the Global Fund to Fight AIDS, Tuberculosis and Malaria, and UNAIDS.

Although competitive regime creation is a new concept, existing work has documented many cases where states take the lead in creating new multilateral forums to affect the rules or mission of existing institutions. In the area of migration, for example, wealthy states have sought to change their obligations to accept migrants as refugees by creating a migration regime complex that limits the impact of their obligations under the 1951 UN refugee convention and the practices of the UN High Commissioner on Human Rights (Betts 2009). In the area of biodiversity, developing countries wanted to preserve more autonomy to regulate genetically modified organisms (GMOs) in the face of the creation of the WTO in the 1990s. These countries took the lead in negotiating the Cartagena Protocol on Biosafety in 2000, which had a "disruptive" effect on the WTO-based regime (Oberthur and Gehring 2006: 14). In Morse and Keohane (2014), we discuss the creation of the IRENA and the development of the PSI both initiated by powerful states; and the reaction to the Convention on Certain Conventional Weapons (CCW) by a large European-led coalition, leading to the conventions on land mines and cluster munitions.

Institution-Led Competitive Regime Creation

IGOs can play key roles in regime shifting, and they can also be pivotal in the creation of new institutions to challenge a regime complex. Our case studies in our longer paper of what we call "institution-led competitive regime creation" focus on how coalitions of states and non-state actors have challenged the WHO over the last 30 years, leading to a proliferation of regime complexes in global health. The example that we use here is that of the GAVI.

Beginning in the early 1980s, many public health officials became committed to the idea of harnessing advances in biotechnology to produce revolutionary vaccines for debilitating diseases in the developing world. As the central multilateral institution for global health issues, WHO was the natural place to coordinate the endeavour, but its divided and uncoordinated efforts generated dissatisfaction, and in 1990 a coalition of five non-state organizations (UNICEF, WHO, UNDP, the World Bank, and the Rockefeller Foundation) reached an agreement to form a new Children's Vaccine Initiative (CVI), designed to advance the full continuum of vaccine development. WHO at first resisted the CVI, but once it became clear that the initiative was inevitable, WHO managed to make the CVI a subordinate entity within WHO (Muraskin 1998). At this point, therefore, counter-multilateralism was avoided.

But the CVI did not thrive within WHO, which prioritized its own vaccine programs, constrained the CVI's attempts to partner with private industry, and eventually announced its intention terminate the CVI entirely. In response, civil society organizations, public health advocates, and some elements of the vaccine industry created GAVI outside the structure of WHO, with significant support from the Gates Foundation (Muraskin 2002). GAVI has been much more successful than CVI was in working with industry and civil society (Harman 2012).

GAVI emerged because of organizational resistance by WHO and incomplete information that prevented WHO from accurately gauging the seriousness of the challenge. WHO's resistance to the CVI in the face of a powerful supportive coalition helped generate counter-multilateralism—the creation of GAVI, which challenged WHO's dominance of vaccine development and delivery. WHO has continued to function as a partner in GAVI, but the challenge created a regime complex that significantly reduced WHO's authority over vaccine coordination.

Conclusions

Having developed the umbrella concept of "counter-multilateralism," we now see a wide variety of examples of it, even apart from those referred to above. Control over multilateral development finance has long been contested between the World Bank, with weighted voting, and various vehicles controlled on a one-state, one-vote basis within the UN structure, such as the UN Special Fund. The Nuclear Non-Proliferation Treaty (NPT) has been supplemented by more or less informal institutions such as the Nuclear Suppliers Group or the International Nuclear Fuel Cycle Evaluation, which shifted the effects of nuclear proliferation policy in the direction favored by the United States and other established nuclear powers. Such challenges to existing multilateral institutions are often multilateral rather than unilateral or bilateral. As noted above, some of these challenges focus on the rules governing a set of activities—for example, more stringent intellectual property or due process standards; other challenges—such as the PSI—focus on the actual operation of a regime complex; and still others focus on organizational missions, as in the cases of IEA/IRENA and the WHO. States or coalitions of states, IGOs, and non-state actors may support or create multilateral institutions with rules and practices that contradict those of established multilateral institutions to which they belong, or with different missions. Such attempts at counter-multilateralism are remarkably common, and they are most interesting and surprising when they are led by powerful states. When successful, they typically create, reinforce, or expand regime complexes. And counter-multilateralism may create losers as well as winners.

Table 2.1 Aspects of counter-multilateralism by issue

CM Process Issue:	Challenged institution	Challenging coalition	Principal sources of dissatisfaction	Focus on rules, practices, or mission	New or selected institution	Implications for regime complex
TRIPS	WIPO	Developed countries	Exogenous: IPR pressure in rich countries	Rules	GATT/WTO	Redistribution of authority in regime complex
Kadi case	UNSC	ECJ and EU countries	Exogenous: ECJ challenge to UNSC, resulting from ECJ rights activism	Rules	Greater role for European human rights standards	Creation of regime complex with role for ECJ
Land mines and cluster munitions	CCW	West Europeans and many others	Exogenous: new activist pressure	Rules	Ottawa Convention (Anti-Personnel Mine Ban Convention) and Oslo Convention (CCM)	Creation of regime complex, less centrality for CCW
Renewable energy	IEA	Germany and partners	Exogenous: new activist pressures undermined IEA	Mission	IRENA	Redistribution of authority in regime complex
PSI	UN Law of the Sea Treaty (LOS)	US and allies	Exogenous: aftermath of 9/11	Practices	Informal PSI network	Creation of regime complex
WHO issues	WHO	Developed countries and NGOs	Endogenous: WHO organizational barriers to action	Mission	GAVI, UNAIDS, Global Fund	Creation of regime complex

Table 2.1 (p. 25) illustrates how the concept of counter-multilateralism helps us analyze seemingly dissimilar cases and understand their effects on the international system. The table summarizes the cases discussed in this paper and several others discussed in Morse and Keohane (2014), the sources of dissatisfaction, and the implications of each case for regime complexes. In our examples, the challenging coalitions all consist of developed countries, but this is not a general rule: if we had selected developing countries' contestation of World Bank dominance over multilateral development issues, or of US dominance of internet governance arrangements, we would have cases of contestation by developing countries. Four of our cases focus on contestation over rules; two focus on contestation over the missions or practices of established organizations. The newly selected institutions range from international legal conventions and formal organizations to informal networks or organizations including civil society organizations, such as GAVI and UNAIDS. Significantly, in each case, there were implications for the regime complex, redistributing authority or creating a regime complex when there had previously been a dominant treaty or organization. Counter-multilateralism thus provides a framework for understanding the growth of regime complexes across a variety of different issue areas.

We study the phenomenon of counter-multilateralism because it seems to be a significant and common process, and also to throw light on issues of institutional change. When interdependence is high and power is widely dispersed, multilateral institutions are essential tools for states and non-state actors. When coalitions are dissatisfied with existing institutions, they seek to shift the focus of rule-making to other institutions or to construct new institutions for that purpose. States, IGOs, and other non-state actors act strategically, using alternative multilateral organizations to pursue their interests when established institutions fail to do so. The result is a change in the configuration of multilateral institutions, often leading to, or expanding and reinforcing, regime complexes as opposed to integrated international regimes. The phrase, "counter-multilateralism," helps us to understand both the persistence of contemporary multilateralism and the major changes that it is currently undergoing.

Whether or not negotiations on the TTIP represent another example of counter-multilateralism is one of the key questions explored in the subsequent chapters in this volume. If they do, as a result, the newly created institution will challenge the established ones that are governing the transatlantic financial and commercial relations and which have historically been central to the transatlantic relationship. The concept of counter-multilateralism raises an important question: will the TTIP constitute continuation and strengthening of the global trade regime and the strategy of regime maintenance or, in contrast, will the TTIP lead to a fundamental departure, involving a profound contestation of the established rules, norms, and practices?

Chapter 3

Transatlantic Partnership and Global Governance from the EU's Perspective

Mario Telò

The Historical Background of the Transatlantic Economic and Security Dialogue since the Second World War: Between Americanism and European Autonomy

Contrary to US policy in the Asia-Pacific, transatlantic relations quickly evolved from a bilateral partnership with the UK (1941) towards a multilateral relationship. Since 1943–47, the common global context of the Bretton Woods and the United Nations (UN) multilateral organizations framed the transatlantic partnership (Clark 2011, Patrick 2009, Telò 2014b), while a regionalist option still inspired the 'hemispheric' organization 'Panamericana' as the first regional/interregional institution (Nye 1968) and bilateral relations were favoured with the East-Asian allies, such as the alliance with Japan.

In the post-war (originally Rooseveltian) Grand Design, the transatlantic multilateral/regional partnership (e.g. the 'Marshall Plan') and the Organization for Economic Cooperation and Development (OECD), and the North Atlantic Treaty Organization (NATO) complemented the global multilateral set-up led by the US: on the one hand, the UN system and, on the other hand, the monetary system based on the dollar, the World Bank and the International Monetary Fund (IMF). Such a framework seemed to be the best for an 'embedded capitalism' (Ruggie 1993), combining the transatlantic market and military alliance on one side with national Keynesian macroeconomic policies and regional integration in Europe on the other. Since 1947, the GATT Article XXIV was the concrete symbol of this complementarity where regional arrangements (notably the European Common Market) were legitimized as derogation, or an intermediary step, towards global market liberalization. As a result of the start of the Cold War in 1947, the scope of the partnership was limited to Western Europe and the Cold War changed for several decades the hierarchy between security and civilian/trade issues.

From 1947 to 1973, a European competition took place between the British vision of a free trade area (since 1960, the European Free Trade Association or EFTA) and the vision of the founding fathers of the European Communities (EC) – notably Monnet – i.e. integration through supranational institutions. The early EC project (from the European Coal and Steel Community (ECSC) to the European Economic Community (EEC)) was paradoxically autonomous from the

US to a lesser and, at the same time, to a larger extent than EFTA: to a lesser extent, because it only included NATO members (with the single exception of Ireland which became an EC member in 1973). The EC therefore welcomed the overarching role of the transatlantic security community and did not include neutral countries such as Sweden and Austria. However, the EC was simultaneously more autonomous from the US than the UK-led free trade area because its emphasis on a deeper regional integration which was called for by the EC's supranational institutions; it created a fledgling political project that was potentially able to foster the development of a new political actor expressing a European political international identity, characterized by a more equal transatlantic partnership.

European integration combined exogenous factors stemming from the Cold War and US hegemony with internal factors. How did the main European political cultures understand the balance between the European integration process and the transatlantic partnership? Two poles emerged as a perennial dichotomy, balancing continuity and change. Following the Second World War, on the one hand, the deeply rooted and pluralist tradition of thinking that identified the US with modernity enjoyed a sort of revival. Based on the dynamic interplay between the American and French revolutions and the seminal work of Alexis de Tocqueville on 'Democracy in America' along with the new wave of 'Americanism' which spread during the early decades of the twentieth century, as described by Siegfried (see Allen 1953), Philip (1927), De Man (1919), Gramsci (1978) and others,[1] the US was the symbol of modernity and democracy which was understood as 'an expansion of the European civilization' even according to critical thinkers. To understand commitment to the transatlantic unity by, among others, Monnet, Spaak, de Gasperi and Spinelli without taking into account such an 'Americanist' pluralist background would be impossible.

On the other hand, after 1945, several critical junctures in the area of geopolitical and economic interests as well as values fostered an emphasis on the need for enhanced European political autonomy. This need for greater political autonomy would crystalize in several national and transnational political cultures: from de Gaulle's policy of *grandeur* to emphasis on the '*exception culturelle*' and, more largely, the Catholic accent on the distinctive 'European social model' as well as from the transnational peace movement of the 1970s–80s to the theory of the '*Geschiedene West*' by Jürgen Habermas (2006), underpinning the massive bottom-up mobilization against the Iraq War. These various political and cultural streams seeking more European autonomy grew over time, and keep growing, far beyond the old protectionism and the extreme right- and left-wing anti-Americanism. The 2013–15 public debate on TTIP is conditioned by this controversial and dialectic background.

---

1   The two-way interplay was shown by D. McCullough (2011).

The EC/EU Approach Combining Regionalism, Globalism and Transatlantic Relations

The international literature does not often enough emphasize the fact that the European project since its very beginning includes not only a distinctive concept/ practice of the relationship between the state and market but also a critical approach to globalism. The main distinctive feature of the European project is its *"finalité politique"*, and interest in regional integration which saw the creation of a multidimensional regional entity with its own varied set of regional priorities and regulations and a special focus on interregional relations.

It is evident that this project has, since the time of its 'founding fathers', entailed the idea of combining it with a transatlantic alliance as a two-step 'security community' (as termed by Karl Deutsch, see Deutsch et al. 1957) and *de facto* symbiotic economic integration with the US. However, deepening and widening of regional cooperation in the context of global multilateralism (even beyond the GATT Article XXIV) inevitably fostered political dynamics of discontinuity as well as several critical junctures. For instance in 1971, in the context of the end of the Bretton Woods monetary system, the first project of a European currency would take shape. After the end of the Cold War in 1989–91, distinct European geopolitical interests emerged: in the context of the 'liberal peace' (see Gamble 2012 and Gamble's chapter in this book), with the end of the Soviet nuclear threat, incentives for security alliance with the US have obviously decreased. Moreover, during the presidency of George W. Bush, the EU showed its wish for enhanced political autonomy in the context of aggravating transatlantic rifts and trade conflicts (i.e. the steel industry).

All in all, notwithstanding trade deviations, from the EC as a regional common market, including a distinct regulatory system, to the euro as a regional monetary stability project, the EC/EU has developed an alternative model with an increasingly autonomous set of regional priorities. Since the 1957 Common Market (and, since 1992, the Single Market), the EC/EU has offered an alternative to an FTA model: a model which is supported by common institutions and shared norms and codes (North 1991, Damro 2012). In fact, territorially and regionally regulated capitalism interplays in very complex ways with globalization in the context of an evolving Westphalian system (Clark 1999).

Furthermore, European market-based regionalism gradually became a model for deeper regional cooperation abroad and, directly or indirectly, supported regionalism on other continents both through other regional groupings 'mimicking' European regionalism and through the EU's conscious interregional policies along a hub-and-spoke model. These evolving interregional efforts included institutional relations with: the African, Caribbean and Pacific (ACP) countries (from Yaoundé to Cotonou Conventions), fostering regional cooperation on the African continent (Economic Community of West African States or ECOWAS, Southern African Development Community or SADEC) and in the Caribbean (Caribbean Community or CARICOM); and the EU's expanding influence in Asia

(Association of South-East Asian Nations or ASEAN, South Asian Association for Regional Cooperation or SAARC) and Latin America (Southern Common Market or MERCOSUR, Andean Community of Nations or CAN). In parallel, two systems of cooperation emerged, often driven by 'domino-effects' (Baldwin 1993), combining globalism, regionalism and conscious policies of 'competitive inter-regionalism' (Hettne 2007). These EU- or US-led competing platforms included the Single European Act (SEA, 1987–92), the North American Free Trade Agreement (NAFTA, 1994), the Free Trade Area of the Americas project (FTAA-ALCA, 1994), the 'Rio Process' (1999), the Asia-Pacific Economic Cooperation (APEC, 1993, started in 1989) and the Asia-Europe Meeting (ASEM, 1996). In the context of the scramble for 'emerging markets' (Bergsten 1994), both the EU and the US were looking for competitive regional and interregional arrangements shaping globalization according to their respective interests.

The literature largely agrees on similarities and differences between both approaches: according to the soft 'NAFTA model' (Sbragia 2007), the US-centred partnerships are more asymmetrical and limited to supporting soft regional trade liberalization (FTAs), but nothing more than that. Furthermore, in case of any problems, these partnerships rapidly revert to bilateral arrangements. The competitive EU-centred model favours deeper and multidimensional regionalism abroad (cf. MERCOSUR, ASEAN). This kind of regionalism, i.e. supporting inter-regional relations, became an 'identifier' of the EU's external relations in the 1990s. This is understandable since bloc-to-bloc relations play into a mirror effect which strengthens the EU's internal integration and cohesion. For the past decades, this approach was compatible with the global GATT-WTO negotiations. However, since 2006 the EU is increasingly favouring bilateral 'preferential trade agreements' (PTAs) with single countries, interregional negotiations and bilateral 'Strategic Partnerships' with emerging powers[2] The WTO deadlock may be considered a critical juncture explaining the end of the previous era. It sets into motion a new set of path-dependencies (Jupille et al. 2013), affecting both US trade policy and, in 2006, the consequential decision by EU Commissioner Mandelson to re-orient the EU's trade policy. However, as a regional actor, the EU is perhaps better equipped than others to adjust itself to the potential WTO (and, politically, the UN) deadlocks by way of a possible regionalist piecemeal change, paving the way to a reformed multilateralism.[3]

---

2   The EU's strategic partners include the US, Canada, Russia, China, India, Brazil, Japan, Mexico, South Africa and Korea. Each Strategic Partnership is based on political dialogue and economic and cultural cooperation (see Grevi 2013).

3   Pascal Lamy stated that 'although 80 [per cent] of the job is done, negotiations are considering the remaining 20 [per cent], staring at each other waiting for the other side to move first. Obviously nobody wants to move first by fear that its moves could be pocketed by others without obtaining anything in return' (WTO 2010).

The Changing Post-Cold War Security Alliance from George W. Bush to Barack Obama

In the period after the end of the Cold War and the Soviet nuclear threat, observers stressed the oscillating European approach to the transatlantic security partnership. In the context of NATO's post-1991 identity crisis, Europeans did not agree on what kind of relationship with the US they wanted. They oscillated between, on the one hand, reviving and widening while rebalancing NATO and, on the other hand, a vague quest for an autonomous *'Europe security identity'* (Howorth 2013).

The quest for transatlantic complementarity was symbolized by the NATO Berlin plus agreement (2002). The NATO-EU security agreement included: an exchange of classified information under reciprocal security protection rules, access to NATO planning capabilities for the EU-led Crisis Management Operations (CMOs), availability of NATO assets and capabilities for the EU-led CMOs and the mutually reinforcing capability requirements, incorporation of the military needs and capabilities within NATO's defence planning which are required for the EU-led military operations and the EU-NATO consultation arrangements in the context of EU-led CMOs. On the other hand, the quest for rebalancing of the Western alliance was represented by the Western European Union (WEU) and the European Security and Defence Policy (ESDP) as a presumed hard core of an EU autonomous security identity (Helsinki European Council 1999). This second model evolved into a competitive political pole at the height of the worst transatlantic rift and as a reaction to the National Security Strategy and 'preventive war' (2002–05) by George W. Bush. The Franco-German-Belgian-Luxembourgish Joint Declaration on European Defence (29 April 2003) was a symbol of this rift (and of the EU's internal divisions): it was published as the Blair, Berlusconi and Aznar governments joined the Bush-led 'coalition of the willing'.

During Obama's era (2008–16), the US and the EU have set out a revived common transatlantic security discourse. The US started by a clear break with unilateralism and announced its 'return to multilateralism'. Obama has also been the first US president to accept a multipolar world while maintaining US military spending levels at about 640 billion dollars (Stockholm International Peace Research Institute 2013). A relative shift to the Pacific ('Pivot to Asia') is the direct consequence of the global economic trends and not only of US trade and financial bilateral interdependence with China. In contrast, perception of a US-China 'duopoly' after the Copenhagen UN Conference (2009) was exaggerated, as demonstrated by the revived bilateral tensions, notably around the Trans Pacific Partnership (TPP) which excludes China, and the revived Pacific bilateral alliances with Japan and other Asian countries (see the US Defense Strategic Guidance, US Department of Defense 2012).

In the post-Lisbon Treaty context, Europeans moved from an early 'Obamania' to repeated misunderstandings with the US regarding both low and high politics. The US cancelled the EU-US bilateral summit in 2009 while the 2010 Lisbon NATO Summit which widened its membership to 28 was an apparent success thanks to NATO's restructuring, withdrawal from Afghanistan and a new concept addressing terrorism and cyberterrorism. Furthermore, the impact of the financial and economic crises was also complex and ambivalent. Regarding the G20, the EU shifted from an initially leading role in London (2008) to that of a 'sick man' of the global economy in Cannes (2012).

Burden-sharing still represents a serious transatlantic cleavage. Even more so after the sovereign debt crisis, the European states continue to cut their national defence budgets and the Common Foreign and Security Policy (CFSP)/ESDP shows a low profile despite US expectations. In qualitative terms, budgetary trends are not improving; declining R&D spending is combined with lower coordination among EU Member States. The US-EU Strategic Partnership did not perform badly on several international issues (Road Map for Iran; the 2013 deal between Serbia and Kosovo). However, the NATO-led Libya intervention (2011) is a matter of controversial evaluation on both sides of the Atlantic (Howorth 2013). In any case, it illustrates the CFSP's paralysis when France and Germany diverge. The 2014 crises in Ukraine and Syria/Iraq have exposed different perceptions of (in) security, including energy security. However, the US and the EU combine convergent and divergent orientations within the current unstable multipolar environment. In such a transitional context, the transatlantic economic and trade dimensions are returning to the forefront with the TTIP negotiations process.

All in all, a policy opportunity may change the balance between Atlantic solidarity and the EU's autonomy as illustrated by the Libyan and Syrian conflicts (2011 and 2013) as well as by the Ukrainian conflict with Russia (2014). However, in this context, the most relevant piece of news is that Germany is no longer the 'stalwart ally' which it once was (see also Mayer's chapter in this book). Berlin has outgrown its status as NATO's junior partner and has gradually become the leader of a low profile, trading and civilian EU foreign policy which is characterized by military budgets of on average about 1 per cent of the GDP (1.38 per cent in 2013). Hence Germany plays a key role in the entire process of the TTIP negotiations.

The EU and TTIP (2011–15): Four Political Challenges

TTIP represents both continuity and change: the previous 'New Transatlantic Agenda' (NTA, 1995) and the 'Transatlantic Business Dialogue' (1994) (see Hocking and McGuire 2004 and, notably, Peterson's contribution) were conditioned by the transition from the post-Cold War context to the 'unipolar momentum' (2000–05). TTIP should be explained through the systemic change which occurred over the last decade (from the second George W. Bush mandate to both Obama administrations) towards a multipolar world order. It combines an exit strategy out of the worst post-war economic and financial crisis with a geopolitical dimension regarding the relationship between the 'West' and the 'Rest'. The bridge between the two dimensions is clear when an opportunity for a joint action of relief out of the recession and fostering growth, trade and jobs by exploiting the strong transatlantic economic potential (representing 40 per cent of global trade and 50 per cent of global GDP)[4] is combined with a global power stake: is it possible to maintain Western traditional primacy in global rule-setting and standardization (Sapir 2007) in the new challenging multipolar context where global trade negotiations are in a deadlock (notably the WTO Doha Development Round (DDR)) and the growth trend is strongly in favour of the Asian giants? This major political challenge is complemented with five political issues which have been addressed both in the public debate and by the academic literature and set the context around TTIP:

a. Is the negotiation structurally uneven since the EU as a non-state polity is being disadvantaged when bargaining with the sole remaining superpower? Is the EU necessarily the loser of a competitive zero-sum game? This assumption has been disproven by comparative research. Although the EU is subject to a fragmented decision-making process, it is not the case in this policy field: according to the Treaty (TFEU Art. 207), the Commission negotiates on behalf of 28 EU Member States on the basis of a Council decision (June 2013).[5] Obviously, the EU's institutional complexity matters and the Commission delivers its reports on a regular basis to a special Council committee, i.e. to 28 Member States, and the European Parliament (EP) committees under the co-decision procedure. Furthermore, coordination by DG Trade with several other Commission DGs is required and interventions by the High Representative for Foreign and Security Affairs (who is, as a Vice-President of the Commission, also in charge of coordinating the entire array of the EU's external relations) are possible. Finally, EU governance must take into account the voices raised by NGOs and the critical public opinion as well as repeated calls for enhanced transparency. During the EP elections campaign in April–May 2014, TTIP proved to be a very challenging topic. The EU's institutional set up, however, limits the internal complexity through the selectiveness of roles of both the Council of Ministers and the Commission.

On the other hand, international literature on Foreign Policy Analysis states that the US also faces an internal challenge of fragmentation in its foreign policy in general and in its commercial policy in particular. Many

---

4   Joint Statement following the EU-US Summit, 28 November 2011; 'We must intensify our efforts to realize the untapped potential of transatlantic economic cooperation to generate new opportunities for jobs and growth ... To that end, we have directed the TEC [Transatlantic Economic Council] to establish a joint High Level Working Group on Jobs and Growth ... We ask the Working Group to identify and assess options for strengthening the U.S.-EU economic relationship, especially those that have the highest potential to support jobs and growth' (White House 2011).

5   The negotiation mandate includes four chapters: market access, regulatory issues, trade-related rules and trade multilateralism.

tendencies towards a 'fragmented authority' exist in the US. The decision-making process is marked by institutional complexity (Allison and Zelikow 1999) and socio-economic lobbying (Milner 1997, Löwy 1964). If we take the three-level classification of foreign policies (fragmented, elitist and poly-archic) into account, we can talk about two comparably poly-archic negotiation processes on both sides of the Atlantic: the EU Commission and its DGs play the role of a strategic actor comparable with the US administration, while the Council of Ministers and the EP/national parliaments are comparable with the classical role of the US Congress (Schattschneider 1935). Moreover, the fragmented and critical pressures by domestic constituencies (both private and public) are numerous, decentralized and split in the EU, but still present in the US as well. The fast-track procedures of any kind look equally problematic on both sides of the Atlantic. All in all, if Athens cries, Sparta does not laugh: both the EU and the US have huge internal problems of foreign policy consistency and coherence.[6]

Furthermore, the US-EU negotiations are not hierarchical. The US cannot unilaterally assert its standards and rules, particularly those concerning parts (b) and (c) of the negotiation agenda (non-tariff barriers, or NTBs, and 'regulatory issues'). Any US arrogance would not be 'irresistible' because the EU's standards are generally much more sophisticated thanks to the fact that they are a product of long *internal* multilateral negotiations. To forecast an inevitable end of the EU's regulatory distinctiveness underestimates that the EU has the following cards to play. The EU's market power is based on a solid background of rules, institutions and values. True, the European socio-environmental regulations can only survive provided they are able to compete and expand beyond EU borders. But the EU may show that only if it is framed by socio-environmental rules which are sophisticated and institutionalized (not national, but European and, to some extent, transatlantic), a common market can provide the expected benefits.

To conclude, even if partially uneven, negotiations are not as imbalanced as to necessarily give birth to a kind of 'leonine pact'. TTIP is much less asymmetric than other US-led negotiations such as the Bretton Woods arrangements of 1944, the recent FTAA and APEC or the current TPP (although here, too, Japan and the ASEAN countries proved able to resist the overwhelming pressures of the US more than in the past). By scrutinizing the negotiation process, its rules and procedures, a complex mix of bilateralism and multilateralism emerges, while the 'general principles of conduct' stop any unilateral arrogance. Of course, many

---

6　For example, the second round of negotiations (scheduled for 7–11 October 2013 in Brussels) was cancelled because of the consequences of the US government 'shutdown'. The first round of negotiations (Washington, DC, 8–12 July 2013) covered 20 areas and included a meeting with 350 stakeholders.

variables will influence the final TTIP outcome: from the European side, the EU's internal vertical and horizontal cohesion and the controversial degree of legitimacy among national public opinions.

b. Are 'issue linkages' necessarily in favour of the US? The US still provides the EU with military security within NATO and, potentially, in case of tensions – notably those provoked by Putin's Russia – with a possible energy security. Both these asymmetries matter, but they do not change the systemic framework, making a post-hegemonic multilateralism possible (Keohane 1984). It would be a paradox to acritically revive the theories of US 'empire' or 'hegemony' within the current multipolar and uncertain global context.

Furthermore, European states are also able to raise possible issue linkages of political nature against any arrogant move. For example, private data protection is such a sensitive political issue that bipartisan pressures from the EP and the German Bundestag asked for a suspension of the TTIP negotiations until the US provides serious guarantees and firm commitments to stop such humiliating practices. Such demands showing European political autonomy should not be underestimated because they are particularly strong precisely in the country which has traditionally been more in favour of TTIP, i.e. Germany, led by conservative Chancellor Angela Merkel (see Mayer's chapter in this book).

Germany matters in the transatlantic negotiations more than any other European player and more than any time before. Between the French economic and trade protectionist approach to TTIP, combined with a revived political understanding with the US (see Libya, Mali and Syria) on the one hand and, on the other hand, the UK's approach which is characterized by an economic and political symbiosis with the US, Germany seeks to combine its traditional support for transatlantic economic and trade integration with enhanced political autonomy in the areas of both external (Libya, Syria and Ukraine) and internal security (private data protection). Germany's provisional rejection of the Comprehensive Economic Trade Agreement (CETA) with Canada was warning a strong opposition to the American understanding of the investor-state dispute settlement mechanism (ISDS, see *Neue Gesellschaft* 2014). Moreover, Germany is not isolated: convergences with Italy, Belgium and the Scandinavian countries are emerging and this approach is likely to become the EU's mainstream.

Accordingly, the acceptance of TTIP by domestic public opinion is only possible provided that: firstly, a critical stance is taken by EU institutions regarding the most sensitive transatlantic issues, i.e. ISDS and the private data protection of EU citizens (by the US National Security Agency (NSA) and based on the Foreign Intelligence Surveillance Act (FISA)); secondly, TTIP does not weaken the Eurozone's internal cohesion which is going to be strengthened after the sovereign debt crisis under Merkel's pressure and in the interest of Germany, France, Italy and other EU Member States who are favouring a 'hard core' approach to EU integration. Of course, the expected changes in the EU's internal trade flows will be uneven, which is another explanation of variations in national perceptions from Germany and Italy to France and other Member States. However, internal divergences are not going to develop only along the lines of Northern vs Southern Europe. The political will towards an enhanced and closer cooperation among 19 Eurozone members will be the crucial variable. Thirdly, a modest impact on CFSP is expected (and a clear stance by the HRVP would be needed), but TTIP should not have any military implications for transatlantic relations, concerning the burden-sharing and military intervention in the out of area. Fourthly, TTIP should not be presented as a 'civilization project' against the BRICS, and notably China, but as a concrete, business-focused, open and potentially inclusive agreement. Such political acts would seriously contradict any superficial perception of a *revanche* of the UK's traditional vision of the EU as a mere FTA through the TTIP.

c. The third political issue focuses on the implications of the fact that the US, as the sole remaining superpower, is leading the global game while shaping the international trade by way of two parallel negotiations, i.e. TTIP and TPP. Does the US have the second best choice (TPP as a leverage for shaping the global rules), while the EU cannot play the role of a global player by isolating the US. According to the leading scholarly literature, the international system has since the 1970s and 1980s entered into a 'post-hegemonic era' (Keohane 1984). Obama cannot stop this *longue durée* tendency; in contrast, he is adjusting to a multipolar world. Within such an emerging multipolar context, is the US the single global and 'polygamist' trading power? The opposite is, however, true: the EU is also extending a series of interregional and bilateral trade arrangements worldwide in its capacity of first global trading power. For instance, with the Republic of Korea, Columbia and Peru, agreements exist; with Singapore and Canada, the negotiations have reached their very advanced stages; while with Japan and MERCOSUR a roadmap exists. Similar deals are likely to emerge with more regions, such as ECOWAS, SADEC and the Eastern African Community. Starting in 2005–06, both economic giants decided to look for alternatives to the WTO-DDR deadlock. For both of them, the process of 'downgrading' after the Doha Round paralysis meant diminishing their ambitions and finding temporary side routes through regionalism, inter-regionalism and bilateralism, perhaps towards new global multilateral negotiations. On the one hand, this shift towards a mix of the hub-and-spoke model and, on the other hand, possible degradation towards a kind of 'spaghetti bowl' mix is similar for both trade giants. The key difference from the perspective of EU Member States is their spontaneously shared belief that an alternative to an inefficient global multilateralism may be set through regional and interregional arrangements which is a belief that is directly linked to the EU's own nature as a regional entity.

d. The fourth political issue at stake is internal legitimacy, depending on the electoral cycles and social consensus in both the EU and the US. In the twenty-first century, contrary to the twentieth century, an answer to the strong call for an enhanced legitimacy can no longer simply be addressed by arguing about the democratic nature of the contracting states. Particularly in the EU what is needed is a supplementary supranational legitimacy which can only be provided by combining the roles of the two levels of the European parliamentary system (the EP plus national parliaments, see European Parliament 2013) with the direct involvement of NGOs. Many indicators have highlighted that TTIP suffers from a democratic deficit: see, for instance, the controversy about the initial negotiating mandate, demands of transparency during the negotiations process, the shared distrust of lobbying by private companies and the revival of protectionist reflexes, anti-Americanism and various domestic pressures and cleavages. This challenge is stronger in the EU, although it is not absent in US domestic politics. On both sides of the Atlantic, an enhanced regulation of trade through new rules and supranational procedures inevitably raises multiple demands for information, participation, accountability and democratic control by the democratic public opinion, trade unions and national parliaments. This is the reason why the European Commission promoted a large public consultation in 2014. The twenty-first-century governance cannot omit the challenge of enhanced legitimacy without affecting its own credibility in providing an efficient performance (Keohane 2006).

The New Scenarios: Contested Multilateralism and/or 'Peace by Pieces'?

An integrated post-hegemonic Western approach may be fit for a multipolar 'no one's world' (Kupchan 2013) only as long as the TTIP negotiations and an eventual agreement are consistent with one of the two alternatives for the forthcoming multilateralism: a contingent, minilateral, cooperation or a virtuous 'peace by pieces' scenario. Rather than simply downsizing and downgrading the trade negotiations, the relationship between TTIP and the WTO is a typical example of 'contested multilateralism through competitive regime creation' (see Keohane and Morse's chapter in this book). What is distinctive is that the new coalition is combining a state (the US) with a regional grouping of states (the EU).

The umbrella concept of 'contested multilateralism' emphasizes a change in the international system. The TTIP process revealed such large internal and external difficulties that we can only observe that the official discourse which combines the transatlantic agreement with a worldwide perspective of TTIP as benefitting everyone[7] is realistically replaced by multi-layered, controversial and

---

7   The 2012 report, *A New Era for Transatlantic Trade Leadership: A Report from the Transatlantic Task Force on Trade and Investment*, states that the 'revival of bilateral trade

uncertain negotiations. The previously integrated trade system will be replaced by new regime complexes, including interregional arrangements. Nobody can, however, so far predict the outcome of TTIP. The elites on both sides of the Atlantic have invested so much in TTIP that its failure is excluded; TTIP's failure is also excluded because of its likely implications for the deepening of internal divisions within the EU.

TTIP is not a simple FTA: while cutting down tariff barriers is relatively easy, difficulties soon emerged in 2013–14 as NTBs and regulatory issues were touched upon (for example, public procurement, transport, issues covered by the 'Reach' directive and/or linked to the EU's environmental standards, car emissions, public health issues, agriculture, phytosanitary issues, services, explicitly value-driven issues such as GMOs, food safety and, in general, all issues where different histories, public perceptions and culture matter). The creation of an ISDS arbitration court emerged as a highly controversial issue in 2014, notably because of the German opposition to the marginalization of national courts.

Now that the early rhetorical goal of concluding the TTIP in 2014 has already been missed, the more realistic alternative scenarios for 2015 are: firstly, the classical 'long harvest for a little corn', with only tariff reductions along with some progress in harmonizing regulation of new issues such as ICTs, while leaving an open door for future steps. In case of such an outcome which can be defined as a contingent mini-lateralism[8] not much will change in either the transatlantic or global power balance even if the political impact of a transatlantic agreement should not be underestimated (e.g. a 'domino effect' for other negotiations). Alternatively, a more comprehensive arrangement can be reached. Which one?

The international response to the current stage of negotiations (at the time of writing, the latest, 6th round took place in Brussels in July 2014) is showing ambivalent signals. Some of these responses allow for dark forecasts about the strengthening of competing trading fortresses (Gilpin 2000) which have been called by Jagdish Bhagwati and others the 'stumbling blocks scenario', while others recalled a possible revival of the cleavage between developed and developing countries that could have been observed at the Cancun WTO Meeting in 2003. The BRICS countries are expressing their worries and China's leadership (Xi Jinping and Li Keqiang) is restyling its Asian policy by upgrading the 'ASEAN plus 1', 'ASEAN plus 3' and the Regional Comprehensive Economic Partnership (RCEP), all of these regional groupings excluding the US and the EU (see Zhang's chapter in this book), while reviving the problematic energy alliance with Russia

---

and regulation partnership between the United States and the European Union ... can create jobs and growth' on the one hand and, on the other hand, 'can play a necessary and unique leadership role in promoting economic welfare both within the transatlantic marketplace and worldwide' (GMF and ECIPE 2012).

8   The contingent mini-lateralism can be defined as: 'getting together the smallest possible number of countries needed to have the largest possible impact on solving a particular problem' (Naim 2012).

(May 2014). Moreover, India, after the 2014 elections that brought Narendra Modi to power, has surprisingly refused to ratify the Bali WTO Agreement (December 2013). Lastly, the Trade in Services Agreement (TISA) negotiations on services liberalization among 23 parties, including the EU, is getting out of the WTO context.

However, in the case of TTIP as a more comprehensive arrangement, the magniloquent perspective of an 'economic NATO' as an opposition of the West *vis-à-vis* the Rest is unlikely. Several possible intermediary scenarios may emerge beyond the sole tariff barriers reduction. The current situation of 'contested multilateralism' may pave the way for various complex, fragmented and instrumental mini-negotiations and *ad hoc* regimes, mixing the regional, territorial, functional, sectoral, bilateral and interregional levels and modes.

In a more optimistic outlook, 'contested multilateralism' may open the door to a win-win game, benefitting not only the two Atlantic giants but also a large majority of the global trade players. However, this would be very difficult and totally unlikely without the following three conditions:

- Firstly, a clear choice in favour of openness means a commitment to change, through targeted diplomatic action, the ideational negative perceptions of TTIP as a Western defensive and fragmented approach to trade governance (which would provoke trade diversions and where the two main global economic powers would be further seen as marginalizing the global multilateral fora in favour of mega-regionalism/bilateralism/ inter-regionalism while jeopardizing the WTO framework by the BRICS nations, South Korea, Mexico, South America and others). However, openness does not mean widening membership but sharing the best outcomes with other regimes.
- Secondly, a political endeavour to manage in an appropriate way the large geopolitical implications of trade and investment rule-setting. Since de Tocqueville we know that trade policy is the first step in foreign policy and that trade rules entail power implications. In a post-hegemonic era, interpolar links will matter very much: the transatlantic link has to demonstrate its potential role as a driving force for fair and even global regulation and for fostering concrete gains for other players and regimes.
- Thirdly, a clearer rejection of any kind of a Western 'civilizational option' (based on Huntington's concept of 'clash of civilizations') against the Rest would be consistent with both the EU's vision and Obama's policy. Provided that TPP also limits TTIP's conflicting potential as a global strategy containing China, the option of an 'alliance of like-minded democracies against authoritarian regimes' (Kagan 2012) is not the mode of the current US leadership, aware that it is impossible to recast the classical US singular hegemony: the US does not want and cannot pursue such a strategy also because of the weight of many domestic factors. In any case, this option would be impossible for the EU: the strategy of a closed Western bloc is

neither the EU's preference nor interest and would be rejected by internal oppositions, notably in Germany. However, since misunderstandings are spreading, multiplying the communication ties with China, India, Brazil and other partners and keeping them informed on a regular basis about the progress and obstacles will be a crucial variable. The positive interplay of TTIP with the US- and EU-led negotiations with other Asian[9] and American partners[10] will also be extremely relevant; will the EU be able to mobilize its special approach of combining trade negotiations with a comprehensive issue linkage (including environment, climate change, financial regulation, public procurement, research etc.)?

Such a 'peace by pieces' strategy would not amount to a replication of the past 'stepping stone scenario' that combined the complementary global and regional market liberalization (see the GATT Article XXIV and the context of the 1940s–80s world): this option is now challenged to multilateralize a multipolar world. A dynamic multi-layered, regionalist and interregionalist approach to global governance could maybe emerge: while soft arrangements such as NAFTA and FTAA tend to fail, a deeper regional integration appears as the method possibly paving the way towards a new multilateralism. Contrary to a 'spaghetti bowl', there is room for various coexisting modes of innovative regional governance, including 'experimentalist global governance' (De Burca, Keohane and Sabel 2013, Zeitlin and Sabel 2011) and a less contingent multilateralism (Telò 2014a) which is open to the general principles of conduct, a deeper integrationist agenda and diffuse reciprocity.

This new multilateralist perspective would see the EU to have a special twofold role to play, stemming from the solid background of its regulated market and deep regional cooperation. On the one hand, the EU, provided a successful internal consolidation, should update its regulatory framework and embedded capitalism in order to make them more sustainable within the global liberalization/competition. On the other hand, it should revive the collective leadership of the multilateral network (G20, WTO and the UN Security Council) as a strong pressure balancing both fragmentation and *Realpolitik*, the new medievalism and the logic of hard power balance.

However, also the external variables would play a crucial role. How could the WTO, its 160 Member States in this complex context, re-start the DDR after only controversial progress at its Bali 2013 Ministerial Conference (see Mavroidis' chapter in this book)? Will it be possible to somehow overcome the rigid

---

9   The EU is about to give relevant signals for an 'EU-China Investment Agreement' (including market access, legal security, nondiscrimination etc.). The negotiations of an FTA with Japan are ongoing and were also fostered by the completed FTA with South Korea. On the contrary, the EU-India Annual Summit was cancelled in 2014.

10   The bilateral FTA negotiations with the EU are ongoing: a quasi-agreement was reached with Canada in October 2013 while negotiations remain problematic with Brazil.

unanimity rule and other Westphalian legacies? Will it be possible to coordinate any serious reforms of the WTO and international organizations (representation rules, rotation on a regional basis etc.) while enhancing their legitimacy and accountability? Without any new collective leadership, nothing will be possible. Only in this context, non-governmental networks, advocacy groups and epistemic communities may play a major role by multiplying the links and communication for a better multilevel global governance. New initiatives are needed, thus reviving a multi-layered, more efficient and more legitimate multilateralism. New ideas are also needed:[11] new actors should intervene both before the multilateral agreements are concluded and during their implementation.

We can define such a virtuous process, where the states and regions jointly select their converging priorities across multilateral fora, as a 'peace by pieces' scenario, i.e. a regional way towards a possible multi-layered multilateralism and, furthermore, an opportunity for a more progressive, social and environmental shaping of the globalization (*Neue Gesellschaft* 2014). 'Contested multilateralism' does not mean the end of multilateral global governance. By contrast, it may open the way to alternative scenarios, i.e. either a spreading of the unstable, contingent and merely functional forms of cooperation, or a more complex and mixed array of various dynamic arrangements where some of them are instrumental and *ad hoc*, albeit combined with a lively framework for further progress, including the diffuse reciprocal forms of multilateralism both of a functional and territorial kind. The current process is open-ended and demands further theoretical work by deepening the complex features of the forthcoming multilateral cooperation: when interdependence is high and power widely dispersed, multilateral institutions are the essential tools for both state and non-state actors. Similarly to the uncertain interaction between the 'Chiang Mai Initiative' or the European Stability Mechanism (ESM) and the IMF, the complex interplay of TTIP and TPP with the WTO may provide evidence of an institutional change that is occurring and changing the balance between territorial, regional and global multilateralism. How do they coexist?

Deeper, territorially-based and multilateral regimes that are inspired by diffuse reciprocity may establish a competitive or collaborative framework with contingent, functional, instrumental and *ad hoc* multilateral cooperation arrangements and regimes. The conditions for complex balances between regionalism, interregionalism and globalism exist today much more than they did in the 1930s and in the post-Second World War hegemonic era. Regional blocs, interregional arrangements and large national players may coexist and pursue both cooperative and competitive policies within a shared global framework.

Are the global multilateral arrangements and organizations definitely the losers of contested multilateralism, characterized by their declining authority and status? While states and regions are looking for alternative options, it is hard to imagine that

---

11   For example, see Zhang's chapter in this book suggesting the creation of a new 'forward thinking trade policy group'.

global governance could only develop out of a bottom-up process of aggregation of regional and interregional agreements, a kind of 'club of clubs'. In this evolving context, the benefits of regional and interregional arrangements still look larger than their costs, but a multilevel regime complex, including the stabilizing global dimension, is needed. The role of international global institutions and fora (such as the G7 or the G20) remains crucial: they are there to provide more than a meeting point and common language. They need to offer a realistic collective strategic leadership for the agenda-setting, the identification of priorities and their sequencing, indicating the long-term objectives while keeping the possibility of a compromise permanently open so that member states or regional actors can reach an agreement on specific issues and their common challenges. Since most of the international institutions have specific missions to carry out, the issue linkages and interplay among different institutions in a post-hegemonic world could be driven by the convergence of the leading players, ultimately consolidating the emergence of global multilateral networks and multilevel regimes complexes. A neo-regionalist agenda should not be confused with a mere deregulating liberalization agenda. In this perspective, TTIP may perhaps contribute to opening a new multilevel, pluralist and multilateralist era.

PART II
Negotiations, Actors and Agencies

Between 'NATO for Trade' and 'Pride in Angst': The German TTIP Debate and its Spill-over into Wider Transatlantic Concerns

Hartmut Mayer

Introduction

> I have travelled all around the Member States, from the United Kingdom, to Spain, Poland or Bulgaria. Everybody is interested in TTIP. But nowhere in Europe is the debate as lively as in Germany. (Karel De Gucht, European Commissioner for Trade and Europe's Chief TTIP Negotiator, 2014)

When on 11 February 2013 the High Level Working Group (HLWG) on Jobs and Growth of the Transatlantic Economic Council (TEC) recommended to the US and the EU to aim for a most ambitious and comprehensive trade agreement, it revived the old idea of a transatlantic free trade area that had been around for more than two decades. Similar ideas had originally been proposed as 'TAFTA' in the immediate post-Cold War era in the 1990s (Piper 1995). Germany, from its very inception, had always been at the heart of the negotiations of a transatlantic free trade area. For example, Foreign Minister Klaus Kinkel pushed the idea in a much publicized speech in Chicago in April 1995 (Businessweek 1995). When the newly united Germany searched for its place in a domestic debate 20 years ago (Mayer 1997), an integrated transatlantic economic area was seen as both an engine for growth and as the revival of the transatlantic partnership as the indispensable anchor of stability in a rapidly changing world order. It is therefore no surprise that the idea resurfaced in 2006/7 under the German EU presidency. Today, TTIP became the latest concrete reincarnation of a strategic vision that saw Germany integrated both into the EU and into a wider common Western economic space. It would allow Europeans, embedded into a newly strengthened community of liberal values and economic practices, to engage and trade with confidence and security with the rapidly emerging powers and regions in the twenty-first century.

Having been an unsuccessful aspiration for more than 20 years, no one expected easy rounds of negotiation at the start of formal TTIP talks on 8 July 2013. Nonetheless, despite such serious obstacles, there was a strong political will to succeed and huge optimism about the mutual economic benefits on both sides of the Atlantic. In addition, TTIP from its very inception stood, as it did in the 1990s, for a larger transatlantic integration and for the re-affirmation of the liberal centre within a fluid global order. The old TAFTA labels, such as 'Economic NATO' (Piper 1995, Flockhart 2013), 'NATO for the World Economy' (Steingart 2006) or 'NATO for Trade' (Piper 1995) were immediately transferred to TTIP. The German term '*Wirtschafts*-NATO' (Haendel 2014), used by proponents and opponents alike, symbolizes that TTIP was seen in Germany as high global geo-politics as much as big business.

Naturally, Germany and the United States were central anchors in the project. In the words of Ambassador Miriam Sapiro who had directed the launch of TTIP in 2013, its success would 'require serious engagement at the highest level, in particular by President Obama and Chancellor Merkel. They and other leaders will have to provide clear guidance and deadlines to the negotiations, and start explaining to the public why this agreement and this partnership matter' (Sapiro 2014: 7). The truth and the curse of this statement are the starting point of this chapter.

What difference did a year make? After more than 12 months into the negotiations, political enthusiasm in Germany had completely faded. President Obama and Chancellor Merkel had lost significant trust in one another. Furthermore, much wider issues of global security and individual freedom had overshadowed the narrow trade agenda of TTIP. As far as the public debate in Germany was concerned, it was by no means prudent politicians who drove the agenda but the critical public that drove the politicians. A highly critical TTIP debate had sprung up in the media, both on- and off-line, and in many public forums to which the politicians, in silence mode for far too long, then gradually reacted with an increasing intensity. At the end of July 2014, it culminated in the German government's provisional rejection of the CETA (Gammelin 2014), the free trade agreement which has been negotiated between the EU and Canada since 2011. CETA had widely been seen as a blueprint for TTIP. When key provisions of the CETA agreement, meant to be fully confidential, were leaked in August 2014, the German daily *Süddeutsche Zeitung* dubbed it '*Stoff für Zoff*' (material for trouble) (Rexer and Brühl 2014), thereby lifting the German TTIP debate once again to a new plateau. A further intensification began in September 2014 after the European Commission announced its rejection on legal grounds of the official registration of the European Citizens' Initiative (ECI) 'STOP TTIP' that an alliance of more than 200 civil society groups had proposed to the EU in July 2014. Proponents and opponents within Germany once again sharpened their rhetorical weapons after this verdict. In the words of a German MEP, the European Commission obviously intended to 'shut out citizens from TTIP decisions' (Giegold 2014).

Due to its central economic and political position in Europe and due to its government's obvious willingness to reach autonomous decisions, an understanding of the German debate on TTIP is essential for the future of TTIP. It has clearly proved to be a 'trade agreement with side effects' (Mildner and Schmucker 2013: 1). This chapter analyses such side effects. It aims to identify the key parameters of the German debate on TTIP and its wider implications for transatlantic relations and global security. Berlin is bound to remain the decisive European voice and force in the process. German thinking and policies will clearly influence the direction and general prospects of the project. However, it is important to highlight that the German TTIP debate developed a very unique dynamic that integrated a wide-ranging set of overlapping concerns. These included narrow questions of technical trade standards, investor relations and consumer protection. These were then also blended with much wider notions of varieties of capitalism, Germany's new foreign policy and the general place of the transatlantic alliance in the new multi-polar global order. Finally, it touched upon philosophical concerns about the relationship between the state and the individual, freedom versus security and fundamental concerns about privacy, personal freedom and data protection in the age of big data global business. TTIP gradually and unintentionally became a part of what the Germans call a '*Grundsatzdiskussion*', an essential and fundamental debate. It is the purpose of this chapter to analyse the various aspects of this debate and to assess its potential impact on the ongoing TTIP negotiations.

The Substantive Issues and Concerns in the German Debate on TTIP

Within the complex German TTIP debate, trade experts, business communities, political activists, politicians and the media have together provided a vast spectrum of views. German attitudes about TTIP have been shaped by three wider underlying trends. While there is, first, still enthusiasm about the potential economic benefits, there is criticism of the US and its role in global affairs and the belief that the US is mainly trying to use TTIP to force generally lower standards on Europe. Secondly, there is to some extent an anti-globalization stance within the German opposition movement. Deeper reservations about the Anglo-Saxon form of capitalism as opposed to the traditional social market economy in Europe play a significant part. This is then, thirdly, combined with a growing anti-Brussels attitude and the notion that the EU has not been transparent enough about the TTIP negotiations at all. In order to paint a balanced picture, I identify objective technical and legal challenges of TTIP before analysing the larger strategic and political issues surrounding those perceived obstacles. As in other European countries, even the most favourable voices within the German TTIP debate agree that there are real substantive challenges.

*The Perceived Economic Benefits of TTIP and its Potential for
Adverse Consequences*

The essential starting point for all debates in Germany is the perceived benefit of TTIP and its projected stimulus for the European economy. Once completed in all its aspects on tariffs, regulatory barriers, services and procurement, TTIP is estimated to generate a permanent increase in the size of the European economy resulting in significant job creation (see e.g. CEPR 2013, de Gucht and Lambsdorff

2014). The forecasted economic benefits were particularly interesting for Germany with its export-oriented automotive industry which would likely benefit the most. Also the chemical industry, machine tool engineering and electrical industries are supposed to gain disproportionally, creating altogether up to 200,000 new jobs (CDU 2014).

While the global financial crisis since 2008 had lowered the level of trust in the general reliability and the predictive power of all economic models, there was also a significant set of arguments by economists who suggested an adverse economic impact of TTIP. Critics claimed that TTIP raised economic expectations that 'will be impossible to fulfil' (Dieter 2014). One of the reasons was the fact that the benefits of ending tariffs was always included in the interest-driven optimistic scenarios while the actual costs were ignored. The most important new costs in return for waiving taxes is the need for companies to fully document the origin of the products by issuing 'certificates of origin', a significant administrative and financial burden on small and medium-sized companies (Dieter 2014), traditionally a stronghold of the German economy. The big global multinationals on either side of the Atlantic would benefit from TTIP (Merz 2014) but there was more reluctance to extent the rosy picture to Germany's vast majority of small and medium-sized firms.

Investment Protection

The objectively most concerning issue across the entire spectrum of the German debate is the so-called investor-to-state dispute settlement (ISDS) likely to be built into the treaty. It has been the major *casus belli* for the German government in CETA as well and was used as the main reason for the government's provisional rejection of the draft CETA treaty in July 2014. The fear across Europe has been that US companies and investors could challenge EU governments directly in the private international tribunals lying outside normal state legislation. Even though EU companies investing in the US would have the same privileges, many in Europe widely perceive this as a 'massive Trojan Horse' (MEP Yannick Jadot cited in Atlantic Community 2014) for multinational companies to threaten and whittle away European legislation across a wide spectrum of policies. Critics highlight that if the threat of costly legal disputes was to prevent elected governments from enacting progressive legislation, this would be a major drawback for democracy as such.

Regulatory Standards

If one looks for symbols of the German debate on TTIP, 'hormone-cattle' and 'chlorine chickens' are the most prominent front-runners. These illustrative examples refer to differences in American and European regulatory standards in agriculture. As with every trade agreement, these standards naturally have to be re-negotiated and the bulk of the work of the trade negotiations lies in such regulatory issues. Proponents of TTIP paint an optimistic picture arguing that all such challenges can be solved in TTIP without compromising on German standards and societal values. Opponents, however, fear the 'Americanization' of public life, which would bring lower citizen protection as the unavoidable and regrettable consequence of TTIP. In the market for media attention, the 'apocalyptic versions' often carried the day even in the serious press as, for example, the front cover of *Die Zeit* ('Will we soon be dominated by America?', *Die Zeit*, Issue 27, 2014) showed. Whatever the pros and cons of regulatory harmonization might be, the lack of transparency on these issues became a source of suspicion in the German TTIP debate.

Transparency

As in other European countries, a major point of the criticism in Germany has been the lack of transparency and the generally secretive nature of the TTIP and CETA negotiations. First, as a result of the resistance of some EU Member States to publish draft texts, they are to remain secret until TTIP is concluded. Secondly, the fact that it was business communities and regulators who met in these secret meetings was interpreted by critics as evidence that mainly a corporate agenda and a predominantly pro-corporate mandate was negotiated at the expense of consumers and public life (Sawatzki 2014). Thirdly, people took issue with the fact that the negotiations were conducted mainly through Brussels, thereby feeding into growing general concerns that too much power was transferred to EU executive bodies that were not subject to democratic scrutiny. Although this is not a sentiment normally associated with pro-integrationist Germany, since the financial crisis began in 2008 there has been a steady decline in public support for the idea of further enhancing the power of the EU. In addition, various recent Constitutional Court decisions and the handling of the EU financial crises mechanisms have made the public much more aware of the delicate balance and the boundaries between German and European decision-making authority.

Cybersecurity, Data, Privacy and 'Brutal Information Capitalism' (Gabriel)

A substantive issue in 2013–14 turned out to be a very formidable game changer in the German debate: the rapidly growing public debate in Europe over big data, cybersecurity, citizens privacy and the generally diverging viewpoints across the Atlantic on the vices and virtues of the global digital economy. This general debate overlapped with the discussion on the concrete TTIP agenda. The anti-TTIP campaign made it a key point of their strategy by claiming that TTIP would, on the one hand, open 'the way for even more monitoring and surveillance of internet users' (Campact 2014) while, on the other hand, restricting users freedom through 'excessive copyright regulations' (Campact 2014) with regard to culture, education and science. However, the issue of appropriately regulating the Internet is a widespread concern across the spectrum of society in Germany. It certainly provided the environment for an increasingly critical stance in Germany with regard to TTIP and beyond.

While a dispute between Europe and the US over the role of US-based firms such as Amazon, Apple, Facebook and Google and their alleged aspiration to dominate the global digital space had been brewing for some time, 2014 clearly saw the EU being further galvanised against 'Silicon Valley's creeping global power' (Garside 2014). In May, the Court of Justice of the EU upheld the plea of a Spanish citizen who wanted pages hidden from any Google search in his name and won the 'right to be forgotten' (Garside 2014). The Court ruling had a positive reception in Germany. General fears about an unregulated Internet that would be dominated by a few US digital giants accumulating and selling vast amounts of citizens' personal data worldwide have deep roots in Germany. The lack of effective Internet governance and regulation and the general concentration of power and knowledge in the hands of a few IT giants has led to a system that generally favours profit maximization over citizen protection and cyber security (Gaycken 2014).

There is a wide agreement across the political spectrum in Germany that more needs to be done internationally to address the problems related to Internet governance. For example, SPD-party leader Sigmar Gabriel called to action in *Frankfurter Allgemeine Zeitung* by stating that Europe must protect itself against 'brutal information capitalism'. He went on to juxtapose two alternatives:

> Either we defend our freedom and change our policies, or we become digitally hypnotised subjects of a digital rulership. … It is the future of democracy in the digital age, and nothing less, that is at stake here, and with it the freedom, emancipation and self-determination of 500 million people in Europe. (Gabriel cited in Garside 2014)

Gabriel's forceful and amplified statement symbolizes a key feature of the German debate. Parts of the government embraced the apocalyptic language of the anti-TTIP campaign and therefore made dialogue with their American counterparts more difficult. Nobody in the transatlantic business or political community denies the importance of the digital debate. The question remains what the best channels are to address such issues. Meetings such as the so called US-German cyber dialogue which occurred in late June 2014 could be a way forward. A systematic forum is certainly needed but TTIP is a double-edged sword in this context. It could foster solutions as well as amplify the worst fears. The most ironic aspect of the spying saga with regard to TTIP were reports in the European and German press that the US had been spying in Brussels itself to find out about the European strategy for TTIP.

Financial Regulation and Banking Disputes

As in France, the German TTIP debate was also influenced by the coverage of high-profile cases brought against German banks in American courts. The willingness of the US to bite European banks really grabbed the headlines in 2014. The French BNP Paribas Bank was fined 8.9 billion US dollars for violating US sanctions against Iran, Sudan and Cuba without having broken any French or European law. French officials had unsuccessfully lobbied against draconic fines and had generally opposed the US principle of simply extending its legal reach over every foreign bank that deals in US dollars. For them, it was a threat to French sovereignty. Among other European banks facing scrutiny and possibly similar fines for alleged US sanctions busting are currently Italy's UniCredit, France's Société Générale and Germany's Deutsche Bank and Commerzbank. While the stories were still unfolding, media coverage in Germany joined the French criticism of US unilateral law enforcement in this field. It was the French government, backed by German officials, who in August 2014 urged the G20 to put the matter on the agenda of its November 2014 meeting (Stothard et al. 2014).

Geo-Strategic Considerations

TTIP has always been more than a trade agreement. In German eyes, it was clearly part of a geo-strategic and geo-economic vision that has been alive ever since the end of the Cold War. The essential question has been whether the strengthening of the transatlantic alliance was the centrepiece of the preservation of the liberal world order. Secondly, how would Europe position itself in a multi-polar global order – as a strong pillar of a united Western world or as a more independent second but non-American 'liberal voice'? Such strategic ambivalence is symptomatic of the current mindset in Germany and certainly has implications for an evaluation of TTIP.

All three geo-strategic views on TTIP were present in the German debate. First, there was the idea that Europe could enhance its political and economic interest by expanding its world-leading standards through the transatlantic alliance to the rest of the world. Many saw the big geo-economic picture as the key benefit of TTIP. As Karel De Gucht phrased it in a speech in Germany: 'Perhaps the biggest value of an agreement will be our relations with the rest of the world' (de Gucht and Lambsdorff 2014). Second, there is the notion that even if some sacrifices of the European standards had to be made, it was only the combined strength of a common Western approach that would secure high standards and liberal values for Europe in a fierce competition with the non-Western world. Third, many saw TTIP combined with TPP as an American vehicle for preserving first and foremost US interests *vis-à-vis* China in an emerging G2-world. This would certainly go against European geo-strategic and geo-economic interests, in particular for the export-oriented German economy that was so successful in Asia because of its world-leading standards and product quality. Any flavour of anti-Asian trade protection within TTIP would certainly amount to an own goal for Germany and Europe. Lastly, those who generally favoured an open world trade system based on the WTO saw TTIP as an American-led departure from a serious attempt to complete the Doha Round (Dieter 2014, see other chapters in this book).

The Decline in Trust in US-German Relations

Against the background of these several objectives and substantive concerns, the main factor in the development of German attitudes towards TTIP in 2013–14 was the general state of transatlantic affairs and the gradual decline of trust in German-American relations. As a result of a series of events in the last decade, public attitudes towards the US have become less favourable than in the past. A recent poll in 2014 suggested that only 38 per cent of Germans look favourably at the US (Donfried 2014), a surprisingly low figure even in European comparison. However, while views tend to be exaggerated during immediate crisis, there can be no doubt that German-American affairs have soured since the beginning of the twenty-first century.

Since 2013, this trend has even worsened. German-American relations deteriorated in at least three steps. The first chapter opened in the spring of 2013 and focused on the National Security Agency's (NSA) bulk collection of metadata. In order to mend wounds, President Obama actually visited Berlin in June 2013 and spoke about it at length at a press conference in the Chancellery but could not overcome 'genuine transatlantic dissonance' (Hawley and Warner 2013). The second step hit in October 2013 with allegations that the US had tapped Angela Merkel's mobile phone. The third major blow came in the summer of 2014 with allegations about possible US double agents in Germany. With great outcry from the political class, this led to the expulsion of the CIA station chief in mid-July 2014. In particular these new allegations of the US conducting espionage operations against its German ally 'brought bilateral tensions to a full boil' (Donfried 2014). A further twist in the saga then occurred in August 2014 when it became public that the German intelligence service, the Bundesnachrichtendienst (BND), had allegedly spied on US Foreign Secretary John Kerry and his predecessor Hilary Clinton. Having accused the US of violating trust among NATO allies by spying on Germany, it was then revealed that the BND had also systematically kept a NATO member under surveillance, i.e. Turkey (Vasagar 2014). The fact that Germany was 'caught' (Joffe 2014) lowered the tone and raised questions about the general nature of the relations between democratic governments and their intelligence services.

For the purpose of this chapter it is important to emphasize that the spying dispute and the German perception of TTIP became inseparably intertwined. On several occasions, politicians explicitly linked the two spheres. For example, Justice Minister Heiko Maas (SPD) in July 2014 publically questioned the fact that TTIP could succeed since such an agreement would require a minimum of societal approval in Germany which had been completely undermined by the US spying activities (Zeit Online 2014b). Sometimes politicians saw TTIP as a vehicle through which the fundamental differences over spying could be resolved, using it as either a stick or a carrot. In 2013, Germany wanted a bilateral no-spy agreement, a naive demand as the Obama administration made it clear that the US would never sign no-spy agreements with any nation. During the most heated weeks of the debate on US surveillance activities, some German politicians called for an end to the TTIP negotiations (Zeit Online 2014a). Some had earlier called for a pause until there was a no-spy agreement while others suggested a transatlantic 'no-spy-declaration' as a document attached to a future TTIP treaty. SPD parliamentary floor leader Thomas Oppermann called the spy affairs not only a huge political mistake by the US but a self-made 'promotion programme for anti-Americanism' across Europe (Zeit Online 2014a). Whether one could take all such statements at face value is debatable, but the criticisms of the German public had at least some impact on the US administration. It is undeniable that the general erosion of the trust between Berlin and Washington was a major driver for the increasingly intense debate and criticism of TTIP. It continues to provide a real challenge for Germany's political class and is unlikely to fade away in the foreseeable future.

The Intensity of the Critical Public Debate and the Ambivalence within the Political Class

While most of the substantive issues with regard to TTIP feature in all European debates, the sharp decline in US-German relations explains its unique intensity and the somewhat ambivalent responses of the political class. Across the political spectrum, politicians had difficulties in positioning themselves in the TTIP debate as the growing public concern and the overlap with deep worries about big data and 'big brother' (USA) made TTIP hardly a winner for most politicians. As one prominent but unnamed politician described it in a background discussion with this author during the European election campaign in April 2014: 'I am fully in favour of TTIP but it is a nightmare for me as a campaigner. In small events, I do mention it in passing but I hope it will not be noticed. If you have a TTIP-person in the audience, you know that the evening is over' (background talk, 12 April 2014). According to this politician, TTIP opponents tend to radicalize the room and would leave no more space for any other topic. Moderate but informed people generally express their reservations towards the US and Brussels. Business people would ask what it would mean concretely for their firms. Since politicians lack the detailed knowledge that only experts and negotiators have, 'we look silly either way. All in all, TTIP is a real loser for any politician right now in Germany' (background talk, 12 April 2014).

While TTIP was a challenge for all politicians from its start in 2013, it was the sudden pace and the dynamics of the public debate in 2014 that caught the

Christian Democrat (CDU)/Social Democrat (SPD)-led government wrong footed. The coalition agreement between the CDU/CSU and the SPD clearly states the commitment towards a speedy conclusion of TTIP. Until early 2014, this consensus had been sustained. Both parties generally praised the potential benefits of the treaty and supported its aims in the run-up to the May 2014 European elections. Outside the narrow political arena, however, the TTIP debate started to gain momentum.

Firstly, the Federation of German Industries (Bundesverband der Deutschen Industrie, BDI), consistently supported TTIP and sustained a professional and well-designed campaign in favour of the agreement in its existent form. BDI's President Ulrich Grillo became a prominent face for the pro-TTIP voices in the German campaign. Industry representatives engaged with the criticism mainly by trying to show that the fears of the anti-campaign were exaggerated and that the benefits clearly outweighed any potential harm. The existing challenges could all be addressed in the negotiations and would be solved through reasonable and sensible compromises (BDI 2014a, BDI 2014b, BDI 2014c, BDI 2014d). Secondly, the trade unions also heavily engaged in the debate from its inception with a first agreed position paper published in April 2013 (DGB 2013). The stance of the Confederation of German Trade Unions (Deutscher Gewerkschaftsbund, DGB) was generally a half-way-house at the beginning, asking to improve the agreement rather than opposing it. The DGB believed that an agreement could indeed potentially bring valuable economic benefits but warned not to exaggerate them. Furthermore, TTIP did not, as politicians claimed, 'constitute an effective remedy against the crisis in the Euro area ... This would require other measures, completely different in both scope and focus' (DGB 2013). Pure liberalization, so argues the DGB, would not generate the desired welfare effects. What was needed was a comprehensive transatlantic co-ordination of macro-economic policies, including the stabilisation of euro-dollar exchange rates, the strengthening of the joint struggle against fiscal evasion and tax avoidance and the introduction of a global financial transaction tax.

In addition to this wish list, the DGB highlighted a very concrete criticism of the US that appealed to traditional trade union audiences. It concerned workers' rights:

> The German Trade Union Confederation, DGB, views with grave concern the non-ratification by the USA of six out of eight basic core labour standards of the International Labour Organisation (ILO), including conventions 87 and 98, on the freedom of assembly and the right to collective bargaining ... From a union perspective, one of the objectives of the agreement with the USA must be an improvement of labour rights everywhere. (DGB 2013: 4)

In the beginning, the unions started from the assumption that the treaty should be concluded with that improvement. While their stance on substantive issues remained stable, the general tone sharpened within a year and policy recommendations have gradually shifted over time. In the summer of 2014, a new position paper called for suspending or abandoning the negotiations as there should be 'no agreement at the expense of workers, consumers or the environment' (DGB 2014a, DGB 2014b). The radicalization was a typical example resulting from the above-described decline in US-German relations and the general shift in public discourse.

Thirdly and most vigorously, civil society activists from different traditions, including environmental, anti-globalization and civil rights groups across Europe, launched a sophisticated online campaign (see also Strange's chapter in this book). Some NGOs which normally represent a wide range of issues chose to make 'defeating the TTIP' their new primary concern. TTIP was a convenient 'one-size-fits-all' vehicle for many societal concerns which made it perfect for a concentrated campaign. It was an easy mobilizing tool as it could actually deliver a concrete result. 'Stop TTIP' became both the slogan as well as the somewhat realistic goal of a new political movement. It was certainly more likely to stop TTIP than previous 'stopping targets' such as the classic 'Stop War' or 'Stop Atomic Energy'.

With campaigns from all relevant actors and with the media enjoying the sudden hype over TTIP, positioning for the political parties was a challenging act. It was easier for the Greens and the Left who had argued against key provisions of the TTIP mandate from day one. It was as early as at the beginning of the TTIP negotiations in 2013 that the German Greens had formally positioned themselves against TTIP by embracing most of the arguments of the civil society campaign (Bündnis 90/Die Grünen 2013). Die Linke (The Left) did the same and, as the largest opposition party, constantly questioned the government over TTIP throughout 2014, finally culminating into a *'Grosse Bundestagsanfrage'* in the German Parliament with 125 specific questions on TTIP's impact in the summer of 2014 (Deutscher Bundestag 2014). The Free Democratic Party (Freie Demokratische Partei, FDP) provided a mixed picture. Generally in favour of TTIP and in line with the core arguments of the BDI with regard to economic gains, the FDP was nevertheless very critical when it came to big data, surveillance and the protection of privacy and civil liberties. As a result, there was an attempt to separate the two issues clearly and to avoid mixing too many things into a toxic brew. However, the FDP provided a range of views. At the height of the frantic debate over spying, voices such as FDP's veteran-rebel Wolfgang Kubicki called for an end to TTIP (Kubicki 2014). Ex-interior minister Gerhart Baum (FDP), still highly regarded across the party spectrum, provided one of Germany's debating highlights when he published an article stating that he was truly 'proud of the German Angst' with regard to the matter (Baum 2014).

However, most importantly, the government parties CDU/CSU and SPD fully represented the general German ambivalence across the political spectrum. The SPD was the most undecided and torn player. Party leader and economics minister Sigmar Gabriel struggled with a double act. He was supposed to advocate TTIP as a member of the government while responding to his increasingly critical party and the shifting views of the trade unions. Already in March 2014, the conservative daily *Die Welt* dubbed TTIP 'Gabriel's loser-topic' (Greive 2014), while the left-wing *Die Tageszeitung* in May brought it down to the essentials. The SPD, the paper wrote, was clearly and simultaneously in 'favour of and against' TTIP (Reinecke 2014). The party's strategy then became to play for time. In May 2014, economics minister Gabriel established an official external advisory council on TTIP, including experts across the range of relevant actors and stakeholders in the debate (BDI 2014d). The strategy was to delay the substantive issues for a period of further reflection whilst allowing SPD politicians to punch for and against TTIP in different forums and on different aspects of the TTIP debate.

While the CDU was less divided than the SPD and generally promotes the conclusion of TTIP as planned, the shift in the public's general mood certainly had an effect on Germany's 'catch-all party' as well. One of the most symbolic incidents in the European election campaign, witnessed by the author of this chapter, was Chancellor Angela Merkel's return to Hamburg in May 2014, the city where she was born. Instead of providing a warm welcome, the event was specifically targeted by the anti-TTIP campaign which turned up in high numbers and clearly overshadowed the gathered crowd of CDU supporters. The reaction of the official speakers was symbolic of the ambivalence within the CDU. One speaker wanted to avoid TTIP as a topic and tried to duck the issue, whilst another stuck to a generalist praise of the economic benefits as a minor topic in a wide-ranging speech on Europe. However, the Chancellor grabbed the opportunity and abandoned her manuscript in order to directly address the critical audience. Merkel had defended TTIP in the Bundestag in a major speech in March 2014 and promoted TTIP in Washington in May 2014 in a speech at the Chamber of Commerce (CDU 2014). It was now time to make a much bigger effort to defend the project in the general German public as well. As a result, ever since the European election, the CDU has clearly upgraded its information campaign and has plans to launch a new narrative in favour of TTIP in the autumn of 2014. Back in Hamburg in May, it was not only Merkel who was in a fighting spirit. Her opponents were clearly ready as well. Watching both sides raising the game, one must suspect that a new and most decisive phase in the German TTIP debate was about to begin.

Conclusion

When the US and the EU in 2013 launched negotiations to conclude a TTIP, Germany had been optimistic and supportive of TTIP. However, German public attitudes on TTIP soon and rapidly became quite negative over the period of negotiations. The decline in support for TTIP in Europe's central economy was essentially due to objective problems of TTIP which are shared by many Europeans. It was then intensified by a sharp decline in trust between the US and Germany with a bleeding over the NSA spying issues and a frantic civil society campaign against TTIP. This resulted in generally more and more ambivalent responses by the political class, essentially undecided between the potential for economic growth and the potential for political dissatisfaction in Germany. This genuine uncertainty combined with growing uneasiness about the larger geo-economic and geo-strategic consequences of TTIP created a toxic brew among the German public spilling over into the political arena. It reached a state where the government seemed to reconsider its general position towards the project with voices within the government echoing both optimism and fear about TTIP. All in all, it has clearly made Germany increasingly reluctant to put its considerable weight behind the project. The German TTIP debate has been Europe's most vibrant, touching upon crucial concerns far beyond the treaty's mandate. It remains to be seen whether the potential cure for European economies promised through TTIP will eventually prevail over its severe side-effects which were so clearly pronounced in the German debate.

Chapter 5

EU Institutions, Member States and TTIP Negotiations: The Balance of Power and EU Foreign Policy

Tereza Novotná

Introduction

Although the Transatlantic Trade and Investment Partnership (TTIP) between the United States (US) and the European Union (EU) is primarily an economic agreement focused on trade and regulatory issues (as discussed by other chapters in this book), if TTIP is concluded, it is likely to have broader political and, in particular, foreign policy implications for the EU, its institutions and Member States. By focusing on empirical data, this chapter therefore sheds light on how the conclusion of TTIP can affect the balance of power within the EU, particularly through different ways in which the EU conducts its negotiations of international agreements, including TTIP.

Firstly, TTIP is not an agreement between two nation states. Even though EU Member States and particularly Europe's 'Big Three' (i.e. the UK, France and Germany) have a key say in setting the strategic direction of the EU's position on TTIP and, from time to time, may have become vocal if any issues which are sensitive to them are included (or left out) in any deal, this chapter argues that, taking a sporting metaphor, all EU Member States are essentially substitutes on the bench waiting while the negotiations are conducted between the American and EU authorities. In the first section, the chapter therefore asks this question: what impact do TTIP negotiations have on the role of EU institutions and their weight in international settings *vis-à-vis* EU Member States?

Secondly, the 2010 Lisbon Treaty created a new post of the High Representative/Vice-President of the European Commission (HRVP) and a new diplomatic body, the European External Action Service (EEAS) with its 'EU embassies', or EU Delegations, bringing together the EU's foreign and security policy with the external competencies of the Union into a single 'comprehensive approach' (European Commission and High Representative of the European Union for Foreign Affairs and Security Policy 2013, Council of the European Union 2014). Yet at the TTIP negotiating table, it is not the HRVP and EEAS who are representing the EU, but the European Commission (and its directorate for trade, or DG TRADE, in particular). Drawing on the negotiation literature and literature on the EU and its foreign policy (Howorth 2011, Bátora 2013, Telò and Ponjaert 2013) as well as a number of semi-structured interviews and background discussions conducted with EU and US officials, including senior members of the negotiating teams, the second part of the chapter therefore inquires: what implications do TTIP negotiations have on EU foreign policy *vis-à-vis* the US? How can EEAS shape and be shaped by TTIP negotiations?

The chapter argues that unless HRVP and EEAS particularly through its EU Delegation in Washington, DC gets more involved in TTIP negotiations, the negotiation process may in fact sideline the EEAS and hinder rather than encourage the comprehensive approach in EU's foreign policy. Despite the fact that TTIP negotiations may lead to increased clout for EU institutions at the expense of EU Member States at the international level, it may be the European Commission rather than the EEAS which has greater input in setting the direction of TTIP and transatlantic relations in general, particularly since it is the Commission rather than EEAS which is in charge of the nitty-gritty aspects of TTIP negotiations.

Although the low emphasis on effectiveness of the comprehensive approach and on the 'Vice-Presidential' half of HRVP's role has been one of the most criticized aspects of Catherine Ashton's 2010–14 tenure (Lehne 2013, Marangoni and Raube 2014), the chapter nonetheless suggests that the shift in the balance of power from HRVP to the Commission through TTIP is, however, not a foregone conclusion. It can be substantially changed with Juncker's incoming Commission where, thanks to its restructuring into 'project teams' of groups of Commissioners who are led by the Commission Vice-Presidents, it is indeed the incoming High Representative who in her role as the Commission's Vice-President controls the foreign policy cluster which includes the Commissioner for Trade and DG TRADE (European Commission 2014b). Yet it may all in the end depend on the personal chemistry and working arrangement between incoming HRVP Mogherini and Commissioner Malmström with her trade portfolio as well as on Commission President Jean-Claude Juncker and the extent to which he will run his 'Team Juncker' (King 2014) with a tight fist and get involved in one of the most significant Commission agendas of the next few years – TTIP.

Who is in Charge of TTIP Negotiations? The European Commission vs EU Member States

Before we can embark on unravelling the first question of this chapter, i.e. how TTIP negotiations and their (successful) conclusion may shift the balance of power between EU institutions, and the European Commission with its DG TRADE in particular, *vis-à-vis* EU Member States, it is necessary to explore how TTIP negotiations were launched, how they are prepared and how they are conducted at the European (as well as the American) side.

In contrast to other EU-led negotiations, such as on EU enlargement, which has been widely examined by an 'enlargement' and 'conditionality' literature as well as documented by participants in these talks (see e.g. Novotná 2012, Novotná 2015, Ludlow 2004, Telička and Barták 2003, Vassiliou 2007, Haughton 2007, Schimmelfennig 2001, Schneider 2008, Vachudova 2005), TTIP negotiations do not take place within an intergovernmental conference with EU Member States sitting on one side of the table with the negotiating partner (such as a candidate state) on the other and the European Commission playing a role of a technocratic expert and mediator, but not of a direct participant. In TTIP, all EU-28 Member States are represented by a single authority i.e. the European Commission which is primarily represented by the negotiating team coming from DG TRADE.

The prominent role of the Commission is given mainly by the fact that trade policy is an exclusive power of the EU (e.g. Young 2002). This EU's trade and investment policy is set down in Article 207 of the Treaty on the Functioning of the European Union (TFEU) and includes trade and investment relations with non-EU countries that are managed through the Commission. As DG's TRADE website puts it: '... so only the EU, and not individual member states, can legislate on trade matters and conclude international trade agreements'.[1] Of course, and perhaps even more importantly, in TTIP negotiations in contrast to EU enlargement, the power (a)symmetry between the negotiating sides is strikingly different: the US is not an applicant, or 'entering entity', and the EU is not an 'accepting entity' (Novotná 2015), but the EU and the US are more or less on the same footing as two equal partners. In other words, neither of the two wants to join the other's club, but both want to get a mutually beneficial deal.

So where did EU Member States disappear from the equation? Was it not France which initially threatened to stop the launch of the TTIP discussions due to its concerns over the 'cultural digital agenda' (i.e. the rules on TV, movie and other cultural production)? Later on, was it not one of the German coalition partners (the Social Democratic Party – SPD) which wanted to temporarily suspend the EU-Canada Free Trade Agreement (CETA), a treaty that has been widely considered a template for TTIP, if the investor-state dispute settlement (ISDS) issues are not dropped from CETA and, consequently, from TTIP (see Mayer's chapter in this book on the German TTIP debate)?

As one of the interviewees[2] pointed out to the author of this chapter, at the strategic level, the impetus to initiate TTIP negotiations with the US came from EU Member States. In fact, according to the official, some Member States even pushed the Commission into the launch of the talks despite the fact that there was seemingly no clear consensus within the Commission that the negotiations should commence as quickly as they did. The Council has adopted several conclusions in which it called for the work of the Commission to be expedited and for the negotiations to be launched. At the top political level, influence of EU Member

---

1   DG TRADE, http://ec.europa.eu/trade/policy/policy-making/ [accessed: 28 September 2014].

2   An interview with a senior official, DG TRADE, Brussels.

States was therefore very high and the major strategic orientation was fully co-decided between the Commission and the Council.

Nevertheless, following the EU-US summit in November 2011, preparatory work was at the European side done by the Commission with DG TRADE in charge. The summit established a High-Level Working Group on Jobs and Growth (HLWG) which was led by US Trade Representative (at that time Ron Kirk) and EU Trade Commissioner Karel De Gucht. The HLWG published its interim report in 2012 (High Level Working Group on Jobs and Growth 2012) and the final report in February 2013 (High Level Working Group on Jobs and Growth 2013). During this exercise, any influence of EU Member States was limited. As one of the Commission officials put it: 'WE informed THEM'.[3] Yet the final report must have been endorsed by all three Presidents – of the European Commission, of the Council of the European Union and, of course, President of the United States.

Between March and June 2013, the Commission launched procedures to obtain a negotiating mandate. The Commission proposed a draft mandate and submitted it to EU Member States for their approval. Since the negotiating mandate was a highly political and sensitive issue, EU Member States amended it quite significantly by, for instance, removing the audiovisual services from the mandate. Because a number of Member States still do not wish to make the original mandate public, we can only speculate which countries pushed for what amendments. It seems, however, clear that it was not just France that took a critical stance on the audiovisuals, but a number of other states were happily hiding behind it.[4] In the end, the Council (2013) approved the mandate and thus gave a green light to the launch of TTIP talks on 14 June 2013.

Given the fact that the European Parliament (EP) must in the end assent to any negotiated deal, it is rather surprising that EP entered the game rather late albeit with all the more greater force. Even though the EP has been very vocal on issues related to private data protection provoked by the NSA spying scandal (see Mayer's and Telò's chapters further in this book) and, as a response, some MEPs called for suspension of TTIP talks (EurActiv 2014), this may have only been the result of the pre-election campaigning and realization that jumping on the bandwagon of a general dissatisfaction with TTIP among the European publics may bring electoral points. The EP has in fact so far adopted only one resolution (European Parliament 2013) clearly related to TTIP on 23 May 2013 i.e. two months after the Commission drafted its negotiating mandate and a month before the Council's decision on the launch of the talks.

Once TTIP negotiations were launched, DG TRADE, which is in most of the cases the Commission's lead Directorate-General (DG) on the TTIP agenda, strictly follows the inter-service consultation process.[5] Before taking any official position on a TTIP item, particularly if in writing, DG TRADE clears it with

---

3   An interview with a senior official, DG TRADE, Brussels.
4   An interview with a senior official, DG TRADE, Brussels.
5   It is also possible to split the issues between the lead and co-lead DGs.

other services (DGs) concerned. For instance, if DG TRADE makes a proposal on public procurement, it consults it with DG Internal Market (DG MARKT) and DG Enterprise (DG ENTR), while proposals on sanitary and phytosanitary (SPS) issues are jointly prepared with DG Health and Consumers (DG SANCO). Although the negotiators do not in the end have to accept amendments by other DGs to the draft position proposed by DG TRADE, the aim is to reach consensus among all the Commission services involved. As one of the members of the TTIP negotiating team explained: 'If I think that what they are proposing is rubbish, I can say no ... We argue but we work it out ... that is the governing way how we work'.[6]

In contrast to the comprehensive consensus-seeking intra-service method within the Commission, the working method with EU Member States is different, partly because the Treaties provide for such different working arrangements. All TTIP draft positions and other papers are submitted to Member States for their comments. Moreover, all trade decisions are accompanied by the Council's Trade Policy Committee which meets weekly at the technical and once a month at a senior political level. Member States also have an opportunity to provide their views in writing on TTIP or ask for a meeting with anyone on the negotiating team. As a rule of thumb, the negotiators always accept such requests for meetings.

Yet when it comes to official approval, Member States are not required to agree to any of the TTIP materials that are submitted to them. Or, vice versa, the Commission negotiators are not obliged to accept any of the suggestions made by EU Member States. Although DG TRADE officials claim they would take on board issues that Member States ask for to the extent that the negotiators think that the requested change is possible or a good idea, a number of times, however, they do not bow to the pressure of Member States and do not accept their proposals. Clearly, though, officials then need to explain to the Member State 'demandeur' why an issue was off the TTIP table. The negotiators after all know that, at the end of the day, any TTIP deal which will be agreed on will need support by Member States. Similarly, after each TTIP negotiations round, the Commission officials report to Member States through information sessions and answer numerous questions of Member State representatives in order to make sure that they are fully on board and understand both what the Commission is proposing and what the US position is. In the words of one of the TTIP negotiating team members, 'it is a subtle exercise'.

A special case of Member State-negotiating team collaboration relates to the role of the Presidencies of the EU throughout the process of TTIP negotiations. When negotiations are conducted within an intergovernmental conference, as in the case of accession negotiations, the Presidencies can become main drivers of the entire process by clearly setting the negotiation agenda, finding consensus among fellow Member States and pushing both sides to accept a compromise (Ludlow 2004). Moreover, they tend to compete and show off what was achieved under their helm. In trade negotiations, including TTIP negotiations, however, the

---

6   An interview with a senior official, DG TRADE, Brussels.

Presidencies play rather a marginal role. It is not up to them to propose next steps and draft texts, but up to the Commission. Since Member States do not sit at the TTIP negotiating table, the Presidencies do not run the show. They are more or less only involved to the extent that they chair meetings of the Council and the Trade Policy Committee.

Moreover, the intensity of the relationship with the Commission's TTIP negotiating team varies depending on the issue at stake and a specific moment during the negotiation process. When the Presidency is lucky enough to be in the chair when it comes to decision time, the TTIP negotiators may work with it very closely. On the other hand, during the more routine periods, the relationship is looser and is basically limited to reporting by the DG TRADE negotiators on the TTIP negotiations' state of play. As with other issues related to the clout of Presidencies, they come and go every six months and, depending on their own priorities and quality of the resources, they may be more (as the Irish in the first half of 2013 who worked hard on getting the negotiating mandate) or less (as the Greeks in the first half of 2014) active on TTIP-related issues.

To better compare the TTIP negotiation process on both sides of the Atlantic but without going much into the detail, it suffices to say that the US negotiating position goes through a triple consultation process.[7] As with the inter-service consultations within the Commission, the American draft position papers firstly go through an internal 'inter-agency' process. Once a draft is complete, it is sent to the US Congress where it is looked over by the House and Senate staffers and experts. In the third step, the US TTIP position paper is submitted through a secured website to the Advisory Committee for Trade Policy and Negotiations (ACTPN) whose advisors have about five to ten working days to provide their feedback.

Only after this sophisticated and, to some extent, even more complex than in Europe process of consultations with the additional third layer of trade advisors is complete, the US negotiating position on TTIP is presented to the European counterparts. Interestingly though, and in contrast to other negotiating partners that the EU is involved with in trade talks, the US side does not allow the sharing of its position papers with EU Member States. Since any final TTIP agreement will be an EU (rather than EU Member States)-US deal and it is the Commission who represents the Union at the TTIP talks, from the American perspective it is logical that only EU officials should have access to the key documents. As a Commission official indicated, Member States are unsurprisingly unhappy about this situation but none of them has so far told the Commission TTIP negotiators to stop the talks and otherwise 'what else you can do about it'.[8]

All in all, this section of the chapter demonstrated that TTIP negotiations are on the European side clearly led by supranational institutions, the European Commission with its DG TRADE in particular. Although EU Member States get involved in the strategic political aspects of TTIP by, for instance, pushing for the

---

7   An interview with a senior official, USTR Office, Brussels.
8   An interview with a member of the negotiating team, DG TRADE, Brussels.

start of TTIP talks, throughout the negotiation process they are bystanders rather than key players. Their side role is well understood and reflected by the wish of the American partners who ban them from seeing the US negotiation positions. As a result of a potentially successful conclusion of TTIP talks, the balance of powers between EU institutions and EU Member States can shift towards the EU side. A TTIP agreement will after all be an EU deal with the US rather than a treaty among EU Member States with a third party.

Yet the question remains: will this potential swing towards the clout of EU institutions be replicated in transatlantic relations in general or will it be limited to the transatlantic trade and investment relationship? In other words, how can TTIP impact on the EU's foreign policy *vis-à-vis* the US? The second section of this chapter will examine these questions.

Who is in Charge of Transatlantic Relations throughout TTIP Negotiations? The European Commission vs European Diplomatic Service

The partnership with the US and transatlantic relations have traditionally been at the forefront of the EU's foreign policy. Not only is the US one of the EU's key Strategic Partners, but the EU (and previously the Commission) Delegation to Washington, DC has been the first representative office of the European Communities since the 1950s in a third country outside the EU (Maurer and Raik 2014).[9] The EU Delegation to Washington is also one of the most active EU offices around the world whose work is generally welcomed and supported by the US administration and enjoys good access to senior US officials (Novotná 2014). Moreover, since the creation of the EEAS, a special division covering North America has been created within a managing directorate for the Americas.

Despite having a good pool of resources when it comes to TTIP, however, neither EEAS with its head, HRVP, nor EU Delegation get much involved. Yet once concluded, a TTIP treaty will have not only economic but also political and geostrategic implications (Hamilton 2014a, Hamilton 2014b) which should not be overlooked by the EU's foreign policy machinery. To some extent, the ambiguous stance of EEAS, HRVP and the Delegation on what to do about TTIP reflects the hybrid structures and lacking consistency in the EU's foreign policy-making as well as EEAS's ambivalent cooperation with other EU institutions, the Commission in particular.

Although the head and deputy head of EU Delegation to Washington follow TTIP closely and the press and political sections offer a useful analysis of the American situation, their role is more or less limited to providing input in terms of intelligence gathering. The trade section within the EU Delegation in Washington, on the contrary, is a part of the DG TRADE's negotiation team and

---

9 The first EC Delegation was opened in London, but the United Kingdom has since then joined the EC/EU.

reports directly to the Commission's deputy TTIP negotiator.[10] The coordination on TTIP within the Delegation thus does not go through a single person, i.e. the head of EU Delegation, but through two Brussels channels that are separate from one another – EEAS and its North America division on the one hand and the North America Trade Relations unit in DG TRADE on the other.

The practical aspects of inadequate coordination on TTIP among EU institutions are also illustrated by practical issues, such as the logistics for trips of the negotiating teams to both sides of the Atlantic. Since the logistical aspects, such as flights and accommodation for TTIP negotiators, are supposed to be taken care of by the host negotiating country, it is DG TRADE's negotiation unit which handles these issues when the European negotiators visit the US rather than the locally-based EU Delegation. The communication and coordination between EEAS and the Commission is thus left to personal contacts: the heads of both North America sections in EEAS and DG TRADE meet for a weekly coffee to discuss the latest developments in TTIP negotiations and transatlantic relations. It is the sad truth that the North America unit is the only unit in DG TRADE which meets its geographical counterpart from EEAS on such a regular and frequent basis.[11]

Conclusion: TTIP and the Balance of Power in Brussels

Even though TTIP and TTIP negotiations are primarily about getting the best trade deal between the EU and the US, there are broader political ramifications related to TTIP which are worth exploring. This chapter focused on two factors tapping into TTIP negotiations. Firstly, at the European side, who is in charge of the negotiation process: do we see EU Member States leading the direction of the talks or can we observe EU institutions and the European Commission in particular having the main say? Secondly, the chapter examined the input and participation of the EU foreign policy-making bodies in TTIP negotiations.

Despite the fact that EU Member States spurred the launch of TTIP negotiations, it is primarily the Commission with its DG TRADE which is in control of the TTIP process. Thanks to the fact that EU Member States are not required to approve any negotiation positions and do not directly participate in TTIP talks, their influence on the final outcome has rapidly decreased, particularly in comparison to other types of negotiations which are led at the EU level, such as EU enlargement. Therefore, the chapter argues that thanks to the negotiation process but mainly if TTIP agreement takes place and a common transatlantic market is created, the balance of power between EU Member States and EU institutions may be significantly shifted towards the supranational side, at least in relationship to the US.

Nevertheless, a word of caution needs to be spoken here: all EU Member States are adamant to keep their bilateral relations with the US, which is evidenced by

---

10   An interview with a member of the negotiating team, DG TRADE, Brussels.
11   An interview with a senior official, EEAS, Brussels.

the fact that all EU-28 keep their national embassies fully staffed in Washington. Moreover, some Member States allegedly complain about the Commission's negotiators directly to the American side (USTR). This, however, undermines the EU's negotiating position instead of strengthening it. As a result, the US officials can play a good cop-bad cop double act: a good cop *vis-à-vis* EU Member States and a bad cop *vis-à-vis* the Commission negotiators, thereby exploiting the desire of Member States to maintain their bilateral relations and be appreciated by them.

The foreign policy aspects of TTIP have not yet been fully explored by academic literature. This chapter therefore analysed to what extent and how the EU's diplomatic service (EEAS) with its EU Delegation based in Washington participates in and is shaped by TTIP negotiations. The chapter highlights that despite having promising means of influence that could ensure better impact and coordination both on the ground in Washington and in the Brussels HQ, EEAS with its current (at the time of writing of this chapter) head, HRVP Catherine Ashton, does not seize upon its possibilities and, in a way in contrast, distances itself from TTIP. Although it is understandable that EEAS does not want to get in the way of the Commission's prerogatives and increase already tangible tensions between these two Brussels-based EU bodies, it is a shame because TTIP provides a unique chance for HRVP to make full use of her Commission's Vice-Presidential hat and lead the way in terms of strategic thinking about TTIP and transatlantic partnership. In fact, TTIP offers an exceptional opportunity for the 'comprehensive approach' combining management of foreign policy with the EU's external policies (trade in particular) to be implemented in one of the most significant partner countries for the EU. On the other hand, a reluctant approach is hazardous for EU's diplomacy because once the TTIP train is set in motion and the Commission is one of the two principal drivers, it will be hard to become at least a substitute driver.

Not all is lost for EEAS and HRVP, however. Much will depend on agencies and actors rather than structures which are coming into place. Firstly, David O'Sullivan, former Director-General in DG TRADE and Catherine Ashton's chief operating officer overseeing the set-up of EEAS, has been selected to be a new head of EU Delegation in Washington. Perhaps his past experience and credentials will be the best asset for the EU Delegation to establish itself on the TTIP negotiation stage. Indeed, he has himself confirmed that TTIP will be his top priority in his new post.[12] Moreover, once the Commission President-elect Jean-Claude Juncker gets his team confirmed and the restructuring of the Commission services into 'clusters' or 'project teams' receives the go ahead from the EP, it will be incoming HRVP Mogherini who will oversee the foreign policy cluster and who will be responsible for the new Commissioner for Trade. Last but not least, given the significance of the transatlantic partnership, the new Commission President may decide to make TTIP a *Chefsache* and get personally involved. In any case, TTIP will impact not just on trade and politics, but also on how the foreign policy business is done in Europe.

---

12 An interview with a top official, EEAS, Brussels.

Chapter 6

Business Interests and the Transatlantic Trade and Investment Partnership

Andreas Dür and Lisa Lechner

Introduction

Much business lobbying takes place on the Transatlantic Trade and Investment Partnership (TTIP) on both sides of the Atlantic. Early on, both European and American business representatives contacted the European Commission to influence the agenda of the negotiations (Hakim 2013). In the United States (US), broad-based business associations such as the US Chamber of Commerce, sectoral associations such as the American Farm Bureau and individual companies such as Time Warner have been active in lobbying on TTIP.

What do business interests want to see in TTIP, and what are the chances of success of these lobbying efforts? To answer these questions, we first discuss how trade policy lobbying works in the European Union (EU) and the US. We briefly compare the European and American lobbying styles and also review the literature on trade policy lobbying success in both entities. We then empirically investigate business lobbying on TTIP, relying on 222 contributions to consultations held on TTIP in both the EU and the US. The evidence shows a strong lobbying effort by business, stark variation across sectors in which topics are seen as essential in these negotiations and some areas of high conflict between European and American business groups.

Trade Policy Lobbying in the EU and the US

Business interests possess many channels of influence in both Europe and the US. In Europe, interest groups can try to influence trade policy formation via the 'national route' or via the 'Brussels route' (Greenwood 2007: 25). The national route entails lobbying the national government or the national parliament with the expectation that these actors then defend business interests at the European level, for example in the Council of Ministers. The Brussels route, by contrast, means directly addressing the European Commission or the European Parliament. Lobbying the Commission has been important since the early days of the European Economic Community (see Dür 2010), as it is the Commission that makes a proposal for the start of trade negotiations and that represents the EU in the negotiations. Specifically for the TTIP negotiations, the Commission set up an expert group that offers formal access to a wide range of societal interests, including business associations but also trade unions and non-governmental organizations (NGOs). Influencing the European Parliament in matters of trade policy has become more important as a result of the increased powers of the Parliament in this domain with the entry into force of the Treaty of Lisbon on 1 December 2009. Following this latest revision of EU treaties, the Parliament's approval is needed for the ratification of international trade agreements.

Neither the European Commission nor the European Parliament is a unitary actor. In the Commission, although the Directorate-General (DG) for Trade takes the lead, various other DGs also play a role in preparing and conducting international trade negotiations. Not all of these DGs are considered 'business friendly'. DG Environment, for example, may be more open to lobbying by environmental NGOs than business actors (Pollack 1997). Similarly, in the European Parliament several committees play a role in approving international trade agreements, with some being more (International Trade) and others less (Development) business friendly. Moreover, members of the European Parliament (MEPs) tend to vote in line with their party groups. Some of these party groups (e.g. the European People's Party) take a more business-friendly position than others (e.g. the European United Left).

In the US, too, business interests benefit from several channels of access. The Office of the United States Trade Representative (USTR), which is part of the Executive Office of the US President, is responsible for the conduct of trade negotiations. Many other federal agencies and offices are involved in formulating US trade policy, including the Council of Economic Advisors and the departments of State, Agriculture and Commerce. The US National Economic Council, which is chaired by the US President, also sometimes deals with issues related to international trade. The US International Trade Commission is a final executive agency that can be the target of business lobbying. It not only administers the US's trade remedy laws, but also offers information to the US President on trade policy issues.

Business interests thus have many targets for their lobbying efforts in the US administration. They can either approach these institutions informally or have their voices heard via the trade policy advisory committee system. This system currently consists of 28 advisory committees that bring together representatives from companies, business associations, labour unions and a few NGOs. Business interests clearly dominate most of these committees.

Business interests also address Congressional committees (e.g. the House Committee on Ways and Means) and individual members of Congress. Formally, the regulation of trade and the setting of tariffs is a constitutional prerogative of Congress. Indeed, until the early 1930s Congress mostly unilaterally determined US tariffs on imports. The 1934 Reciprocal Trade Agreements Act, then, delegated competences to negotiate trade agreements to the President (Dür 2010). Congress, however, did not abdicate its trade policy powers. For one, trade agreements signed by the President could only enter into effect with the approval of a simple majority in both houses of Congress. Moreover, the delegation only happened for a limited period of time, with Congress repeatedly renewing the delegation. The last piece of legislation that delegated trade policy authority to the President, the Trade Act of 2002, expired in 2007. If no legislation is passed prior to TTIP being signed, any agreement negotiated between the EU and the US will have to be ratified by a two-thirds majority in the US Senate (as required by the US Constitution for all international treaties signed by the President). With many Democratic members of Congress currently taking a critical view of international trade agreements, and (at the time of writing) the Senate dominated by Democrats, such a two-thirds majority may be difficult to reach.

A European and an American Lobbying Style?

It seems plausible that the different institutional structures of the EU and the US may result in a transatlantic divide in lobbying styles (Woll 2012). In the EU, most decisions require the approval of many different actors, most importantly the Commission, a qualified majority of member states in the Council of Ministers and the European Parliament. By contrast, in the US many decisions just require simple majorities in both houses of Congress (and consent from the President). The requirement for having many actors on board may make business lobbying in Europe less adversarial than in the US. The US political system is also more reliant on money from interest groups to finance election campaigns, meaning that financial contributions play a larger role in lobbying in the US than in the EU.

Especially for business interests, however, the transatlantic differences in lobbying style should not be exaggerated. On both sides of the Atlantic, business actors mainly engage in inside lobbying, that is, direct contacts with decision-makers to convey the interest groups' demands (Gais and Walker 1991, Dür and Mateo 2013). In such contacts, adversarial tactics are necessarily of limited use. This is particularly so because, again in both the EU and the US, interest groups have most contacts with 'friendly' decision-makers, that is, politicians who are favourably disposed towards the groups (Hall and Deardorff 2006). In both entities, moreover, lobbying is mainly a case of strategically transmitting information to decision-makers. Business actors possess both political information (i.e. information about constituency preferences and the preferences of other decision-makers) and technical information (i.e. information about the feasibility of a proposed policy). While certainly some differences in lobbying styles exist, the expectation is for business actors trying to influence the TTIP negotiations and ratification process to behave in broadly similar ways in the EU and the US.

Business Influence in the EU and the US

Several studies suggest that the EU's institutional structure insulates trade policy-making from lobbying by societal interests (Meunier 2005b: 8–9, Woolcock 2005: 247, Zimmermann 2007). In the EU, the argument goes, the chain of delegation from societal interests to decision makers is long. Together with the EU's complex institutional structure, this long chain of delegation creates information asymmetries between politicians and interest groups that favour the former. For example, decision-makers may tell interest groups that they fought as much as possible for their interests, but that they were unable to pull other actors to their side, even if in practice they barely considered the groups' position. The insulation of the trade policy-making process in the EU may have been a conscious effort by the designers of the EU to keep protectionist interests at bay. In the words of Sophie Meunier (2005b: 8), European policymakers 'chose to centralize trade policymaking in order to insulate the process from protectionist pressures and, as a result, promote trade liberalization'. What worked for protectionist business interests should also be effective in reducing influence from business interests that favour trade liberalization. Following this strand of literature, therefore, business influence over EU trade policy should be low.

Several factors, however, cast doubt on the insulation thesis. Most importantly, considerable evidence shows that the EU's trade policy is largely in line with interest group demands (van den Hoven 2002, Coen and Grant 2005, Dür and De Bièvre 2007, Dür 2008). Illustratively, in the Doha Development Agenda, the currently on-going round of trade negotiations in the World Trade Organization, the EU has consistently taken a position in line with business demands (Dür 2008). On topics such as services liberalization, investment protection and intellectual property rights, where European business has taken offensive positions, the EU has demanded far-reaching commitments at the WTO level. With respect to agricultural trade and trade in audio-visual services, where European business takes a protectionist position, also the EU has tried to slow down the process of liberalization. The theoretical reason for this coincidence between business positions and the EU's position in international trade negotiations seems to be that the EU's institutional structure actually facilitates lobbying. The EU's many access and veto points make it relatively easy for societal interests to have their demands heard.

Nevertheless, public opinion can act as a restraint on business influence over trade policy. The case of the failed Anti-Counterfeiting Trade Agreement (ACTA) offers an illustration of this effect (Dür and Mateo 2014). Most European business interests supported this agreement which promised to improve the transnational enforcement of intellectual property rights. Only very few sectors of the economy, most notably internet providers, opposed provisions contained in ACTA. Dür and Mateo (2014) empirically show that only when NGOs and informal networks managed to increase the public salience of this agreement, both national governments and MEPs changed opinion about ACTA. Even a concerted business campaign in favour of ACTA could not deter the European Parliament from voting down the agreement. Public opinion, if mobilized by organized groups, thus seems to be a greater obstacle for business lobbying than the EU's institutional structure. With issues such as the treatment of poultry with chlorine dioxide having the potential to mobilize public opinion in Europe, this point may become crucial if the agreement reaches the stage of ratification.

For the case of the US, the extent to which business interests can influence trade policy formulation has also been hotly debated. Little doubt exists that business interests were key in determining US tariff levels when Congress set these rates unilaterally. The Smoot-Hawley Act of 1930, which led to an across the board increase of tariffs, has become a prime example of how lobbying by concentrated interests can affect legislation (Schattschneider 1935). Some authors, however, have suggested that the delegation of trade policy competences to the President limited the influence of protectionist interests over US trade policy (Destler 1986, Ehrlich 2008), creating the basis for the subsequent liberalization of US trade policy. Business interests may also be trumped by geopolitical considerations. With the executive playing a key role in the negotiation of trade agreements, and the executive also having strong foreign policy preferences, these preferences may spill over into the trade policy domain (Milner and Tingley 2011).

Similar to the case of the EU, however, there are good reasons to be sceptical of the notion that business interests have little influence over US trade policy. In fact, several studies found that interest group pressures play a major role in shaping US trade policy (Chase 2005, Fordham and McKeown 2003, Milner and Tingley 2011). Moreover, references to foreign policy aims in trade legislation may simply be a rhetorical ploy to enhance support for the legislation (Dür 2010), as the likelihood of Congress passing foreign policy legislation is higher than of it passing domestic legislation (Fleisher et al. 2000). For both the EU and the US, therefore, the expectation is for business interests to play a major role in shaping the TTIP negotiations.

TTIP: The Business Position

So what is the business position with respect to the TTIP negotiations? To answer this question, we draw on contributions that business actors on both sides of the Atlantic submitted to public consultations. Eleven stakeholder meetings, hearings or calls for written contributions took place between January 2012 and March 2014, including two joint EU-US solicitations. Although for most of the events a list of attendees is available, written submissions or transcripts of the meetings can only be accessed for four rounds of consultations, namely the EU's initial general public consultation completed in April 2012, the joint EU-US solicitation in October 2012, the – US organized – US-EU high level regulatory cooperation forum from 10 to 11 April 2013 and the US public hearing on 29 and 30 May 2013. In addition, the EU conducted a survey with 114 respondents for which 77 responses are available online. Because the European Commission designed the survey and thus set the agenda of contributed issues by asking specific questions, the results of this initiative cannot be used for the purpose of this analysis, namely assessing business actors' issue priorities.

Consequently, we analyse 222 contributions submitted to the four rounds mentioned above. These 222 documents or speeches were addressed to either or both the US (Office of Information and Regulatory Affairs, USTR) and the EU (DG Enterprise and DG Trade). For our analysis, we coded the contributors' profiles (sector,[1] headquarter, size) and the issues the stakeholders want to see tackled in the TTIP agreement. Because we hardly found statements where business stakeholders plead for an exclusion of specific issues from the trade agreement, we did not consider negative approaches in our coding scheme.[2] Furthermore, we coded the contributors' preferences in terms of overcoming the regulatory discrepancies between the US and the EU. Suggested mechanisms of the industries were mutual recognition, application of international standards, establishment of a new bilateral standard, unilateral EU or US adjustment, provision of an investor-state dispute settlement (ISDS) body and regulatory harmonization among EU Member States.

We proceed as follows: first, we assess how much business lobbying we see relative to lobbying from other actors. Second, we present the number of contributions to a certain issue per sector to show which issues business actors want to see tackled in a transatlantic trade deal. Our data allows for a comparison of the preferred scope of the trade agreement both between the EU and the US and across different industries. Moreover, we discuss preferences regarding mechanisms, such as mutual recognition, harmonization and unilateral adoption of the EU or the US. Finally, we conclude by comparing the business demands with the trade policy positions of both the EU and the US to get an idea of business influence or success.

How Much Business Lobbying Can We Observe with Respect to TTIP?

Business associations and companies were the main contributors to the four stakeholder events. They dominated with 87 per cent among the European, 67 per cent among the US and 76 per cent among the transatlantic stakeholders. The stakeholders' profile varies the most for the US-based contributors, ranging from NGOs (16 per cent), trade unions, citizens' representatives, academics, governmental institutions to companies and business associations.

By contrast, the profile of EU stakeholders is restricted to companies, business associations, citizens' representatives and governmental institutions (the two EU-

---

1   From 26 sectors with which we started, 19 applied to our sample: there were no submissions from business stakeholders representing the arms and ammunition, computer and IT equipment, railway equipment, waste management, construction, maintenance service and architecture sectors.

2   In fact, import-competing interests hardly contributed. The multinational companies and exporting interests that contributed want a broad and encompassing agreement.

based NGOs submitted together with a US NGO and presented themselves as a transatlantic interest group). Case selection – which includes one joint solicitation, one EU- and two US- based submissions – explains this evidence. As (a) the analysed consultations primarily took place in the US and (b) stakeholders tend to communicate their interest to their own political representatives, the American submissions are greater in terms of number and also variance. Moreover, the US hearings took place later in time which could also lead to a more intense NGO and academic participation as the public debate became more intense over time.

Furthermore, 20 per cent of the 222 consultation documents presented their position as a transatlantic one. These 45 submissions primarily came from business interests (76 per cent) followed by NGOs (17 per cent) and governmental institutions or regulatory authorities (7 per cent).

Overall, business submissions dominate clearly in terms of delivered speeches and written advices addressed to the negotiating parties. Hence our sample is big enough to assess the extent to which business interests differ across sectors. Moreover, the similarly strong presence of business in the EU and in the US allows for a comparison of the business positions on both sides of the Atlantic.

Do EU and US Business Interests Pursue the Same Aims?

Overall, business is much more concerned about non-tariff barriers – such as technical regulations, standards, intellectual property rights, investment and procurement regulations – than about tariff barriers. In this regard, the EU, US and transatlantic business interests agree. Furthermore, the need to remove barriers in trade in services (especially with respect to financial services) was emphasized on both sides of the Atlantic.

Not on all issues, however, do EU and US business interests agree. Based on the intensity of claims, we found that US business pushes strongly for the inclusion of sanitary and phytosanitary as well as intellectual property provisions in TTIP, but the European-based firms and business associations stressed procurement and investment regulations. The stakeholders that represent both US and EU interests care most about double-testing procedures. Hence, they asked for mutual recognition of certifications and standards. By contrast, US industries favour approximation via the adoption of international standards. Moreover, some US business interests demanded that the EU should unilaterally adopt US regulations and standards. By contrast, EU business interests want the US to apply EU rules. Both agree, however, that the differences in standards are mainly caused by political preferences rather than technical reasons. Mutual recognition is for 21 per cent of businesses in the EU and 23 per cent in the US a goal worth striving for. Moreover, new bilateral rules and standards are favoured by 21 per cent of the business stakeholders.

Even though some consistent similarities and differences between US and EU business interests were identified in the paragraphs above, we must differentiate between industries in order to understand the business interest patterns on either side of the Atlantic. The following section deals with this issue.

Is Business a Homogenous Actor?

In the EU as well as in the US, the food sector (food, beverages and other agricultural products) dominated in terms of contributions, but in the US it is far above all other industries (accounting for 40 per cent of all contributions). This explains the intense debate on sanitary and phytosanitary regulations in the US. The financial service sector was in the EU in second position and in the US in third. American IT service firms and associations submitted frequently. Moreover, the European car industry contributed nine submissions to the TTIP debate wherein they emphasized unfair procurement regulations. The chemical sectors (including pharmaceuticals, rubber and plastic) were equally strongly engaged in the EU and the US, but preferably submitted jointly, partly reflecting the fact that key companies in these sectors are active in both of these entities. This industry primarily addressed testing procedures, claiming that mutual recognition of product assessment results would decrease their costs significantly.

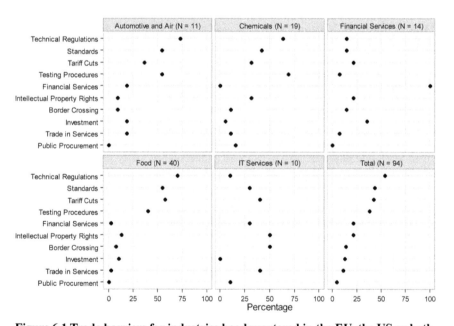

Figure 6.1 Trade barriers for industries headquartered in the EU, the US or both

Note: The N indicates the number of submissions (in total 94 submissions from the five major sectors shown).

Figure 6.1 shows the number of contributions across five major industries (the automotive and air transport, chemicals, financial services, IT services and nutrition sectors) to the debates concerning tariffs, trade in (financial) services, technical regulations, standards, assessment procedures, border crossing, intellectual property rights and investment and procurement regulations.[3]

Technical regulations are an important barrier to trade for all sectors besides the financial services and IT services industries. The same is true for standards, an issue mainly pushed by US food producers that worry about the EU's sanitary and phytosanitary regulations. Tariff cuts are most important for the food sector; interestingly, this issue is also of concern to the IT services sector. Investments, trade in services (with the exception of the question of financial services) and public procurement are issues that come up in only very few contributions. Investments are an important issue only for the financial services sector. Interestingly, with the exception of the IT services industry, there is no big push to protect intellectual property rights in TTIP. The representatives of the chemicals and pharmaceuticals industries are concerned about testing procedures and demand a common product assessment system.

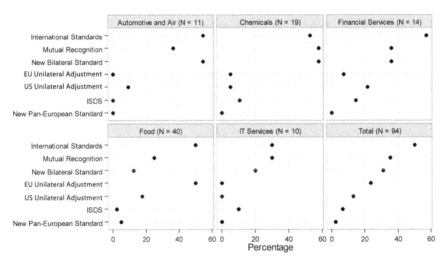

Figure 6.2 Industries' preferred approach to trade liberalization

Note: The N indicates the number of submissions (in total 94 submissions from the five major sectors shown).

Concerning the mechanism used to establish common laws, exactly half of the groups prefer the adoption of international standards (see Figure 6.2). This demand

---

3   Because sanitary and phytosanitary concerns were only discussed by the food sector, this issue is not included in Figure 6.1.

is particularly strong from the financial services sector. Mutual recognition is the next preferred approach to deal with divergent standards. Nevertheless, there is much more support for mutual recognition from some sectors (the chemicals sector) than others (the food industry). The (US-based) food industry has a preference for a unilateral adjustment of EU standards, whereas a substantial proportion of the financial services sector would like to see a unilateral adjustment of US standards.

The discussion has so far shown which issues business actors want to see tackled in an EU-US trade deal. The following section discusses business influence on the trade policy positions of the EU and the US with respect to TTIP.

Business Influence in the EU and US during TTIP Negotiations

The evidence shows that both the US position and the EU position in the TTIP negotiations are in line with business demands. Tariff cuts, technical regulations and standards serve as examples for the strong links between business and policy-makers.

One major divide across the Atlantic concerns the extent to which tariffs should be liberalized. Whereas the EU negotiators have called for further tariff cuts, the US representatives have paid little attention to this issue (ViEUws 2014a). This reflects the relative importance given to this issue by business interests in the EU and the US. Whereas the EU-based business interests emphasize the necessity to cut tariffs for their US counterparts this is not a major topic. Moreover, the chief negotiators have not yet reached an agreement on technical regulations and standards. For the US food industry, technical regulations and standards cause major trade obstacles. Consequently, the US negotiators repeatedly addressed this problem during the (at the time of writing) four rounds of negotiations. By contrast, EU representatives focused on (financial) service regulations and investment protection, thus paying heed to the strong lobbying effort by the financial services sector in Europe. Furthermore, the European Commission continues – despite public opposition – to push for the inclusion of ISDS in TTIP (ViEUws 2014b). Again, this reflects demands voiced by European business interests.

This brief discussion casts doubt on the insulation thesis discussed above. Both EU and US business groups play a major role in the TTIP negotiations and benefit from the many available channels of influence. On both sides, they have excellent access to key decision-makers. In fact, decision-makers actively reach out to business interests, as their input and expertise are needed in the negotiations. To understand the launch of the negotiations and the issues on the agenda, studying business lobbying is thus crucial.

Conclusion

We have discussed business lobbying on TTIP. Business actors in both the EU and the US have many access points to have their voices heard. Their lobbying styles, while different in degree, are largely similar: they mainly rely on inside lobbying, targeting friends rather than foes and relying on the transmission of information to wield influence. For both the EU and the US, some studies have argued that the influence that societal actors can exert on trade policy-making is limited. There are good reasons to doubt this assessment. Indeed, we expect business actors to be quite powerful unless the public salience of the TTIP negotiations strongly increases over the course of the negotiations.

A brief empirical study that relies on contributions to public hearings in the EU and the US has illustrated the extent of business lobbying on TTIP. According to business interests, the planned EU-US trade deal must be comprehensive, including a wide range of issues and consequently leading to a far-reaching liberalization of trade. Business sees the reach of the TTIP far beyond the territories of the EU and the US. Applying and – where not available – setting new international standards is at the top of the agenda of companies and business associations on both sides of the Atlantic. The trade policy positions of the EU and the US largely reflect these business interests. Any analysis of the TTIP negotiations without close attention to business lobbying is thus likely to be seriously incomplete.

Chapter 7

Implications of TTIP for Transnational Social Movements and International NGOs

Michael Strange

Is there a public sphere which is able to influence the TTIP negotiations? This question summarizes a key puzzle at the heart of trade politics which becomes even more salient as the definition of 'trade' has expanded significantly to impact an increasing range of politically sensitive areas of human society. The public face of international trade negotiations varies between, on the one hand, a technocratic 'club-like' process which is of interest only to those who have the relevant economic expertise and, on the other, a highly politicized struggle that was most forcefully epitomized in the now legendary battle that took place on the streets of Seattle during the World Trade Organization's (WTO) Ministerial Conference in December 1999.

At the core of this lies a paradox: as the range of governmental policies subject to trade negotiations has expanded, so too has the degree of specialist knowledge which is required to comprehend and engage with those negotiations. Translating trade agreements to national-level politicians is a challenge that, as civil society campaigners have often noted, is not always successful, leading to the fact that the democratic oversight of negotiations is imperfect. Groups looking to excite a public towards spending time and energy to question the suitability of what is being negotiated face an additional struggle: draft texts are rarely made public until they have been formally concluded and so lie beyond the realm of an effective public contestation. The expansion of what is discussed in trade negotiations represents a part of a broader shift in which policy decisions that were previously taken at lower levels have now increasingly shifted to the supranational level.

This shift has not, however, led to a significant reconfiguration of the supranational level where those who are impacted by the growing range of policies that are decided at that level might effectively contest these policies. There is no global demos, as it has often been stated (Elsig 2007: 79, Clark 2007: 193). International trade negotiations, and the functioning of international trade law, rely almost exclusively upon the practice of international politics as a world of necessarily closed doors and private meetings. Despite this, since the 1980s, there have been growing attempts by civil society organizations to open the closed doors of international trade politics. These attempts can be seen, as argued in this chapter, as the emergence of a public sphere (Castells 2008) in global trade governance. There are, at the time of writing, efforts by civil society organizations on both sides of the Atlantic to form a public sphere to contest the TTIP negotiations. It is too early to say whether these efforts will be successful and certainly not whether they can indeed directly influence the TTIP negotiations.

However, what we can observe is a process of forming new identities and political demands that provide the basis for alliances connecting groups both across the Atlantic and within the US and the EU towards an embryonic TTIP public sphere. This chapter is structured as follows. First, to contextualize the TTIP as a case of trade politics, it is necessary to provide a historical overview of civil society in global trade governance. Second, the chapter compares how groups in the US and EU have, respectively, campaigned on trade politics and how this is reflected in their current work on the TTIP. The discussion turns to what attempts have been made to form transatlantic coalitions between these groups to contest the TTIP. Finally, the chapter examines, assuming the TTIP is concluded and its regulatory bodies set up, how it might impact the future structure of the trade-related social movements.

Global Trade Governance and an Emergent Public Sphere

Since the late 1980s, trade negotiations have, with varying degrees of politicization, moved out of the 'club-like' atmosphere that was so characteristic of the original General Agreement on Tariffs and Trade (GATT) by, for example, moving to the centre of public contestation and street protests.

Campaigning critical of the GATT was largely limited to targeting negotiators and politicians and was only able to attract public attention in early 1991 when Mexico brought a complaint to the GATT over the US restrictions on imports of tuna caught with nets that were arguably lethal to dolphins (Danaher and Mark 2003: 111, Wilkinson 1996). When a GATT dispute settlement panel ruled the restrictions to be in violation of the United States' obligations under international trade law, this was seen as undermining a hard-fought victory by US environmental groups to legislate nationally for 'dolphin-friendly' tuna. A similar experience occurred in the case of 'consumer' groups such as the US-based Public Citizen, with lobbying on such matters as pesticide control and foods labelling that were subject to the expanding GATT (Wallach and Woodall 2004: 3). Public Citizen established a research and campaigning unit called 'Global Trade Watch' which focused on the high-profile case of the tuna-dolphin dispute, articulating it as evidence of a GATT 'assault' on the democratic process on the basis that an unelected panel was able to overturn a publicly-supported domestic legislation (Danaher and Mark 2003: 231).

Given the complex knowledge required to criticize global trade governance – to identify issues as well as engage with negotiators in public and media debates – many groups focus less on public campaigns and more on creating special units and employing personnel who are able to understand global trade governance as negotiations at various levels creating a rapidly expanding and more complicated series of mechanisms. North American groups acquired perhaps the most experience in the 1990s as many different types of demands by social movements became linked together into a critique of global trade governance through two of the most far-reaching trade agreements of that period – the Canadian-United States Free Trade Agreement (CUSFTA) and the North American Free Trade Agreement (NAFTA). Negotiations towards the CUSFTA politicized a broad swathe of social movement groups, including those focused on labour, gender and, in particular, Canadian cultural sovereignty (Huyer 2004: 49).

In the case of NAFTA campaigning, there was a significant tension within the environmental movement: whilst the more ecologist groups were highly critical, some of the larger conservation groups were supportive, seeing the agreement as a means to improve environmental regulation in Mexico (Hogenboom 1996: 993–9, Dreiling and Wolf 2001: 34). To facilitate trilateral networking between groups based in Canada, the US and Mexico, there was an effort to avoid criticizing NAFTA on 'nationalist' grounds so as to prevent alienating foreign groups (Stillerman 2003: 590).

Experience with CUSFTA saw Canadian groups take an initial lead in forming a trilateral alliance with their US and Mexican counterparts to organize against NAFTA, choosing to highlight common concerns such as the 'Maquiladoras' – the establishment of US factories on the US-Mexican border which were seen as a threat to both US and Canadian jobs as well as to Mexico's environment and public health (Stillerman 2003: 585, 590–91, Bandy 2000: 232, 240–41). Strategically, these activists saw the US public sphere and Congress as the two arenas in which the fate of NAFTA would be decided and so they chose to focus their resources on supporting the US campaign as well as on providing testimony to US politicians (Cook 1995: 78–88, Stillerman 2003: 584–5, Hogenboom 1996: 992–5). Although the campaigners failed to prevent NAFTA, there were two positive outcomes for them: NAFTA put global trade governance on the radar of a number of other social movement groups more than ever before, thus increasing public concern. Moreover, it helped establish an infrastructure of relations that would help further campaigning.

The impact of the earlier work became clear in the response to OECD negotiations for a Multilateral Agreement on Investment (MAI) as well as the WTO's Ministerial Conference in Seattle – both taking place in the late 1990s. In the case of the MAI, campaigning began after the head of a Malaysian-group, Third World Network (TWN), spoke at an event in North America where veterans of the CUSFTA and NAFTA campaigns were present and where he passed on information that he had acquired via contacts within the governments of unspecified developing countries (Johnston and Laxer 2003: 52–3). Due to the lack of a publicly available copy of the draft negotiating text, campaigners faced a significant hurdle: it was difficult to challenge the MAI's advocates directly.

This changed, however, when Canadian activists acquired the draft text from a Member of the Canadian Parliament who came across the text by coincidence whilst he was on an official visit to Europe. The Canadian activists belonged to the two most active groups in the NAFTA campaign – Polaris and the Council of Canadians – and had relations with North American and European groups that were established through the earlier campaigns. These relations facilitated dissemination of the draft text to other groups but also led to the rapid production of a report criticizing the text as a 'Corporate Rules Treaty' that came to frame much of the campaign amongst the groups at the global level (Johnston and Laxer 2003: 53–7).

Although the dissemination of such valuable information was transnational, aided by use of the Internet, which was then still a new technology, campaigns were targeted at the national level and tailored to whatever aspect of the MAI that was most likely to be politically sensitive within that context (Egan 2001). This strategy of using transnational links to enable national campaigns was most effective in France where campaigners managed to force the French government to withdraw from the negotiations and, consequently, caused the entire negotiation process to collapse (Egan 2001: 88–9, Johnston and Laxer 2003: 58–9).

Even though the anti-MAI campaign successfully built an alliance that would utilize transnational alliances to its advantage, beyond the initial dissemination of the draft text, however, it was not dependent on developing more substantive transnational alliances that would have required excessive resources. Similarly, campaigning was able to link an extremely broad range of political demands and groups, including: development, labour, gender, human rights, indigenous minorities, consumer protection and representatives of local government. These alliances developed in the context of preparations for other trade negotiations which were taking place during the same period, i.e. the WTO's December 1999 Ministerial Conference that was hosted in Seattle.

The 'Battle in Seattle' – as the protests and police response would become known and as also mirrored in the title of a Hollywood film narrating their encounter – drew on the relations developed through NAFTA and the MAI campaigns, cementing a once unlikely alliance between environmentalists and trade unions. A part of this work included the creation of a loose network – Our World Is Not For Sale (OWINFS) – linking the North American and European groups with those based in various parts of Africa, Asia and Australasia. When the Ministerial Conference collapsed due to disagreement between developed and developing countries, the campaigning groups took credit for it. Although the exact cause of the failure of the conference is open to debate, the rallies and street protests – as well as a visibly excessive police response – politicized the institutional heart of global trade governance much more than had been previously achieved, thus greatly limiting the negotiating flexibility of the WTO Member States (O'Brien et al. 2000: 140, Danaher and Mark 2003: 286). The MAI and Seattle have since become parts of a shared mythology for social movements working on trade but also on broader issues related to the perceived threat of 'corporate power' to social concerns, with both events frequently cited in later campaigns.

The creation of the European Seattle to Brussels (S2B) network, which, as its name implies, was a strategic attempt to bring the level of mobilization seen in the Seattle demonstrations to influence the foreign trade policy of the European Union, is a direct legacy of Seattle (Strange 2013). It was created by a handful of social movement groups based in the West European states who were directly responding to the role that the European Commission plays in representing EU Member States in multilateral trade negotiations, with a particular focus on the WTO. These groups included a broad range of interests, but were dominated by those focusing on development, environment and a general critique of corporate influence in public policy. Formed in the early 2000s, S2B served as an effective mobilizing device enabling face-to-face meetings, telephone conference calls, collaborative campaigns, but, most of all, sharing critical information and reports.

The creation of S2B meant that the European groups took the lead in campaigning against the WTO in the first half of the 2000s, choosing to target the negotiations which were supposed to expand the General Agreement on Trade in Services (GATS) for their perceived threat to democratic control over public utilities. More importantly, much of the network rested on the shoulders not only of just a few groups, but also of a few specific individuals. For instance, a member of a UK-based development group took the central role through her initial activity in helping both establish S2B and then develop a critique of the GATS. This critique became the master template for groups across Europe, both for those who were directly involved in the network as well as for groups more on the periphery. Equally, the network was linked to the global OWINFS and made frequent use of both the 'European' and 'global' identity in its campaigning (Strange 2013).

The Canadian groups that had been active in the MAI and in the earlier campaigns were closely involved in criticizing the GATS with S2B, although it is accurate to say that the European groups quickly became dominant. This had in part to do with the creation of S2B, but it was for many also a strategic decision: the European Union's political system, with its potential for disagreements among its Member States and thanks to its heightened political sensitivity to perceived threats to public services, meant that the EU appeared much more open to influence by social movement than a more homogenous political system of a nation-state such as the US. This strategy seemed to work since the European Commission eventually responded by altering some of the more controversial aspects of its negotiating position, such as its demands for developing countries to ensure access to water services.

The S2B network has continued to grow by being used for contesting the subsequent trade negotiations which involved the EU and other states, including free trade agreements with India, Peru and Colombia. The S2B was also active as part of a wider mobilization within the European civil society against the planned Anti-Counterfeiting Trade Agreement (ACTA). The ACTA, which was promoted by Japan and the US, has been signed by the US but has yet to be ratified after a successful campaign that saw the European Parliament reject the treaty.

The history of campaigns described above provides an outline of the infrastructure of the pre-existing transnational relations between social movement groups that, as will be discussed in the next section, are active in the developing contestation around the TTIP negotiations.

The EU and US Trade-Related Social Movements Contesting the TTIP

Thanks to the historical developments through which social movements have emerged to contest trade-related negotiations like the TTIP, the overall differences between the EU and US groups contesting such negotiations are more directly attributable to variations in the policies and the range of agreements discussed by their respective governments than to any ideological divide.

Trying to discern any clear ideological distinction between the two sides of the Atlantic is also difficult because the respective social movements are far from homogeneous within their own territories. Disagreements range across the spectrum, starting with 'radicals' who demand abolition of the multilateral trade regime up to 'reformists' who seek a more selective amelioration of the regime's perceived deficiencies. As a result, there is little to gain academically from asserting a clear US-EU divide in respect to the trade-focused social movements.

Thus, if we compare activities by the TTIP-related social movements on both sides of the Atlantic, there is little discernible difference.[1] These groups, however, face different challenges. This has to do with what other agreements their respective government authorities are negotiating as well as what the local political system means for how the groups must organize themselves in order to influence the local decision-makers.

On both sides of the Atlantic, the criticism of TTIP falls into several overlapping categories. First, the majority of the criticism has to do with the inclusion of an investor-state dispute (ISD) mechanism in TTIP. The ISD is presented as a direct threat to democracy and public accountability in the area of regulations, with social movements critical of the TTIP citing the past and ongoing cases of ISD in NAFTA and other trade agreements. In these cases, corporations have successfully sued states for bringing about regulations that were deemed necessary for public or environmental safety, but that had the potential to undermine the profitability of an investment by a foreign company.[2]

Second, there has been a significant focus on the TTIP as a threat to consumer safety. This aspect is related to regulatory harmonization that is perceived as undermining the existing consumer safety protection as well as posing an obstacle to further safeguards. Following the same logic, there are at least two other issues that are frequently present on both sides of the Atlantic where social movements

---

1   Interviews with social movement activists who represent both the European and US groups, February to April 2014.

2   By April 2014, the campaigners have already produced a small library of reports criticizing both the TTIP in general and its implications in particular areas, such as food security. For examples, see, S2B (2013); FoEE (2013); Hilary (2013).

mobilize against the TTIP, i.e. environmental protection and labour rights. All in all, these overlapping themes come back to a general criticism of the TTIP as an agreement prioritizing the interests of corporations over the interests of society in designing public policies.

This apparent degree of transatlantic unity among social movements that are critical of the TTIP is a product of the past trade-related mobilizations, as shown above, but also due to the production of several global group petitions (Strange 2011) with a series of specific demands to which the groups on both sides of the Atlantic have added their signatures. Although these petitions have been addressed to the EU and US decision-makers, they also act as a means of framing how the individual groups express their own criticism of the TTIP. Having said that, this kind of collaboration does not signify any substantive form of alliance-building, such as the one that might have been witnessed in cases where the financial resources and personnel were directly shared. It is rather the strength of social movements that they are able to deal with ideas that can be easily communicated across the Atlantic.

The Internet owes much of its current form to social movements who were amongst the first groups to use it seriously as a type of communication technology and it remains central to the way in which mobilization around the TTIP is expressed. In addition to the web presence, the TTIP campaigning is supported, both in the US and Europe, by real face-to-face relations. Since the TTIP negotiations were first announced in 2013, there have been several transatlantic meetings both in Brussels and in Washington, although the vast majority of substantive collaboration remains limited to the cooperation within the US or Europe.

In the United States, Public Citizen, a social justice group, and the Sierra Club, a conservation organization, have been the most prominent groups in campaigning against the TTIP. Thanks to their prominence, these groups became most active in forming and maintaining the networks with other groups which were critical of the TTIP, such as a number of smaller consumer rights groups as well as some trade unions.

In Europe, the majority of activism has taken place via the S2B network. Similarly to the US, since the environment has been the main concern, the key role has been played by Friends of the Earth Europe (FoEE), but also by the Corporate Europe Observatory (CEO), which campaigns for a better oversight of the corporate lobbying in the European Union and, previously, had been central to the GATS campaign and to the original formation of S2B. The campaign literature produced within S2B has extensively referenced the material published by Public Citizen and the Sierra Club. The S2B website also contains various petitions expressing transatlantic solidarity which were signed by groups on both sides of the Atlantic.

Moreover, the groups have had a mixed success in attracting significant media attention through which an ordinary citizen would come across the TTIP. The TTIP has received growing attention from both the US and certain European media, even though the activists on both sides of the Atlantic report that it has so far proved very difficult to get their own views expressed. In addition, social movement groups have been facing yet another challenge: many prominent civil society organizations, including some trade unions, have been uncomfortable with being seen as critics of a trade agreement between the EU and the US. Therefore, the critical social movement organizations have avoided treating either the EU or the US as a threat to one another and, instead, articulated a narrative where the TTIP is a 'corporate attack' on both the EU and the US. This criticism has been published in reports that were intended for interested parties, such as trade unions which are uncertain of their position, as well as for politicians and journalists. These reports are presented in a professional format and supported by evidence, such as examples of what the inclusion of ISD in NAFTA has meant for consumer safety (Hilary 2013).

Due to differences in their respective political systems, direct access to negotiators varies in the US and EU contexts. In the US, there is an established tradition that non-state actors are invited to advise on trade policy, with the US Trade Representative (USTR) having a large number of advisory groups focusing on specific aspects of the TTIP negotiations. A formal process governs the access to these groups where individuals are invited only as 'experts' rather than as representatives of their organization. In principle, being a member in such an advisory group means that the member must not communicate anything that has been discussed inside that group, not even to his colleagues in his own organization. This principle can be enforced with a threat of imprisonment. Whilst it remains unclear to what extent this threat would be implemented, it underlines the limits which are placed on access to negotiations. Activists criticize this formalization as limiting their space for advocacy, particularly where corporate representatives dominate the vast majority of the advisory groups.

In contrast to the USTR's formal approach, DG Trade in the European Commission is less formal with respect to its single *ad hoc* advisory group. Whilst the other parts of the European Commission have a long tradition of having advisory groups, DG Trade has not previously tried this approach. An activist who was involved in that group reported that DG Trade tried to impose its control over what those who were invited to attend, including private businesses, could report back to their organizations but failed because the European Commission lacks the enforcement power of a nation-state. The value of these advisory groups has been questioned where, despite its original promises, DG Trade has not provided any access to the draft negotiating text. However, activists have been surprised by the degree to which DG Trade has moved away from its traditionally closed approach to welcoming them to such dialogues. From the perspective of activists, this demonstrates how seriously DG Trade considers the threat by social movements to scupper the TTIP negotiations. Certainly, DG Trade has been far more open than previously in disclosing some of its negotiating positions.

At the time of writing this chapter, the groups still do not have a draft negotiation text. Building on the experience from the MAI campaign, acquiring this draft would greatly help their criticism and engagement with the media. Given the secretive nature of trade negotiations, where each side is reluctant to let the other know what it is willing to concede, a lack of access to a draft negotiating text for campaign groups is perhaps not surprising. However, in practice, any trade negotiations rely on a step-by-step process where different drafts exist with unresolved issues placed in brackets, thus giving valuable information on the development of the agreement. Negotiators are typically reluctant to publish such drafts for fear of putting undue pressure on negotiations. Yet, activists understandably remain frustrated with the lack of such access. Without having a draft, activists can be easily accused of scaremongering. To defend themselves, social movement groups have turned to building a large coalition of diverse interests. Whilst both the US and EU groups have organized meetings to discuss further transatlantic cooperation on the TTIP, the international consumer safety group Consumers International (CI) has helped establish the Transatlantic Consumer Dialogue (TACD) to criticize the TTIP. Its name is a direct reference to the title of the corporate body that allegedly at first helped launch the TTIP negotiations – the Transatlantic Business Dialogue (TABD) (see Dür and Lechner's chapter in this book). TACD has been used to set up several meetings where the US and EU representatives of negotiating delegations have addressed social movements groups, including Public Citizen and several European consumer rights groups.

The groups working on food security have also been active in transatlantic cooperation with increasingly regular meetings, webinars and the co-publication of reports by ARC2020 – a lose network of NGOs in Europe – and by the US-based Institute for Agriculture and Trade Policy (IATP). This is particularly salient given the sensitive issues, such as the EU labelling of genetically modified food, which has been identified as a key issue by the US negotiators. A similar collaboration has developed on the regulation of chemicals, with regular telephone conference calls, the creation of email-listservs and co-publication of critical reports.

There is a clear interest among social movement groups working on the TTIP to mobilize on the transatlantic level, although it seems unlikely that this would go beyond the current level of information sharing and joint signing of petitions. The TACD is an indication of how things might develop further, particularly if the TTIP negotiations are successful. Campaigning on issues such as the environment or labour rights within the EU or the US will always have to take into account the transatlantic level and thus will require some kind of a stable coordination between the EU and the US groups. Even with an ambitious deadline intended for late-2014, TTIP negotiations remain at an early stage. It is allegedly partly so because negotiators fear that with any extension of the deadline, there is an increased risk that the more politically sensitive aspects of the TTIP will attract public attention and hence will limit the negotiations' flexibility. Whether or not this is true remains to be seen. However, a battle is certainly fought by social movement groups to raise public awareness but also to problematize the TTIP among the more conservative civil society organizations and politicians.

In March 2014, the largest transatlantic meeting of social movement groups occurred with 97 registered participants who met in Brussels. The three-day event included a series of presentations on specific topics – environment, health, labour, investment, food and digital rights – as well as strategy discussions, a stakeholder presentation to the European Commission and a small street protest outside of the offices of DG Trade. This structure reflects the broader strategy where lobbying of negotiators and other social movement groups is prioritized over any public protest. This reflects the calculation of these groups as to where they are most likely to influence the negotiations, accepting there is too little time to catch public interest. Significantly, the issues were presented during the March meeting by two speakers each, i.e. each by a representative from each side of the Atlantic. Due to the history of social movements described above, activists are extremely conscious of the relationship between geography and identity when building transnational alliances, which is required in the case of TTIP campaigning. The challenge is not forming an alliance, but communicating the complexities of a trade agreement to the mass public.

Conclusion

If an agreement on the TTIP is reached, social movement organizations in the US and the EU will most likely establish more regular forms of transatlantic coordination, although this would be a continuation of the existing relations rather than something completely new. Much will depend on how any final TTIP deal would function, to what extent there would be regulatory harmonization and how it would be administered. Without knowing the draft text, it is difficult to say what kind of regulatory structures social movements will face in a TTIP world. Looking back to NAFTA and its impact over the past 20 years, this chapter suggests that there will be an increased collaboration but the predominant role will still be played by the nation-states. In other words, it is in the national context that social movement organizations are best able to mobilize themselves (Kay 2011).

The same conclusion can be based on the European experience: the shift of decision-making to the EU level has not been followed by any similarly developed civil society, let alone any kind of a substantive public sphere. Nevertheless, a public sphere has already developed around the TTIP: it is based on the relations between individuals within the different social movements and they are materialized in joint publications and meetings – whether over the Internet, telephone or face-to-face. Given the lack of media attention, this is perhaps a very narrow and shallow understanding of a public sphere, but it is also a more realistic one. For this reason, activists are, instead, focused on building a common criticism among themselves as well as on producing reports as opposed to undertaking the currently thankless task of attempting to mobilize mass protests.

PART III
Knock-on Effects and Unintended Consequences for Third Parties

Chapter 8

An Open Door?
TTIP and Accession by Third Countries

Vinod K. Aggarwal and Simon J. Evenett

Introduction

As the US and the EU continue their negotiations towards a Transatlantic Trade and Investment Partnership (TTIP), key questions arise concerning the rules for accession for countries that are not parties to these talks and whether third parties are likely to avail themselves of any such rules. Senior officials on both sides of the Atlantic have argued that TTIP should set the standards for global commerce in the twenty-first century – with the not-so-subtle implication that third parties will ultimately have to sign up to these rules. Assumptions, it seems, are being made as to the TTIP-induced incentives faced by third parties.

Analysts have come up with differing estimates of the implications of TTIP for third parties with some arguing that the accord will generate increased exports for them (CEPR 2013), while others claim that there will be significant costs in the form of trade diversion to non-participants (Felbermayr, Heid and Lehwald 2013). This, in turn, raises questions as to whether – however unlikely – third parties should have a voice during the TTIP negotiations and whether there should be any procedures for third parties joining TTIP after it has been signed. We argue that the latter matter is linked to both the substantive content of TTIP and to key matters of institutional design.

The first section of this chapter explores the relationship among different elements of trade agreements such as issue scope, the strength of agreements, the degree of liberalism in the accord and other relevant dimensions and characterizes TTIP using these yardsticks. The second section describes five different means by which the provisions of a possible TTIP accord could spread, taking account of the incentives faced by third parties. Since four of those five means do not involve third parties joining TTIP, we challenge the implicit assumption that third parties will necessarily throw themselves at the mercy of US and EU trade negotiators to align with TTIP's new rules for commerce. The third section explores other past examples of trade agreements to consider the different modalities by which norms and rules might spread in practice. Our conclusion argues that the view of some, that TTIP's twenty-first-century new rules and regulatory approaches will lead to greater uniformity in the architecture of trade accords, may be incorrect. Instead, such mega-free trade agreements (FTAs) could well contribute to the further fragmentation of the world trading system in ways going beyond those we have previously articulated (Aggarwal and Evenett 2013).

Designing Trade Institutions: The Interplay of Elements

Institutions, including those in trade, vary on a number of often inter-related dimensions. Trade accords, in particular, can be characterized according to six criteria. These include: (1) membership which refers to whether the agreement is bilateral, minilateral or multilateral; (2) geographical scope which refers to the question of whether countries seek agreements within a particular region or outside; (3) the economic weight of partners, that is accords with large or smaller countries; (4) issue scope, i.e. the range of issues that a policy or arrangement deals with runs from narrow to broad; (5) whether the accord reduces discrimination against foreign commercial interests (generically, the nature of the agreement); and (6) the strength of the arrangement being negotiated, particularly in terms of the degree of institutionalization.[1]

We consider each element in detail before focusing on the likely contours of TTIP. We use the term bilateral to refer to two countries and minilateral to more than two. We reserve the term 'multilateral' to refer to nearly universal coverage although some might prefer the term global. Examples of bilateral agreements include the multiplicity of FTAs that have been negotiated among countries such as the Korea-US or Japan-Singapore accords. Minilateral agreements include agreements such the current Trans-Pacific Partnership (TPP). Finally, the best example of a multilateral agreement in trade is the WTO although some sectoral agreements have essentially all relevant producing countries involved.

Geographical scope differentiates between arrangements that are concentrated geographically and those that in principle bind states across great distances. Thus, while the North American Free Trade Agreement (NAFTA) or the EU are geographically concentrated, arrangements such as TPP (and TTIP) are geographically dispersed. Despite the diverse membership and geography of these accords, analysts often conflate and describe all of these accords that are not bilateral as 'regional'. This usage by the WTO, and often followed by other analysts, as a contrast to multilateral arrangements is misleading. Thus, it is better to use the term interregional when discussing accords between customs unions (such as EU-Mercosur) and the term trans-regional when referring to agreements

---

1   This paragraph draws on Aggarwal and Lee (2011). Earlier work by Aggarwal (1985 and 2001) developed several of these dimensions at length from a theoretical perspective and analysed their interdependence. Other analysts have also looked at dimensions such as the extent of delegation of power from member states to institutional bodies and the centralization of tasks within the institution (Abbott and Snidal 2001, Koromenos et al. 2001). Given the highly under-institutionalized nature of TTIP, we do not focus on these latter dimensions here.

such as the TPP. The case of TTIP is relatively unique as it involves a single market negotiating with a single country, and thus, to differentiate from the others, Aggarwal and Fogarty (2004) have used the terms 'hybrid interregionalism'.

Another useful dimension is the economic weight of partners. Some agreements have mainly small states (for example, European Free Trade Area), whereas others such as TTIP are among large economic powers. One can also have agreements with both small and large states, the TPP being a good example of such an accord.

In terms of issue scope, the range is from narrow (a few issues) to broad (multiple issues) in scope. Over time, the GATT has grown from a relatively narrow accord focusing on manufactured goods to its current incarnation as the WTO with agreements covering a range of different policies affecting business. For example, negotiations in July 2014 were launched among a group of WTO members to liberalize trade in so-called green goods. Sectoral agreements that started out relatively narrowly such as the Long-Term Agreement on Cotton Textiles (LTA) and wide-bodied aircraft have been complemented by others to cover certain information technology products and certain service sectors.

The fifth dimension addresses whether measures have been either market opening (liberalizing) or market closing (protectionist). Most of the agreements in trade have recently been trade-opening but the degree to which they actually call for significant liberalization has varied. For example, the mega-FTA known as the Regional Comprehensive Economic Partnership (RCEP) that involves ASEAN members plus China, Japan, Korea, Australia, New Zealand and India is likely to be less liberal as proposed than the Trans-Pacific Partnership (TPP). It should not be forgotten that many trade agreements include a myriad of provisions to limit or restrict trade such as those relating to antidumping, countervailing duties, intellectual property, safeguard measures (of different kinds) and provisions to reverse prior liberalization.

Lastly, we can look at the degree of institutionalization or strength of agreements.[2] Strength refers to both the precision and obligation of rules. From this perspective, authors have often contrasted the so-called European and Asian models of regional economic integration. The first one is built upon a wide set of specific and binding rules (called the *acquis communautaire* in the jargon of European integration), whereas the second is built upon declarations, intentions and voluntary commitments.

Turning to TTIP, while the agreement is still being negotiated, in our assessment TTIP is: bilateral (considering the EU as a single actor which, at least in terms

---

2   Aggarwal (1985) uses the term 'strength'. Later work such as Abbott et al. (2000) have used the term legalization, but the two are not identical. Of the dimensions discussed here, geographical scope is the most controversial. It is worth noting that this category is quite subjective since simple distance is hardly the only relevant factor in defining a 'geographic region'. Despite the interest that regionalism has attracted, the question of how to define a region remains highly contested. See the discussion by, among others, Mansfield and Milner (1999), Katzenstein (1997) and Aggarwal and Fogarty (2004).

of the Commission's negotiations mandate, makes sense); hybrid interregional (in being transatlantic); with economically large partners, very wide scope, very liberal in intent and slated to be – at least on paper – institutionalized, binding and enforceable.

Along these dimensions our assessment is relatively uncontroversial. The inter-relationship among the last three dimensions is more interesting, however. In terms of thinking about accession issues, the fact that the current negotiations involve two major actors with the intent to create a strong liberalizing binding agreement is of great significance. For example, EU and US negotiators have explicitly noted that the agreement will cover traditional market access issues, regulatory issues, and new rules including intellectual property, investor rights, labour and the environment.[3]

In view of the high standards being sought both in terms of issue scope and strength, and thus the difficulty in reconciling a host of issues, both the US and EU have explicitly ruled out the participation of other members. Karel De Gucht (2013c), for example, referring to TTIP's breadth and complexity, told the Swiss-American Chamber of Commerce on 15 November 2013:

> That is why it is important that the TTIP negotiations themselves cannot be opened up to others. They are simply too complicated to bring in outside partners – no matter how close. Switzerland has made a choice about membership of the European Union. This is one of the times when that choice has a consequence.

It is worth distinguishing here between 'open negotiations' and an 'open agreement'. The former allows third parties to join prior to the conclusion of the accord, whereas the latter would signify that third parties could join following the conclusion of the accord. At this point, the US and EU have ruled out the former but not the latter (see the discussion in the next section).

This rather blunt dig at the Swiss has been accompanied by continuing claims that the TTIP agreement will benefit third countries. For example, the EU has emphasized that 'The TTIP should not only boost trade and income in the EU and US but also in the rest of the world. The CEPR study finds that the agreement would increase GDP in our trading partners by almost €100 billion' (European Commission 2013e). The same study then goes on to criticize Felbermayr, Heid and Lehwald (2013), arguing that their claims about the negative impact of trade diversion on third parties are incorrect.

---

3 Although it should be noted that US and EU officials have hinted that binding disciplines may not be agreed on every matter of joint interest. The EU-US High Level Working Group report, finalized in February 2013, employed softer language when describing joint work in the areas of intellectual property regimes, labour, environmental policies, export restrictions on raw materials, customs and trade facilitation, state-owned enterprises and 'localization' measures (High Level Working Group on Jobs and Growth 2013).

Rather than encouraging other members to join, the EU and US have argued that TTIP should be seen as a template for future global negotiations. As Karel De Gucht has noted (2013c), the EU views 'TTIP ... as a nucleus and laboratory for the next stage of rulemaking at the global level ...'. These sentiments are shared, it seems, on the American side. In a speech on 5 May 2014, the United States Trade Representative, Ambassador Michael Froman, said of TTIP: 'It's about shaping a global system – one with our shared values at the core' (Froman 2014). Let's suppose TTIP is concluded. The question then arises as to how the TTIP commercially-relevant provisions could spread to third parties? We turn to this important matter next.

Five Means by Which TTIP's Provisions Could Spread

EU and US officials have failed to clarify the manner in which any TTIP provisions might be adopted by third parties. One option is that third parties accede to TTIP after the EU and US have signed the accord. It is precisely because this option exists that the matters of accession terms and institutional provisions facilitating accession arise. We first highlight the range of choices and incentives facing third parties once a TTIP is signed. For our purposes we assume TTIP is signed, including provisions that its parties originally identified as negotiating objectives. Moreover, we focus on the mechanisms by which those provisions could spread to third parties – *not* on the important normative matter of whether those provisions *should* spread to third parties.

Before developing the argument further, the insights of the literature on sequencing regional integration provide a useful point of departure, as it speaks to the factors responsible for increasing the membership of free trade areas and customs unions. In particular, it will be useful to revisit the economic incentives that drive Baldwin's notion of 'domino regionalism' (Baldwin 1993).[4] To fix ideas, suppose nations A and B form a FTA, eliminating tariffs on all trade in goods between them. Suppose some firms in a third party, nation C, were the lowest cost suppliers to country A. Assume, as Baldwin does, that those exporters have made investments in product design, distribution etc. so that they can ship their goods to country A.

The introduction of the FTA can result in trade diversion from exporters in C to less efficient exporters in B, resulting in the former losing market share in A. To protect their investments, exporters in C will lobby their government to begin negotiations to join the FTA involving A *and* B, or so the argument goes. In this

---

4   Evenett (2004) surveys and critically assesses domino regionalism and two other explanations in the literature for the sequencing of regional integration, namely, technocratic entrepreneurship and geopolitical dynamics. As will become clear, our discussion of domino regionalism is not meant to elevate that argument above others. Rather, our goal is to highlight the limits of that argument as far as TTIP is concerned.

manner, then, the creation of one FTA sets off falling dominoes that could result in other FTAs being negotiated and signed. In Baldwin's view, these incentives account in part for the expansion in EU membership over time and for US FTA policy towards Latin America after NAFTA came into force.

The chase for preferential market access with its implications for not just exports but also the desirability of an economy as a location for foreign direct investment (FDI) are the central mechanisms at work in domino regionalism. This logic was developed further by US policymakers in the first administration of President George W. Bush when they saw themselves as organizing contests among trading partners for preferential access to the large US market. This gave rise to the strategy of 'competitive liberalization' and, to the extent that access to markets on both sides of the Atlantic is seen by some as a stimulus to third parties to accept TTIP standards, then aspects of the logic of domino regionalism are relevant to discussions of third party reactions to TTIP.[5]

Considerations of space prevent a detailed critique of Baldwin's theory.[6] Yet the question implicitly raised by Baldwin is the right one: what incentives do third parties face once TTIP is signed? When analysing how a third party might respond, it is worth recalling that modern inter-state accords, like TTIP, contain provisions on many areas of government policy, and thus there may be more than one source of harm to third parties. Baldwin's argument emphasized trade diversion explicitly but also mentioned investment diversion. Although it is often argued that regulatory discrimination is not likely (on the grounds that no government would want to maintain two sets of regulations, for signatories to FTAs and for the rest), the possibility of regulatory discrimination against third parties should be acknowledged, not least in the allocation of enforcement resources.

One reaction of third parties to the signing of TTIP might be to seek negotiations to join that accord. This, however, is not the only option available to third parties. This, in turn, raises questions about the relative merits of different potential responses to TTIP. We can identify at least four alternatives. The second alternative may be relevant in cases where a third party loses primarily because of TTIP-induced policy changes in only one of its signatories which, for expositional purposes only, say, is the EU. Then the third party may respond to TTIP by seeking to sign a FTA with the EU but not the US – or augmenting any FTA it already has with the EU. From the perspective of the US, any such FTA between the third party and the EU might see TTIP's standards spread to the third party, but then they might not. Moreover, since the US and EU do not have identical commercial interests, any subsequent FTA between the EU and the third party will not address

---

5   See Evenett and Meier (2008) for a detailed account and assessment of the US policy of 'competitive liberalization'.

6   Not the least of which is Baldwin's more recent assessment that the large emerging markets will not be part of the mega-regional free trade deals that are currently being negotiated, the latter deals being what he refers to as the second pillar of world trade governance (Baldwin 2012).

the same matters as if the third party had sought to join TTIP. To date, nothing in the TTIP negotiations suggests that the US and EU are willing to commit to jointly negotiate FTAs with third parties after TTIP comes into force or to include TTIP provisions in FTAs subsequently negotiated with third parties. We suspect that some analysts and negotiators have inadvertently made assumptions about how the US and EU would negotiate FTAs that follow TTIP.

A third option arises from the reality that a third party harmed by TTIP may find it unappealing to throw themselves at the mercy of US and EU trade negotiators in a full blown FTA negotiation. This observation is particularly relevant under two circumstances. If the harm done to the third party is perceived to be smaller than the cost of acceding to TTIP, or in negotiating a FTA with the EU or US separately, then the third party may decide to wait for the US and EU to seek to 'multilateralize' TTIP at the WTO. The logic here might be that if the US and EU were to become *demandeurs* of TTIP disciplines at the WTO, then in the apparent logic of that organization's negotiations, the EU and US would have to 'pay' for those demands and the third party would benefit from such payment. A third party might argue: why not wait and be paid to take on TTIP's provisions? Yet given the difficulties in negotiating the Doha Round and in defining a new work programme for the WTO, the likelihood of multilateral trade accords being employed to entrench TTIP provisions as global standards may be many years into the future and, therefore, possibly beyond the time horizon of senior political leaders in third parties.

Should a third party conclude that the regulatory provisions of TTIP – said to be an important element of current negotiations – harm its commercial interests, two more options arise. The fourth option is to negotiate with the TTIP signatories and possibly with other interested nations on an accord whose scope is confined to the implementation of a narrower set of rules or regulations than the full scope of TTIP. This accord need not be a binding accord, or even a WTO accord. A fifth option is for a third party to unilaterally adopt regulatory standards equivalent to those in TTIP and then seek mutual recognition from regulators in the EU and US. The latter regulators often prefer dealing with 'their own kind' rather than trade negotiators and may find either of these latter two options appealing. Options four and five represent, therefore, a more surgical response by third parties to TTIP. Of course, both options imply that some TTIP regulatory provisions may spread to some third parties, perhaps to the satisfaction of EU and US officials and commercial interests. But note the repeated use of the word 'some'.

In conclusion, in assessing whether TTIP's provisions will spread, it is important to focus on the incentives faced by harmed third parties. Those third parties have at least five options available to them – some of which may involve ultimately adopting certain of TTIP's provisions. There are no guarantees, however, that the spread of TTIP's provisions will be anything other than piecemeal. Thus, the US and EU claims to be establishing new global standards through TTIP should be treated with some scepticism. Such claims may be founded on erroneous assumptions that the logic of domino regionalism – with its binary (join, do not join) set of choices available to third parties – applies in the context of a TTIP involving a suite of different provisions. That there are numerous options available to third parties cast doubt on any assumptions that they will scramble to join TTIP – with a key issue being how different third parties react to each other's decisions as to how to proceed. Once TTIP is signed, further strategic interaction between third parties, the outcome of which cannot be confidently predicted at this time, cannot be ruled out.

Examples from Other Trade Agreements

In thinking about how trade agreements might spread to third parties, it is worth looking at parallels from both previously negotiated regional and trans-regional accords. This exercise helps us compare our analysis in the previous section with the historical record to glean insights on how the TTIP initiative is likely to impact others. Following the enumeration of options above, we begin with the basic binary option of joining or not joining.

With respect to accession, Kelley (2010) distinguishes between a 'convoy' approach and a 'club approach'. In the case of a convoy, membership is open to a predefined regional grouping without additional criteria.[7] These two approaches provide a useful framework approach to think about accession issues. The EU constitutes the example *par excellence* of a club approach with very specific criteria that have evolved over its history with respect to third party accession. Some examples include the abolition of the death penalty and democratic institutions (Kelley 2010: 15–17).[8] In addition, the EU has engaged in the monitoring of prospective entrants (Kelley 2010: 18–20).

The Asia-Pacific Economic Cooperation (APEC) provides an example of a convoy approach – at least in the first few years of its existence. Since the early 1990s, however, it has increasingly moved to restricting entry, operating with a consensus rule to admit new members. Moreover, after 1997, it instituted a moratorium on membership for 10 years after it had reached a total of 21 economies. Although the moratorium was extended until 2010, since then it has expired but no new members have yet been admitted. Thus, a convoy approach can evolve into a club one.

The second option discussed for TTIP is to create an agreement with one but not both negotiating parties in response to the formation of an accord. The case of a number of Latin American countries signing FTAs with Mexico to receive some

---

7 Surprisingly, Kelley does not discuss how the very concept of 'region' may be contested, as we have noted above.

8 Other criteria for EU accession (i.e. the Copenhagen criteria) include functioning market economy, democracy and rule of law, ability to take on the *acquis* and, possibly, the absorption capacity of the EU. See http://ec.europa.eu/enlargement/policy/glossary/terms/accession-criteria_en.htm [accessed: 30 July 2014].

of the benefits of NAFTA (though not all, of course, in view of regional content requirements) provides a good example of such a strategy. This Latin American effort has been followed by the conclusion of accords between several Asian countries and Mexico as well as the EU's conclusion of an FTA with Mexico which entered into force in 2000.

In terms of the third option of the multilateralization of TTIP's norms and rules, this strategy has also been explicit for agreements such as NAFTA and APEC. The former sought to create rules about new issues such as labour and environmental linkages to trade, intellectual property and the like with the goal of encouraging the inclusion of such measures in the Uruguay Round of the GATT. Similarly, APEC has sought to discuss issues with an eye to encouraging their adoption in the GATT and later the WTO. This 'pathfinder' approach was evidenced in the effort to promote sectoral agreements in APEC through its Early Voluntary Sectoral Liberalization effort in the late 1990s, but which ultimately failed either to garner support in APEC or to be adopted by the WTO. On a less formal basis, APEC also encouraged the notion of 'open regionalism' (Aggarwal 1993, Bergsten 1997). This idea combines both the issue of membership and the question of openness to encourage the extension of APEC's liberalization to non-members automatically. This idea, however, did not sit well with the US which worried about the EU in particular free riding on any liberalization that it might undertake.

With respect to the fourth option of an agreement with narrower scope than a particular FTA, we have seen the negotiation of multilateral sector-specific accords in the late 1990s on information technology, telecom and financial services as a follow on to the Uruguay Round negotiations. These accords, which Aggarwal and Ravenhill (2001) have dubbed 'open sectoral' agreements, come with their own set of benefits and costs. While they may facilitate sector-specific liberalization that meets the interests of firms in a particular industry, they may simultaneously *reduce* political support for multilateral multi-sector negotiations. Because sectoral agenda setting involves a limited and easily polarized set of domestic interests, the margin for coalition building and political give-and-take is much slimmer.

The fifth approach of unilateral measures by third parties to comply with TTIP also has precedence in APEC although in somewhat different form. APEC has encouraged its members to pursue 'Individual Action Plans' (IAPs) which essentially constitute unilateral liberalization. While TTIP clearly does not call for unilateral liberalization on the part of the US and EU, analysts such as Fred Bergsten (1997) have argued that one approach for APEC to extend its membership is to encourage what he terms 'shadow IAPs' to ascertain how committed third parties are to APEC's goals of broad-scale liberalization.

In sum, the options that we have suggested for how the norms and rules of any TTIP accord might be extended to third parties are not theoretical speculations; precedent for variants of them exist.

Conclusion

On several occasions, US and EU officials have asserted that TTIP's provisions will govern not just transatlantic trade in the twenty-first century but ultimately global commerce. At the same time, the officials involved have so far refused to countenance admission of third parties to this negotiation, nor do reports on the state of negotiations refer to the inclusion of a fully specified accession mechanism.[9] Analysts, therefore, are entitled to ask: by what means will TTIP's provisions spread to third parties? Drawing upon experience with other FTAs, we seek to answer this question by examining the incentives third parties have to take on board in TTIP's provisions.

The old expression 'there's many a slip between cup and lip' neatly summarizes our findings. In their rush to negotiate, US and EU officials, as well as other interested parties, may have overlooked key factors. For example, we have argued that the interplay of a number of dimensions of agreements – like TTIP and those that might follow – including membership, geographical scope, the economic weight of partners, issue scope, the discriminatory nature of accords and strength of arrangements all influence each other. Therefore, considering membership in isolation – and by implication, subsequent accession to TTIP – is flawed.

Worse, third parties that feel they must respond to TTIP's coming into force have at least four options to consider – other than joining this transatlantic deal. Moreover, an implication of our argument is that even if TTIP's provisions do spread, it is optimistic, to put it mildly, that the spread will be uniform across space and time. Analysts should be open to the possibility that a successfully concluded TTIP could be another factor fragmenting – as opposed to unifying – the world economy in the twenty-first century.

---

9   At the time of writing, the latest report on the state of the TTIP negotiations was made public by the European Commission in late July 2014, see http://trade.ec.europa.eu/doclib/docs/2014/july/tradoc_152699.pdf [accessed: 30 July 2014].

Chapter 9

The EU and the US at the WTO

Erick Duchesne and Richard Ouellet

Introduction

As long as the EU and the US have not yet concluded the TTIP negotiations and implemented this potential bilateral agreement, their trade relations are mainly governed by the WTO law, their trade talks are largely held under the auspices of the WTO in the Doha Round and the management of their trade conflicts abides by the rules and procedures found in the WTO Dispute Settlement Understanding (DSU). Thus, observing the interactions between those two trading powers in the multilateral forum might give a good idea of what the pace, the tone and the content of the ambitious talks launched by the giant transatlantic economic partners will be. With this approach, we first propose a brief retrospective of the Doha Round negotiations. We then examine the trade preferences expressed by the EU and the US in WTO fora and see what divides them and what brings them closer. We finally have a look at the way the two powers manage their trade disputes.

The Doha Development Agenda (DDA)

The Doha Development Round of multilateral negotiations was launched at the 4th WTO ministerial meeting at Doha, Qatar, on 9–14 November 2001. While on-going negotiations on agriculture were mandated by the previous round of negotiations, some of its members, including the European Union and the United States, wanted to tackle a broader agenda in order to achieve greater liberalization. Contracting parties quickly settled on the idea that the Round should prioritize the common trading interests of developing countries. In the aftermath of the terrorist attacks on the United States on 11 September of the same year and a sagging world economy, trade ministers had faith that they could reach an agreement on an ambitious agenda no later than 1 January 2005. They were met with the harsh reality of coming to terms on intricate issues among members holding contrasting views, under the Single Undertaking negotiating shackles.

The negotiations stumbled over entrenched disparities between the EU, the US and emerging countries over core issues such as agriculture, non-agricultural market access (NAMA), services and trade remedies. The 5th mid-term stocktaking ministerial meeting in Cancun, Mexico on 10–14 September 2003 failed to provide the political guidance required for a successful ending of the negotiations by the set deadline. Despite the impasse, especially relative to the so-called Singapore issues (transparency in government procurement, trade facilitation, trade and investment, and trade and competition), trade ministers agreed to keep the wheels in motion. A glimmer of hope emerged when WTO members approved a Framework Agreement in July 2004, particularly on the prickly issue of agriculture, which represented some basic principles for instituting the modalities of future negotiations. Optimism was short-lived when the talks backslid into multifaceted knotty challenges prior to the 6th Hong Kong Ministerial Conference on 13–18 December 2005. The final Ministerial Declaration revealed a few minor zones of convergence in agriculture (a 2013 deadline to abandon export subsidies), NAMA and market access for least developed countries, an advance that justified pushing the deadline to conclude the DDA by the end of 2006.

In lieu of an agreement by the new set date and despite a flurry of talks and consultations, WTO Director-General Pascal Lamy suspended the negotiations indefinitely on 24 July 2006. Informal meetings between select WTO contracting parties did not yield any serious breakthrough, but fostered enough goodwill to convince Lamy to revive the negotiations in January 2007. After this near-death experience, central players, including the EU and the US, once again pledged to untie the Gordian knot by the end of 2007. The chairs of the agriculture and NAMA negotiating groups came up with draft modalities by mid-summer 2007 but, yet again, the talks foundered a year late, mainly due to disagreement over special safeguard mechanisms for agriculture products. From that point on the negotiations were maintained on life support, with unproductive revised drafts, until the parties reached a deal on trade facilitation at the 9th ministerial conference in Bali in December 2013, the first multilateral agreement since the creation of the WTO nearly 20 years earlier.

It is beyond the scope of this chapter to account for the reasons leading to a DDA stalemate, but a brief review of the literature leads to the following explanations, among a few others: diametrically opposed perceptions of the nature of the Round between developed and developing countries (Cho 2010), the inclusion of non-trade concerns in the negotiations (Martin and Messerlin 2007) and their increasing complexity (Baldwin 2006), discrepant domestic trade priorities (Young 2007, Bhandari and Klaphake 2011), the rapid growth of bilateral and regional agreements (Bhagwati 2008), a resort to murkier forms of protectionism as a result of the 2008 financial crisis (Aggarwal and Evenett 2013) and a geopolitical realignment (Evenett 2007).

In the next section, we discuss the divergences and convergences in EU and US negotiating positions, but we consider here their respective expectations *vis-à-vis* the DDA. In their relatively lengthy opening statements at the Doha ministerial conference, Pascal Lamy and Robert Zoellick, respectively Trade Commissioner for the EU and Trade Representative for the US, disclosed ambitious laundry lists that would set the agenda for the Round (WTO 2001). In subsequent ministerial conferences, a palpable sense of frustration emerged and opening statements by EU and US trade representatives became shorter and shorter.

Starting with the 2005 Hong Kong Ministerial, opening statements reveal a move towards narrower objectives if a successful round was to be concluded.[1] Hollow opening statements with vague and short wish lists ensued, until a restrained sense of optimism re-emerged at the 2013 Bali Conference, as exemplified by these respective testimonials by current EU and US representatives De Gucht and Froman: 'I feel a sense of purpose in the room. This is due to the big steps we have taken toward consensus since our last Ministerial Conference' and '[a]fter two decades of collective frustration, a deal is right in front of us' (WTO 2013b). It is safe to affirm that EU and US officials share the views held by seasoned trade analysts that '[w]hat is now on the table does not meet the expectations that many countries had when the round was launched ... but ... the deal that is likely to emerge is a valuable one' (Hoekman et al. 2009: ii). While we share these authors' wise counsel, we contend that the resolution of a modest DDA will be a welcome outcome only if it is complemented with a successful TTIP.

Concerns with the status of the multilateral negotiations, starting with the Cancun Ministerial and a movement towards a narrower agenda may have served as an impetus for the opening of the TTIP talks. This is not a new development. Before the launch of TTIP, EU and US officials were already on the same path: 'in view of the deadlock at the WTO, the U.S. and EU have come to believe that mega-FTAs provide a better vehicle to advance their commercial interests, at least in the short to medium term' (Aggarwal and Evenett 2013: 555). In the next section we consider how specific EU-US convergences and divergences in trade preferences at the WTO may have contributed to the launch of the TTIP in June 2013.

Convergences and Divergences in EU and US Trade Preferences at the WTO

Trade agreements and conflicts are the upshots of comprehensive trade strategies, such that we cannot offer undifferentiated analysis of regional agreements, such as TTIP, and multilateral negotiations. In other words, we cannot examine the coevolution of the positions held by the EU and the US in the Doha negotiations without first offering a few words on their respective key trading policies. It is these encompassing objectives that motivate, not only what trade officials sought to include on the DDA, but also, more importantly for the aims of this book, which issues can be more easily untangled in a bilateral channel such as TTIP. This forum

---

1   In the July 2004 Package, the EU had already agreed to the removal of three Singapore issues (investment, competition and transparency in government procurement) from the DDA. Facing strong domestic pressures, US officials were initially opposed to a minimal agreement that would not include substantial concessions by their trade partners. When it became clear that a purposeful agreement could not muster strong support in Congress with the presidential Trade Promotion Authority (TPA), the prospects of a 'Doha-lite' accord became more palatable.

transposition is due, according to Martin and Messerlin, to the 'exhaustion of traditional negotiating fuel' at the WTO (2007: 358–9). It is therefore reasonable to speculate on the possibility to 'refuel' the trade tank at the bilateral service station.

It is widely known that EU officials aim to strengthen their internal regulatory framework and magnify its impact on the world stage (Meunier and Nicolaïdis 2006, Sbragia 2009).[2] This strategy involves pushing for the inclusion of its regulatory framework in multilateral negotiations as well as targeting accommodating countries on a bilateral basis. Building on the momentum to expand liberalization as an objective of the DDA, EU trade officials seized the opportunity to embed the negotiations within a more expansive negotiating framework, therefore facilitating 'package deals' (Kerremans 2004: 372, as cited in Sbragia 2009: 5). On a similar basis, US officials wielded their power, through a strategy of 'competitive liberalization' (Evenett and Meier 2008), to open new trading grounds in contemporary FTAs. If we judge by the objectives that they pursued in the Trans-Pacific Partnership (TPP), they are more likely to use regional venues to push for selective benchmarks on intellectual property, environment and labour issues (Aggarwal and Evenett 2013: 553). Issue linkages on these topics in bilateral or regional negotiations among like-minded partners, while a formidable task, are not as insurmountable as they may seem on the multilateral stage.

In our view, no other study better characterizes the main differences between the EU and the US trade strategies in their pursuit of FTAs than Horn, Mavroidis and Sapir (2010). In a monk-like exercise, these authors analyse the precise content of EU and US preferential trade agreements (PTAs) and classify subjects covered by these agreements into two categories: WTO+ corresponding to 'provisions of PTAs which come under the current mandate of the WTO' and WTO-X 'where parties undertake bilateral commitments going beyond those that they have accepted at the multilateral level' (Horn et al. 2010: 1567). Sifting through a wealth of information, one of their main and most interesting conclusions is that European negotiators are more likely than their American counterparts to seek bilateral agreements that expand on WTO coverage, while the latter seek relatively stronger legal enforcement, albeit from a smaller range of WTO-enhancing issues. On the surface, these comprehensive trade strategies may seem opposite, but they are not irreconcilable. We could even optimistically propose that by stepping away momentarily from the troubled waters of the DDA and jumping into the TTIP arena, EU and US trade negotiators find themselves on more stable grounds to find a healthy compromise between their respective stances.

A few scholars have summarized what is still on the WTO negotiating table (Cho 2010, Martin and Mattoo 2010, Hoekman et al. 2009) and space limitation

---

2   For comprehensive reviews of European trade politics, see a special issue of the *Journal of European Public Policy* (2006), as well as Meunier (2005a) and Young (2007). While reviews of US trade policy objectives abound, we consider that the Congressional Research Service produces some of the most instructive summaries. See, for instance, Hornbeck and Irace (2013).

does not allow us to repeat the information here or cover all outstanding issues, but we would like to discuss a few of the unsettled trade businesses in light of the EU-US overall commercial bonds. At the heart of the DDA and TTIP stand contested and controversial agricultural issues. Yet, there are reasons to believe that the DDA served to narrow the negotiating gap between the transatlantic partners. As an informal member of the 'friends of multifunctionality' in agriculture, the EU supports a market-oriented multilateral trading system for this sector, assorted with social and environmental concerns. Common Agricultural Policy (CAP) reforms and concessions on agricultural export subsidies have allowed the EU to play a more offensive role in the DDA. The re-imposition of some EU and US export subsidies for dairy products in 2009 can be perceived as a reversal prompted by domestic protectionist pressures and a 'legal vacuum created by the Doha deadlock' (Cho 2010: 588). A more hopeful perspective would point to a minor setback that will add a useful bargaining chip to the EU arsenal for the TTIP negotiations. The US has also championed an ambitious liberalization agenda in agriculture, but its position has been weakened by its heavy domestic support in the sector.

Despite some opposing views on agriculture, for instance on geographic labelling, the US and the EU have often been on the same side of the ledger, confronting strong resistance from emerging countries. TTIP could serve as a vehicle to find additional common ground between transatlantic trade allies. It is especially on market access for agricultural products, a tractable issue on a bilateral footing, that some potential headway is within reach. The last version of WTO modalities is so wrought with exceptions, special safeguards and sensitive product designations, that even modest gains in the TTIP negotiations would be greeted with satisfaction. On services, the gap is still wide and offers on the table represent no notable liberalization clout. Yet, services represent up to 80 per cent of the EU and US GDP. Where prospects for a breakthrough are meagre at the WTO, this is one area where TTIP could have one of its most profound effects.

We can nevertheless cast some doubts on such an optimistic scenario, considering that the EU and the US were only seeking limited additional service commitments within the DDA. If there is a shred of hope for the EU and the US to open their borders more widely in the sector, it is more likely to come from their partaking in the Trade in Services Agreement (TISA) negotiations that were launched in March 2013. On government procurement, both parties should build on their respective agreements with Canada as a sound base for innovative and liberalizing measures in government services and contracts. On NAMA, few transatlantic obstacles remain and, while some effort will be needed in this sector of activity, it is on trade facilitation that negotiators should concentrate most of their attention, thus jumping on the opportunity to piggyback on the Bali agreement.

Ideally, contracting parties could find common ground on traditional trade issues at the WTO, but mega-FTAs such as TTIP are mostly about 'WTO+' commitments on regulatory and other issues that fall outside the purview of the DDA. These issues are discussed at length in this volume, but it should be mentioned that some of the impetus to seek greater compatibility of EU and US regulations and related standards stem from a strong opposition, especially from emerging economies, to debating these issues within the DDA. Could more coherent EU-US standards through TTIP be used as a multilateral template? Insofar as these economies are central to international commercial and financial markets, greater cohesion could have a profound impact on non-TTIP members, no matter if a multilateral agreement materializes or not. Ironically, it is therefore the DDA snub *vis-à-vis* the Singapore issues that could potentially lead to the most significant commercial breakthrough since the creation of the WTO.

Despite the strength of the bilateral EU-US relationship and some convergence of views at the WTO, policy tensions arise and some contested issues result into trade disputes. One of the deleterious impacts of the stalled DDA is that it leaves too many outstanding issues falling in the grey zone of the DSU. A promising, if not anticipated, outcome of TTIP would be to bring some meaning and clarity to these 'unresolvable' clashes of two trade titans. If only TTIP were to bring the two parties closer on these commercial spats, it could be viewed as a success. It would be adventurous to speculate on the nature of the TTIP's own DSU, but we offer here some thoughts on present-day EU-US commercial misunderstandings.

The absence of significant progress in the multilateral trade negotiations of the last 20 years and the stagnation of the wording of the WTO agreements never denoted an absence of evolution in the content of the legal frame governing the world trade system. With what is widely seen as the most successful system of dispute settlement in international public law (Hugues 2012), the WTO gave itself a powerful instrument to make sure governments fully implement its agreements and comply with them. The extraordinarily efficient procedure provided for by the DSU allowed for the appeasement of hundreds of cases brought before the Dispute Settlement Body (DSB) either by bringing the parties to a mutually agreed solution or by the adoption of a report ending by recommendations to bring national measures into conformity with WTO law. The lengthy reports of the Appellate Body (AB) and the panels also refined the interpretation of many provisions. Therefore, in spite of the failure of the multilateral trade talks, WTO Member States have always kept faith in a system that proved to be predictable and as shielded as possible from political pressures and governed by the rule of law.

WTO Disputes Involving the EU and the US

Of all WTO Members, the US and the EU are far and away the two most frequent users of the DSU. At the time we write this chapter, of the 479 complaints filed before the DSB since the creation of the WTO, the EU has been or is complainant in 92 cases, defendant in 78 cases and a third party in 144 cases. The US is a complainant in 107 cases, defendant in 121 cases and a third party in 114 cases. Of course, volumes of trade partly explain those spectacular figures but they do not provide a fully satisfactory justification for such important involvements in trade disputes. In comparison, China, which has leapfrogged the US to become the world's biggest trading nation in 2013, only filed 12 complaints before the DSB and has been called as defendant in 31 cases since its accession to the WTO in 2001. What is it then that makes European and American authorities come so often before WTO panels? The question becomes even more relevant when we observe that 32 of the 92 complaints filed by the EU were against a US measure and 19 of the 107 complaints filed by the US were against the EU. These last figures point to the biggest 'exchange' of complaints between two WTO contracting parties. Are those indications of fair battles between two giants of the world trade system, querulous attitudes or fundamental divergences on visions of what free and fair trade is? Should we see behind those dispute tensions a dark sky hovering over the TTIP negotiating table? Do specific issues or provisions of a particular agreement open up a gulf or deepen the ocean between future TTIP partners?

A first look at the agreements invoked in the disputes between the EU and US is quite reassuring in this regard. Generally, what opposes the US and the EU is also, in comparable proportions, what opposes other Members of the WTO. Of the 51 EU-US disputes, nine (18 per cent) are related to dumping. Overall, 102 of the 479 (21 per cent) complaints filed before the DSB since 1995 touch the same category of issues. The same similarity of proportions can be observed with at least three of the most commonly invoked arrangements: the Subsidies and Countervailing Duties Agreement (20 per cent vs 21 per cent), the Agriculture Agreement (16 per cent vs 15 per cent) and the Safeguards Agreement (10 per cent vs 9 per cent). This observation about the use of four agreements whose spirit and letter of the text are closely related to market access tends to reveal that the EU and the US, like any other WTO members, are primarily concerned about opening foreign markets.

Nevertheless, trade conflicts between the EU and the US are not that typical. Those two trade powers are divided over issues and trade preferences that are specific to dominant economies. A close look at the complaints filed by the US against the EU reveals that the American authorities are bothered by the way the EU tries to reconcile free trade disciplines with some non-trade concerns. This was especially true in the *Hormones* case (WTO 2014a for all cases cited here). In this SPS dispute, parties deeply disagreed on the necessary breathing room left for the precautionary principle in the risk assessment upon which a measure applied to protect life or health is based. This was also obvious in the *Bananas* case where the US urged actions against the European-heavy favouritism for certain developing countries, mainly located in Africa, at the expense of American fruit companies located in Central America. Finally, the way the European authorities tried to provide consumer protection was attacked in the *Geographical Indications* and the *Biotech* cases.

Complaints by the EU against the US are apparently driven by the idea of fighting some US hegemonic attitudes. In almost half of those complaints, the explicit protectionist goal of US federal acts about dumping, subsidies, countervailing duties or safeguards was targeted. Cases against the *Tax Treatment for Foreign*

Sales Corporation, the *Anti-Dumping Act of 1916*, the *Byrd Amendment* or the *Laws, Regulations and Methodology for Calculating Dumping Margins (Zeroing)* and at least five other cases on safeguards or countervailing duties are eloquent illustrations that EU representatives considered US protectionism their number one obstacle to overcome. But the US proclivity to act unilaterally without taking into account their international commitments was also in the EU representatives' cross hairs. Among other cases, the arguments made in the disputes *Sections 301–310 of the Trade Act 1974, Section 110(5) of US Copyright Act, Section of the 211 Omnibus Appropriation Act of 1998* are pleadings for multilateralism.

The *Large Civil Aircraft* case, better known as the Airbus-Boeing affair, responds to different dynamics. This saga, where both the US and the EU complained against the financing methods applied by its opponent, is a classic type commercial war oftentimes seen in domestic areas for the domination of a duopolistic market. Only titans like the EU and the US could clash over this issue.

Lastly, one piece of data about the US-EU trade conflicts speaks louder than any other and helps predict what will be a bone of contention during the TTIP negotiations. The number of arbitrations under sections 21, 22 and 23 of the DSU about the implementation of decisions is a powerful indication of the strong reluctance of the EU and the US to comply with the DSB decisions. Up to now, of the 51 disputes that opposed the EU and the US at the WTO, 22 led to the adoption of a panel report or an Appellate Body report by the DSB. Of those 22 reports, 12 required arbitration about their implementation. Some of those 12 cases are famous for the fierce resistance from the party that was asked to comply with the prescriptions of WTO Law. Cases like *Hormones, Bananas, Large Civil Aircraft, Foreign Sale Corporations, Byrd Amendment* and *Zeroing* immediately come to mind. And one could add to this list at least four cases related to dumping or import measures that are direct follow-ups of cases that were previously left without an agreed and fully implemented solution. Of course, this reluctance to comply is not an attitude proper to the US or the EU, but it seems to be particularly frequent and intense with those powers. We remark that, at the time we write this chapter, six pending arbitration cases under article 22 of the DSU involve the EU and seven pending cases under article 23 of the DSU involve either the EU or the US. If this reflects a trend, American and European representatives negotiating the TTIP must think carefully about the efficiency of the dispute settlement system they will put in place to govern their bilateral trade relations.

Conclusion: The Interlocking DDA and TTIP Relationship

The EU and the US share a common belief in the virtues of open trade and investment, but their objectives diverge on several fundamental issues, for instance, the EU's CAP, competition and investment policies, and geographical indications. As comprehensive as they promise to be, bilateral agreements such as TTIP are modest substitutes for a multilateral agreement. Trade irritants of utmost importance, such as agricultural subsidies, can only be resolved in a multilateral setting. Concessions on those issues within a regional trade agreement would be inconceivable without the assurance that non-members would offer the reciprocity at the WTO. A successful TTIP could nevertheless ease some of the multilateral trade vexations. Both the EU and the US strive to impose their own entrenched regulatory configurations in their multilateral and regional negotiations and, one could argue, it is only through the meeting of minds in the TTIP negotiations that a multilateral breakthrough is even conceivable on this critical topic. In addition, an agreement on government procurement could bring the moribund issue back to life at the WTO. Renewed optimism following the Bali package does not put to rest the question of 'what's next for the WTO?' We are of the belief that Mega-FTAs such as TTIP should run their parallel tracks with on-going WTO negotiations. Mega-FTAs are not only 'second-best' solutions; they are also necessary artefacts of a more complex world economy where no amount of goodwill among 159 trading partners can help solve convoluted beyond-the-border commercial and financial issues.

Chapter 10

China's Perspective: The Perception of TTIP by an Emerging Third Party

Zhang Xiaotong

Economic globalization has entered into a 'GPS' period, meaning 'gated', 'protectionist' and 'slow'. That is to say, major economic powers in the world have set up their own economic camps within which preferential rules are negotiated, causing trade diversions. Protectionism is on the rise and the pace of globalization has largely slowed down. In parallel, multipolarity has become a new trend in international politics. Major power competition is increasing. The TTIP talks have been launched against that background. Once announced in early 2013, the TTIP negotiations immediately attracted the attention of various emerging third parties. Feeling encircled by the US-led Trans-Pacific Partnership (TPP), and now the TTIP, China is watching closely every step of the TTIP negotiations and calculating how it should respond. In many ways, China still sees itself as a developing country and therefore shares many common interests with other developing countries, worrying that the TPP and the TTIP would be game changers, without due regard to the interests of developing countries. But China is more than an ordinary developing country. As an emerging great power, China sees the TTIP from a strategic perspective, worrying that the TTIP would serve as a strategic instrument for containing China or curbing the growth of China's sphere of influence, mainly in Asia-Pacific and the Eurasia continent.

This chapter provides an analysis of China's perspective. The first section considers the TTIP's implications for China as perceived by Chinese intellectuals. The second examines the economic implications of the TTIP for China that were calculated by the author, focusing respectively on trade diversion effects and the rules effects. The third section explores China's potential responses and the chapter concludes with a few policy suggestions.

The TTIP in the Eyes of Chinese Intellectuals[1]

The responses of Chinese intellectuals[2] to the launch of the TTIP negotiations are mixed. Their opinions about the TTIP's impact on China fall into three categories: positive, marginal and negative impact. Nevertheless, the opinions in the category 'negative impact' are more influential than those in the two others.

Positive Impact

Firstly, the TTIP is considered good for global trade liberalization. The pro-TTIP Chinese intellectuals believe that, in the face of the twin crises of the US sub-prime mortgage and European debt, it is indeed good news for the world trading system that the US and the EU, as two of the largest economies in the world, launch free trade negotiations (Mei 2013). They expect the US and the EU to take the lead and shoulder their responsibilities in the world trading system and carry out true reforms and re-adjustments in their own sensitive trading areas, such as regulatory issues, geographical indications and substantive reductions in trade barriers. In so doing, the TTIP will have an exemplary effect on the rest of the world (Wang 2013). The TTIP can equally have spillover effects by putting peer pressure on other ongoing bilateral and multilateral free trade negotiations (Ding 2013). Some Chinese intellectuals even predict that, if the TTIP moves forward smoothly, it might again breathe life into the Doha Round of negotiations (Fan 2013).

Secondly, the TTIP is considered good for China and other newly emerging economies based on the idea that transatlantic economic integration might be able to spur China's external trade, investment and economic growth (Li 2013). This first group of Chinese intellectuals believes that the TTIP can boost the world's economic growth and therefore bring renewed momentum for China's further integration in the globalized world (He 2013).

Marginal Impact

The Chinese intellectuals falling into this category tend to believe that the Chinese export structure is strongly complementary to the US and European structures and that a free trade agreement (FTA) between the US and the EU will not change that

---

1   The author has conducted thorough research on the opinions of Chinese intellectuals related to the TTIP in both Chinese and English. For example, the largest Chinese search engine, Baidu, was used to examine the relevant articles that were published on the topic. Similarly, the Google search engine was used to cover additional ground. The research was completed on 7 June 2013.

2   In this chapter, the term 'Chinese intellectuals' mainly refers to scholars, think tank contributors and journalists. Some of them are economists while others are political scientists. They are either independent or associated in one way or another with the Chinese government or Chinese companies.

complementarity. Since the existing international trade norms and international economic order has been set by the US and European countries for some time, the TTIP will not overthrow the existing global trading rules (Chen 2013).

Other Chinese intellectuals in this category, however, find that, although the US and the EU are attempting to bypass the wide range of newly emerging economies and developing countries and foster higher and newer trading rules through regional trading arrangements while relying on their existing advantages, China needs to be confident and indifferent to what the Americans and Europeans do. With the collective rise of the newly emerging economies and an increasing shift in the balance of power in the world, any international trade issue such as the reform of global trade governance cannot be properly handled without the participation of those newly emerging economies and developing countries (Wu 2013).

Negative Impact

The intellectuals in this category seem to be more influential than those in the other two groups. Even those who believe that the TTIP might boost the world's economic growth tend to caution that there are some negative aspects to the TTIP, particularly in setting the new rules against the interests of China and other developing countries. The Chinese intellectuals who belong to this group tend to have doubts about the TTIP.

Firstly, in their view, the TTIP would cause trade diversion at the cost of Chinese exports. The FTA between the US and the EU, respectively China's largest and second largest trading partners, would have a relatively big impact on China (Jing Ji Can Kao Bao 2013). This is mainly because Chinese exports to some extent compete with European and American exports in, respectively, the US and European markets. This competition is increasing as Chinese products quickly climb up the global value chain.

Secondly, the TTIP will undoubtedly change the existing rules which will in turn create large uncertainties. Opponents of the TTIP believe that, apart from the reduction in trade and investment from China, the most worrying aspect of the TTIP is that the developed economies can make use of the TTIP to accelerate the establishment of new rules and new institutional designs and, as a result, have a profound impact on the whole international trade configuration. The TTIP will set up rules for most of the economies, including developing countries, in the world and create pressure for China to follow these rules (Jing Ji Can Kao Bao 2013, Li 2013). Without the binding WTO rules, the EU and the US can trade more through the TTIP or through the frameworks under which their interests are best catered for. They would have less need to listen to the newly emerging economies that have a structural conflict of interest with them. The developing countries will thus accede to the rules set by the developed economies (Guo Ji Shang Bao 2013). Some Chinese intellectuals call on the US and the EU to make sure, when setting the new TTIP rules, that any 'fruit' coming out of the TTIP negotiations will be shared by as many countries as possible. If the developed economies continue to ignore the reasonable concerns of the developing countries, the globalization process might be reversed and create a 'lose-lose' situation in the North-South model of trade (Mei 2013).[3]

Thirdly, the TTIP might have a negative impact on the Doha Round of talks. There is a risk that the existing WTO multilateral trading system might be marginalized (Ding 2013). The TTIP will prevent the establishment of a new international political and economic order that is fair and open. Once the EU-US bloc is established, it will make the bilateral FTA superior to the multilateral system and, consequently, will weaken the competences and credibility of the multilateral system no matter how open the TTIP is (Wang 2013).

The Economic Implications of the TTIP for China

There are two types of implications of the TTIP for China. One is the so-called 'trade diversion effect' which is mainly focused on diversion of trade in goods. The other effects pertain to the rules.

Trade Diversion

The TTIP would create 'trade diversion effects', meaning trade that occurs between members of an FTA replaces what would have been imports from a country outside the FTA. In other words, if the US and the EU establish an FTA, China's exports to either the US or the EU market risk being crowded out by an increase in the EU's exports to the US market or US exports to the EU.

Specifically, we use the Export Similarity Index (ESI) to calculate the competing relationship between Chinese and European exports as well as between Chinese and American exports. The ESI range is 0 to 100. The higher the ESI, the more competitive the relationship is between the Chinese and European or American exports. Using an ESI index based on the 2012 two-digit Harmonized System tariff code (HS 2) of the US International Trade Commission (USITC) and Eurostat, we found that the similarity index of the Chinese and European exports in the US market is 45, while the similarity index of Chinese and American exports in the EU market is 46.4 (Zhang and Zhang 2013). This result shows that, to some extent, Chinese exports compete with European and American exports in the US and European markets, respectively. We also predict that, as Chinese products continue to climb the ladder of the value chain, the similarities between Chinese products and American and European ones will continue to increase, subsequently leading to greater competition.

---

3 Here, North-South trade refers to the trade conducted between developed and developing countries.

To further analyse the potential 'trade diversion effects', we looked into the top 20 categories of Chinese exports to the US and the EU by comparing them with the top 20 categories of European exports to the US and US exports to the EU. As a result, we therefore have a deeper knowledge of the similarities between Chinese products and American and European ones. We found that in the US market in 2012, 10 categories of Chinese and European exports were the same (see Chapters 85, 84, 94, 39, 73, 87, 90, 29, 40 and 71 of the HS 2, arranged in descending order) (USITC 2013). The top 20 categories represented 89.8 per cent of Chinese exports to the US, and 88.1 per cent of European exports to the US (USITC 2013).[4] Equally, in the European market, we found that nine categories of Chinese and American exports are the same (see Chapters 85, 84, 39, 73, 29, 90, 87, 40 and 71). The top 20 categories represent 87.3 per cent of Chinese exports to the EU and 88.2 per cent of American exports to the EU (Eurostat 2013).[5] The more detailed findings are summarized in Table 10.1 (p. 118).

For the competing categories of Chinese, European and American exports, there are potential trade diversions. But these diversion effects vary depending on the current tariff level. If the current tariff level is very low, trade diversion will be marginal, even after trade in goods is fully liberalized. If the tariff level is high, trade diversion will be higher.

Specifically, in the US market, the tariff level for Chapter 40 (rubbers and articles thereof) is high. Chinese exports would face a significant level of trade diversion once the tariffs are removed for European exports to the US market within this chapter. We estimate the affected value around 5 billion US dollars. The tariff level for Chapters 87 (vehicles), 90 (optical products), 29 (organic chemicals) and 39 (plastics) is between 2 per cent and 4 per cent. It implies that the trade diversion would be considerable, affecting around 39 billion US dollars of Chinese exports. The tariff level for Chapters 84 (nuclear reactors, machineries and computers), 85 (electrical machineries), 71 (pearls and stones), 73 (iron and steel) and 94 (furniture) is low, i.e. less than 2 per cent. Therefore we conclude that the trade diversion effects would be marginal even though those chapters represent major Chinese exports to the US that are worth more than 250 billion US dollars (see Table 10.1).

---

4   Using the USITC statistics, the author finds that the value of China's exports to the US in 2012 was 444.465 billion US dollars, in which, the value for the top 20 export items was 399.108 billion US dollars, accounting for 89.8 per cent of total Chinese exports to the US. For the EU, its exports to the US in 2012 amounted to 389.103 billion US dollars, in which, the top 20 export items were valued at 342.727 billion US dollars, accounting for 88.1 per cent of total EU exports to the US.

5   Using the Eurostat statistics, the author finds that the value of China's exports to the EU was 289.314 billion euros, in which, the value of the top 20 Chinese exports to the EU was 252.621 billion euros, accounting for 87.3 per cent of total Chinese exports to the EU. Regarding the US, its exports to the EU amounted to 204.391 billion euros, in which its top 20 exports to the EU were valued at 180.298 billion euros, accounting for 88.2 per cent of the total US exports to the EU.

Table 10.1 Comparison between Chinese, American and European exports in 2012

US Market (Million US$)				EU Market (Million EUR)			
HS2	China	HS2	EU	HS2	China	HS2	US
85	113,322	84	65,783	85	76,556	84	38,368
84	102,164	87	45,449	84	61,964	27	19,719
94	24,786	30	38,889	62	14,738	30	19,166
95	23,104	27	25,603	61	12,495	90	19,085
64	17,876	90	25,599	94	12,260	88	15,548
61	15,552	29	24,094	95	11,386	85	14,075
62	15,299	85	22,752	64	7,788	29	10,551
39	13,158	98	16,233	39	6,619	71	9,737
73	10,120	22	11,727	73	6,528	87	8,561
87	10,003	88	10,503	29	6,396	39	5,673
90	9,043	71	8,029	90	6,328	38	4,361
42	8,890	73	7,188	42	6,081	97	2,284
63	6,761	39	6,796	87	4,698	99	1,922
29	6,668	97	6,385	63	3,104	73	1,806
40	5,028	72	6,038	89	2,953	33	1,735
83	4,088	33	5,513	40	2,859	40	1,734
71	3,725	28	4,531	72	2,637	8	1,604
44	3,493	38	4,261	83	2,596	26	1,523
82	3,241	40	3,804	82	2,344	28	1,518
48	2,787	94	3,550	71	2,292	48	1,328

Sources: USITC (2013), Eurostat (2013).

In the EU market, the tariff level for Chapters 29 (organic chemicals), 87 (vehicles), 39 (plastics) and 40 (rubbers) are high, i.e. more than 4 per cent. Chinese exports would face a significant level of trade diversion once the tariffs are removed for American exports to the EU market under these chapters. We estimate the affected value around 20.6 billion euros. Since the tariff level for Chapters 84 (nuclear reactors, machineries and computers), 90 (optical) and 85 (electrical machineries) ranges between 2 and 4 per cent, we believe that the trade diversion for these chapters would be considerable, involving 145 billion euros' worth of Chinese exports to the EU. For Chapters 71 (pearls and stones), 73 (iron and steel) and 94 (furniture), the tariff level is low, i.e. less than 2 per cent. Trade diversion effects of Chinese exports to the EU would be marginal, affecting only 9 billion euros (see Table 10.1).

Table 10.2 Implications of TTIP for Chinese exports

Import Tariff Rate	US Market			EU Market		
	HS2 Chapters	Value of Chinese Exports Affected by TTIP (billion US$)	Impact Level	HS2 Chapters	Value of Chinese Exports Affected by TTIP (billion euros)	Impact Level
>4%	40 (rubbers)	5.028	Significant	29 (chemicals), 87 (vehicles), 39 (plastics), 40 (rubbers)	20.572	Significant
2%–4%	87 (vehicles), 90 (optical), 29 (chemicals), 39 (plastics)	38.872	Considerable	84 (nuclear reactors), 90 (optical), 85 (electrical machinery)	144.848	Considerable
<2%	84 (nuclear reactors), 85 (electrical machinery), 71 (pearls and stones), 73 (iron and steel), 94 (furniture)	254.117	Marginal	71 (pearls and stones), 73 (iron and steel)	8.820	Marginal

Sources: USITC (2013), WTO, ITC and UNCTAD (2012: 76, 170).

Generally speaking, the TTIP-induced trade diversion effects on China would be more significant in the EU market than in the US market, largely because the EU market has on average higher levels of tariff than the US.

In addition to leading to the above mentioned 'trade diversion effects', the TTIP would also have trade creation effects which could benefit China. However, a study conducted by the Centre for Economic Policy Research suggests that the trade creation effects on China would be limited to an increase in exports by 0.5 per cent and in the GDP by 4 to 5 billion euros which is equivalent to 0.02–0.03 per cent of China's GDP (CEPR 2013: 82–3). As Table 10.2 on page 119 shows, the value of Chinese exports that would be considerably or significantly affected by the TTIP trade diversion effects would amount to 199.6 billion euros. Even if the actual trade diversions were only 10 per cent, the total value would be as high as around 20 billion euros, i.e. roughly 1 per cent of China's total exports and 0.3 per cent of China's GDP. Therefore, we believe that the costs imposed by the TTIP trade diversion on China are much bigger than the potential benefits of the TTIP's trade creation.

Rules Effect

The Chinese government may also be worried about the trade rules and, more specifically, who controls the rule-setting power. For decades, China, together with other developing countries, has been pursuing a new international economic order. There is a strong push within China to bid farewell to the old days when others set the rules. Through the TTIP, the US and the EU, as suggested by both parties, will develop a new generation of global trading rules concerning state-owned enterprises, subsidies, intellectual property rights, public procurement, raw materials, environmental and labour standards. These are exactly the areas where China is most criticized for not abiding by the global trading rules. Once the transatlantic community has set these new rules, Chinese exports will face additional and new difficulties. Equally, China will find it more difficult to negotiate new trade deals with the US and the EU. All of this might lead to a new flashpoint of trade tensions between China on the one hand and the transatlantic community on the other. Here we offer two examples of the potential rules effects on China resulting from the conclusion of the TTIP: government procurement and state-owned enterprises.

Government procurement
As the initial EU position paper on government procurement states, 'this negotiation (TTIP) would present an important opportunity for the EU and the U.S. to develop together some useful "GPA plus" elements to complement the revised GPA disciplines ... A model text agreed between the EU and the U.S., being the two largest trading partners in the world, could thus possibly set a higher standard that could inspire a future GPA revision' (European Commission 2013b: 1). China committed itself to accede to the WTO Government Procurement

Agreement (GPA) when joining the WTO and, since 2007, started the accession negotiations. Due to differences in the levels of ambition, China's several offers have fallen short of the GPA contracting parties' expectations. The high ambition set by the EU and the US in their TTIP negotiations would make China's accession to the GPA an even more daunting task.

State-owned enterprises
In the TTIP negotiations, the US seeks to establish appropriate and globally relevant disciplines on state trading enterprises, state-owned enterprises (SOEs) and designated monopolies, such as disciplines that promote transparency and reduce trade distortions (USTR 2013: 4). Similarly, the objective of the EU is to create an ambitious and comprehensive global standard to discipline state involvement and influence in private and public enterprises, building and expanding on the existing WTO rules. The EU believes that this could pave the way for other bilateral agreements to follow a similar approach and eventually contribute to a future multilateral engagement (European Commission 2013c: 1). China is well-known for the significant role played by SOEs in its economy. China's model of economic growth is even described as 'state capitalism' (as opposed to free market capitalism) (Bandow 2010). It is foreseeable that in the future, China in one camp, and the EU and the US in the other, might fiercely compete for world market shares based on their own economic growth models. Against this background, the debate on the SOEs rules will be of even greater significance.

China's Possible Responses

As the world trading system enters into an era of 'competitive interdependence' (Sbragia 2010), China accelerates the pace of its own FTA negotiations and might come up with new ideas in response to the developments in the TTIP negotiations and the EU-Japan FTA. China stands alert to any mega-regional deal without its participation. However, if we compare the TPP and the TTIP, China is worried about the TPP's geopolitical implications while it is simultaneously worried about the TTIP's rule-setting implications. Therefore, it is worth discussing what actions China might take.

Question 1: Multilateralism or Bilateralism?

China accelerates its pace in implementing its FTA strategy. Regarding European countries, China recently concluded an FTA with Switzerland, which is a milestone for China since Switzerland is the first major economy in Europe with which China has signed an FTA. In Asia, China has made it clear that it prioritizes the China-Japan-Korea FTA, China-Australia FTA and China's FTA with Western Asia (Yu 2013a). With these many FTA negotiations being conducted at the same time, it seems that China abandons multilateralism and moves quickly towards bilateralism. However, the official rhetoric from Beijing does not support that view. One of China's chief trade negotiators announced that China would adhere to a position where multilateralism is the main avenue of trade while regional (bilateral) trade arrangements remain complementary (Yu 2013b). As China's former WTO ambassador Sun Zhenyu commented, '[t]he pendulum of trade liberalization might swing back to multilateralism at the end of the day' (Sun 2013). He suggested that 'the regional trade arrangements that we are now discussing might be multilateralized and it is necessary to agree on a set of multilateral rules for governing various regional arrangements' (Sun 2013). For many Chinese trade veterans, it is impossible to give up on the WTO as China is one of the biggest beneficiaries of it. They fought hard to make China join the WTO and it is unthinkable to turn away from it now.

What then are the possible explanations for the gap between China's official rhetoric and its actual deeds? At least two are available. One explanation is that China responds to the competing pressures resulting from the FTA talks between the Western powers, including Europe, the US and Japan. Given the potential 'trade diversion effects' and the loss of rule-setting power, China has to accelerate its own FTA efforts as a precautionary move. The typical example is China's interest in signing an FTA with the EU.[6] Moreover, an FTA between China and the US has been suggested by some business leaders and former senior officials in China and the US.[7] Although it is far from certain, we can still predict that some Chinese policy-makers and intellectuals are thinking of using FTAs with major economies, such as the EU and the US, to offset the potential negative effects of the TTIP on China.

The second explanation is that China is using FTAs as geostrategic tools to consolidate its influence in the Asia-Pacific region. This view is supported by the FTA negotiations with Japan, Korea, Australia and the Gulf Cooperation Council.

With these factors in mind, China will most probably continue to build its trade policies on two pillars: multilateralism and bilateralism. Priority might be given to bilateralism as the Doha Round is not showing any signs of revival. Having said that, China prefers not to leave the world with the impression that it has given up on the Doha Round.

---

6   China's former Premier Wen Jiabao proposed a feasibility study for an FTA with the EU at the China-EU Summit in 2012 (see Xinhua News Agency 2012).

7   The Joint Statement of the 4th Annual US-China CEO and Former Senior Officials' Dialogue suggested a US-China FTA (see China Daily 2013).

Question 2: Competing Bilateralism or Harmonious Bilateralism?

The second question is whether the EU's FTA negotiations (including the TTIP, EU-Japan, EU-Canada and others) will create tensions in its trade relations with China. This question is in particular relevant given the fact that the EU and China nearly had a trade war as a result of the solar panel cases which involved over 7 per cent of China's total exports to the EU in 2012.[8] However, the trade war logic might not be able to hold as China's official response still emphasizes the strategic importance of its overall relationship with Europe. In a joint press conference with German Chancellor Merkel, China's Premier Li Keqiang again emphasized that Europe is an important force in the world for safeguarding world peace and prosperity and that China will treat its relationship with Europe from a strategic, long-term and comprehensive perspective. Li promised to give full support to European integration and efforts in handling the debt crisis (Renmin 2013). Although Li hinted at a linkage between the overall EU-China partnership and the solar panel case, it was still China's official position to adhere to its traditional position of remaining a partner to Europe.

However, the official position and rhetoric might not be able to conceal China's real worries about the TTIP. As the spokesman of the Chinese Ministry of Commerce Shen Danyang clearly expressed, it is China's hope that the TTIP negotiating parties will make sure that the TTIP negotiations would remain open and transparent. It is necessary for the TTIP not to be only beneficial to the EU-US economic and trade development interests, but also conducive to pushing forward the Doha Round and global trade liberalization (Chinese Ministry of Commerce 2013).

From the above analysis we conclude that China is concerned about the latest trends in bilateralism which are not very harmonious in character and generate a fairly high degree of tension. China's pursuit of the so-called 'harmonious world' is colliding with the cold facts of 'competing bilateralism'. Against that background, China's possible responses might be pragmatism in action combined with idealist rhetoric. A lack of multilateral governance of world trade may lead to more bilateral trade tensions between China and its Western trading partners.

Question 3: Further Reform or Turning Inward?

The EU's FTA negotiations together with those launched by other industrialized economies are creating external pressure on China's domestic economic reform and opening-up. The timing is opportune, considering the emergence of a new generation of leaders that is more reform-minded. A good example lies in the fact that Premier Li Keqiang can be credited with the launch of the China-Switzerland

---

8   The solar panel anti-dumping case lodged by the EU against China has ended with an amicable solution in the form of a price cap (European Commission 2013a).

FTA when he was Vice Premier and with the conclusion of the FTA during his first trip to Europe after assuming the premiership in May 2013.

It seems increasingly obvious that China's new leadership is cleverly using external pressure to push forward domestic reform. During his meeting with President Obama, China's President Xi Jinping announced that China was considering pushing through a medium and long-term comprehensive reform programme (Xi 2013). China's Premier Li Keqiang's patronage of China's FTA with Switzerland might usher in a new era for China's FTA negotiations with developed economies, such as with Australia and the EU. Li's predecessor, Premier Wen Jiabao, had already proposed a feasibility study for an FTA with the EU in 2012 (Xinhua News Agency 2012). The conclusion of the trilateral China-Japan-Korea trade agreement is also at the top of the list for China. All FTAs are potential 'drivers' for China's domestic reform.

To sum up, the EU's FTA negotiations and their potential implications may not change China's traditional position and its preference for multilateral trade talks. But the pressures arising from the 'trade diversion effects' and the will of the new reform-minded Chinese leadership will probably accelerate the FTA negotiations in the near future. In the meantime, although China's bilateral relationship with Europe and other industrialized economies might enter into a period of 'competing bilateralism', China's traditional diplomatic stance and economic partnerships with these economies will not suffer a great deal.

Some Suggestions

The possible TTIP 'trade diversion effects' on China might be marginal and the new rules that come out of this would-be historical trade agreement between the US and the EU may not be fearsome for China. However, there is a widespread suspicion among Chinese intellectuals about the EU's recent FTA adventures, in particular with regard to the TTIP. Their view may eventually affect the Chinese government's response to the TTIP. Against this background of an increasingly competitive interdependence between the trading partners in the world, and considering that the multilateral trading system is in a crisis, we believe that there is a solid case to be made for the EU and the US to: (1) have a better strategy regarding how to make the TTIP more compatible with the actual trade activities and trade relations with other countries and (2) consider how to see China in the context of a concluded agreement.

The TTIP is better designed and established as a building block rather than a stumbling block for the multilateral trading system. To allow the multilateral system to continue to prosper, China and other emerging economies cannot be bypassed or marginalized, especially given the fact that China is now the world's largest trading nation. It is wishful thinking that China would easily accept whatever is reached at the negotiating table, as some European policy-makers seem to believe (De Gucht 2013a).[9] Our estimation is that China will launch further FTA negotiations in the near future as a response to the changes that are taking place in the increasingly competitive world of trade. If China joins the FTA scramble and there is no minimum consensus about the future of the international trading system, the world will probably be thrown into a 'Cold War' on the trade front with two main camps – one consisting of the developed countries and the other made up of the developing economies – competing against each other. It is therefore advisable that all efforts be made to avoid an FTA 'Olympic Games'. Two specific policy recommendations can be put forward:

- Major developed economies and newly emerging economies including China need to increase information exchange through summits and strategic economic dialogues such as the EU-China Summit, the EU-China High-Level Trade Dialogue, the China-US Economic and Strategic Dialogue, G20 and BRICS meetings.
- A forward-thinking Trade Policy Group needs to be established by world-renowned think tanks to provide analyses and policy recommendations to governments about the current FTA situations.

To conclude, the new round of bilateral FTA talks might be an equally once-in-a-century opportunity for China to move ahead with its domestic reform and 'opening-up' agenda on which progress has been lacking. As Premier Li Keqiang said, 'China's reform has entered into deep waters' (Renmin 2013). It is necessary for the Chinese reform-oriented leaders to use external pressure to push forward domestic economic reform and 'opening-up'.

---

9   EU Trade Commissioner Karel De Gucht mentioned that 'the EU-US combined weight in the global economy means that many who wish to sell into our markets will have an interest in moving towards whatever rules we can achieve' (De Gucht 2013a).

Chapter 11

From Noodle Bowls to Alphabet Soup: The Interactions between TTIP, TPP and the Japan-EU Free Trade Agreement

Frederik Ponjaert

Introduction

Since the 1990s, the growing weight of East Asia and the stagnant Doha Round have conspired to prompt the globe's largest trading partners to reconsider their respective trade policies (Messerlin 2012). The resulting proliferation has been the source of much concern as the resulting "noodle bowl" of crisscrossing FTAs is particularly fragile. Each party's competitiveness increasingly hinges on the free-flow of intermediary goods prompted by way of unilateral tariff-cutting removed from any WTO initiative and often absent any top-down coordination (Baldwin 2008). The various strands of this so-called "noodle bowl" primarily bound smaller economies to larger ones as even limited agreements between larger markets have proved particularly elusive (Table 11.1).

This poor track-record notwithstanding, between March and July 2013 each side of the traditional trilateral dialogue opted to launch separate interregional trade talks bridging the Atlantic, Pacific, and Eurasian spaces respectively—i.e. the Transatlantic Trade and Investment Partnership (TTIP), the US-Japanese Free Trade negotiations embedded within the Trans-Pacific Trade Partnership (TPP/JAP-US), and the Japan-EU Free Trade Agreement (JEUFTA). As the broader trend towards mega-PTAs has snowballed, questions have arisen with regard to how this new alphabet soup of potential agreements would interact.

The sheer size of the economies involved makes a trade agreement linking any two of these economic giants of systemic importance. As PTAs have become both a structural and structuring feature of the global system, the puzzle much trade literature has come to struggle with is what characteristics define the resulting complexity. As Heydon and Woolcock (2009: 5) suggest: "the presumption that preferential deals amongst the willing can somehow compensate for slow progress multilaterally is as inappropriate as the idea that PTAs inevitably undermine wider multilateral efforts. ... The key question in international trade and investment policy today is not about choosing between preferential agreements or multilateralism, but about understanding how the various, interacting negotiating forums are used by the leading countries or regions."

Table 11.1 On-going and concluded PTA negotiations involving G20
**   countries (January 2014)**

G20 Members	Share of Global GDP (%)	EU28	USA	China	Japan
EU28	26.6	N/A	On-going (TTIP)	–	On-going (JEUFTA)
USA	23.9	On-going (TTIP)	N/A	–	On-going (TPP)
China	9.6	–	–	N/A	On-going (RCEP)
Japan	9.0	On-going (JEUFTA)	On-going (TPP)	On-going (RCEP)	N/A
Brazil	3.4	On-going	–	–	–
India	2.8	On-going	–	Concluded	Concluded
Canada	2.6	Concluded	Concluded	–	On-going
Russia	2.4	–	–	–	–
Mexico	1.7	Concluded	Concluded	–	–
Korea	1.7	Concluded	Concluded	Initial step	CKJ
Australia	1.5	–	Concluded	On-going	On-going
Turkey	1.2	Concluded	–	–	–
Indonesia	1.2	Suspended	–	Concluded	Concluded
Saudi Arabia	0.7	Suspended	–	–	On-going
Argentina	0.6	On-going	–	–	–
South Africa	0.6	Concluded	–	–	–

This chapter examines comparatively the underpinnings of three inter-regional trade negotiations. The chapter's central contention is that these high-stakes PTA negotiations are neither a coordinated policy nor a series of directly correlated policy responses, but rather a series of very distinct conservationist adjustment strategies seeking to preserve deeply-rooted "national" trade and policy patterns in view of mounting challenges to domestic political economies. First, the chapter succinctly assesses the relative quality of all three negotiations, be it in macro-economic or discursive terms. Secondly, it explores the policy paths and catalysts which prompted these key trade actors down the road of mega-PTAs. Finally, it concludes by linking its insights into the actor's respective trade policy environments with the exact institutional set-up thus assessing whether hampering interferences or positive spill-overs are to be expected.

Mega-PTAs: The Relative Significance of the Shifts in Scale and Discourse

A first quandary when considering the relative significance of these three potential mega-PTAs is their relative weight within the considered actors' historical commercial policies and future economic prospects.

Is Big Beautiful?

It has been argued that the Doha Development Round's decade-long stalemate has prompted several global actors such as Japan, the EU, and the US to engage in bilateral negotiations out of necessity. The relative advantages attributed to bilateral or regional platforms are: more straightforward and confidential negotiations, a more targeted approach to tariff reduction, and a greater ease in broaching topics associated with the new "twenty-first-century trade" agenda. Nevertheless, most PTAs concluded up to 2014 involved one large and one smaller partner (Table 11.1) where the former is able to foist its agenda onto the latter (Laird 2002). The scope and depth of PTAs are highly variable as they tend to be defined by the strongest party's domestic agenda. Mega-PTAs, where none of the parties can play a hegemonic role, are therefore even more contingent on fortuitous convergences in domestic agendas while stakes are higher and returns on either side even more uncertain.

In 2014, between a quarter and a third of the EU, the US, and Japan's trade fell under the provisions of a PTA. Irrespective of the uneven quality and depth of these various bilateral and mini-lateral agreements, PTAs are still a relatively secondary factor in their overall trade environments. Although each of the considered mega-PTAs would see up to 50 per cent of global GDP linked through facilitated trade and investment flows, the actual share of each partner's trade covered would not be quite so overwhelming. A successful conclusion of TTIP, TPP/JAP-US, and JEUFTA would still only see about 50 per cent of each country's overall trade volume covered by a PTA (Figure 11.1). Moreover, this share would most likely diminish over time as the more dynamic components of all three actor's trade lie elsewhere—e.g. trade with their respective neighbors and/or emerging economies. The apparent tension between the gargantuan size of the trading partners involved and the all-in-all limited share of new trade that would be covered lies at the core of one of the central controversies of all three of these mega-PTAs: the expected benefits in terms of growth.

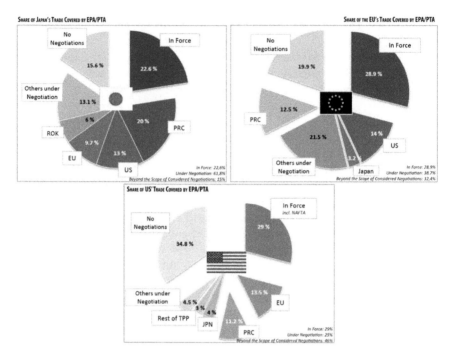

Figure 11.1 Share of trade covered by PTAs (January 2014)

A New Pitch or a New Product?

Trade policies in advanced economies have become a core feature of their overall growth strategies. With their focus on the nature of markets rather than merely on access, third-generation trade agreements can advance both reform- or export-driven[1] growth agendas. This raises the question how TTIP, TPP/JAP-US or JEUFTA would impact potential growth prospects. This has proven a major bone of contention in all three polities involved. Any given agreement's relative gains are necessarily controversial as potential losers and winners jostle for influence; most strikingly the central polemic facing all three of these mega-PTAs is the expected aggregate benefits to overall GDP growth (see Figure 11.2). European, Japanese, and American officials have all argued that these mega-PTAs are potential "boost[s] to [their] economies that [do not] cost a cent of tax payers money" (Barrosso 2013). Nonetheless, expected gains in aggregated growth have emerged as the key stake in legitimizing any agreement despite unavoidable costs and possible

---

1   Large economies can leverage PTAs to capture extra growth either through additional exports or through efficiency gains. In the latter growth windfalls are the result of improved domestic production born of economies of scale and heightened competition; in the former additional growth is the product of a more level international playing field.

unintended consequences (Orbie and De Ville 2014). Since the 2008 economic crisis the world has witnessed a shift in European, Japanese, and American trade policies away from more defensive stances seeking to mitigate the stifling effects of a stagnant Doha Round in favor of more offensive ones "allowing for more attention to the potential of trade to contribute to economic recovery ... as it has the potential to help us pull back to prosperity" (De Gucht 2010). These mega-PTAs are above all a response to the collapse in growth prospects experienced by these advanced economies in the aftermath of the 2008 global crisis.

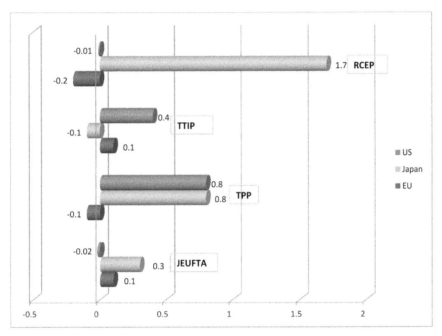

Figure 11.2 Mega-PTAs estimated maximal effects on Japanese, US and EU GDP growth (%)

Source: Kawasaki 2012.

Accordingly, the rise of mega-PTAs marks neither a concerted effort to restructure the Global Value Chain (GVC), nor a significant shift in the political rationale mobilized by advanced economies. On the one hand, the actual share of trade covered by these agreements is a shrinking one as growth in trade is mainly garnered elsewhere, and on the other, discourses surrounding these agreements have remained fundamentally unchanged. Whether one considers the American approach to "competitive liberalization," the Commission's "Global Europe Strategy," or Japan's post-2009 METI (Ministry of Economy, Trade and Industry) White papers, they all offer a conservative vision which seeks to preserve existing trading models in spite of a changing environment. None of these strategies marks a fundamental or structural reappraisal of their commercial policies in favor of protectionist, regionalist, or bilateralist alternatives. They seek to legitimize continuity through considered discursive shifts (De Ville and Orbie 2014). Mega-PTAs are an attempt to preserve the three considered political economies' central position in the GVC's three main hubs—i.e. the US in North America, Japan in East Asia, and the EU in Europe and its neighborhood. Trade policies are no longer primarily a tool for systemic improvements through generalizable tariff reductions favoring the selling of goods across borders, but rather a means to meet the new needs associated with improvements in productivity and profitability in the making of goods and services across borders. As a result, PTAs of all shapes and sizes are tailored to secure a given political economy's competitive position along the GVC, notably in light of shifting technologies and rising powers.

Mega-PTAs: Their Respective Historical Antecedents and Current Drivers

As adaptation and continuity appear to be the underlying logics of these mega-PTAs, the respective path-dependencies each negotiating party brings to bear are of the utmost importance.

Where are They Coming From?

As early industrial and trading powers, Japan, the EU, and the US all have a long history of trade politics. The origins of their contemporary strategies can be traced back to the inter-bellum and post-World War II periods when most of their trade concerns and institutions crystalized.

The United States
The infamous Hawley-Smoot Tariff Act would become a historical watershed in terms of "beggar-they-neighbor" growth strategies and their systemic perils. As a near immediate response, a push for proactive trade liberalization through bilateral agreements saw the Reciprocal Trade Agreement Act (RTAA) voted in in 1934. Based on an unconditional Most Favored Nation (MFN) clause, it established the basis of what would eventually become the global multilateral trade system (WTO 2011b).

As the end of World War II neared, Europeans, and most notably the UK, were confronted with Cordell Hull's insistence on the need to mitigate the adverse effects of Imperial Preferences by seeing the colonial system abandoned in favor of a multilateral one. In November 1943, Hull would state: "there will no longer be need for spheres of influence, for alliances, for balance of power, or any other of the special arrangements." This marked a real sea change in global trade, one where preferential spheres were progressively abandoned in favor of an open system articulated around the MFN-principle, monitored by way of an accepted

Dispute Settlement Mechanism (DSM) and regulated through a multilateral intergovernmental body. These foundational principles of American trade policy remain unchallenged.

"Throughout the post-war period [the US] has been a leader of the multilateral trading system and a *demandeur* of all nine of the GATT and WTO negotiations. For the past two decades FTAs have been pursued both to complement and cajole the progress at the multilateral level" (Schott 2004: 381). The US concluded its first FTA with Israel in 1985, followed by the US-Canada Free Trade Agreement (CAFTA) in 1988, and NAFTA in 1994. Besides the specific case of Israel, these agreements are part of a "second wave of regionalism" (Telò 2014) which saw all major economies develop distinct regionalist strategies. From the 2000s onwards, the US reasserted its distinctive regionalist strategy (Hettne and Ponjaert 2014) as its trade policy increasingly sought to cast the US at the center of the network of privileged partners having signed a standard bilateral FTA reflecting emerging US-readings of the new "21st century trade agenda" (Roderburg 2013) while simultaneously pushing an offensive tariff reduction agenda.

Fred Bergsten would come to qualify this shift in favor of bilateralism as a move towards "competitive liberalization" (Bergsten 1996). The format, objectives, and constraints of "competitive liberalization" were: (1) to necessarily broach the tariff and non-tariff issues Washington was unable to address at the WTO level, (2) respect the founding principles of the WTO such as the MFN-clause, and (3) conform to a negotiation format singularly focused on trade. This left only the choice of potential negotiation partners open to political controversy. The selection of FTA partners has remained a discretionary choice of the executive which has repeatedly proven to be motivated by foreign policy criteria. Nevertheless, despite its pro-active PTA policies, as the US negotiates mega-PTAs with both the EU and Asia, 90 per cent of US exports are directed in roughly equal proportions to the globe's three main economic regions: North America, East Asia, and the EU.

US trade policy has

> ... aggressively been pursuing a variety of commercial and diplomatic interests, both tactical and strategic, that include bolstering local democratic institutions and the processes of economic reform, [and] strengthening US security ties, [however the primary concern remains] accelerating commercial liberalization by allying with regional leaders, establishing new precedents to use as bench markers in future trade negotiations, and otherwise using free trade accords to advance its comprehensive global trade policy agenda. (Feinberg 2003: 1038)

Bilateral efforts focus on expanding US export facilities whilst protecting US investments as new sectors of the economy are opened up to international competition.

The European Union
European reciprocal trade policies emerged in the late nineteenth century when the Cobden-Chevalier Treaty between Britain and France (1860) referenced the

principles of reciprocity, non-discrimination, and national treatment. Although harking back to these early attempts at reciprocal liberalization, the EU's Common Commercial Policy (CCP) is above all a product of the post-war European project. Following two wars, the promotion of free trade within Europe had come to be seen as the catalyst of a possible continental political settlement, and not merely a quest for maximal economic efficiency. The promotion of free trade beyond Europe was both a logical extension of the continent's endogenous peace-building agenda and a necessary consequence of its one-of-a-kind drive towards a customs union as the European political project has inimitably followed the different stages of the Belassa model of integration (1961).

If rather more reactively than the US's hegemonic trade policy, the EEC/EU unprecedented and unparalleled, politically riven exercise in economic integration would also prove a crucial determinant of the multilateral system. The Dillon Round of 1960 was prompted in part by the adoption of the EEC's common external tariff, whereas the Kennedy Round of 1964–67 was a US response to a more unified European market. At the same time, the EEC was also the main force behind the "first wave of regionalism." The EEC signed its first bilateral and inter-regional mixed association agreements in 1961 with Greece and in 1963 with the ACP countries. This early adoption of an (inter)regional trade strategy was the product of the combined effects of the EEC/EU's own founding instrumentalization of preferential trade agreements for political ends and its limited capacity to steer the global multilateral system other than through the leverage it enjoyed in view of the relative weight of its internal market. PTAs emerged as the preferred means of deploying an active and distinctly European external influence (Hettne and Ponjaert 2014).

If the Europeans were the only of the Triad's members to actively engage with the "first wave of regionalism," again from the mid-1980s into the 1990s the EEC/EU's internal and external policies reasserted themselves as a key catalyst of the "second wave of regionalism." The creation of the single market in 1986 laid the foundations of a "Market Power Europe" (Damro 2012) willing and able to leverage the size of its market, regulatory sophistication, and capacity for societal mobilization in favor of its geo-economic interests, while the newly minted Partnership and Cooperation Agreements (PCA) outlined the premises of its comprehensive external action (Rosamond 2014: 218–20). The EU initially centered its PTA efforts on its neighborhood and a set of economically peripheral countries with some political significance such as South Africa (1999), Mexico (2000), and Chile (2002). This reflected the political logic underpinning the first two phases in the EEC/EU's interregional PTA strategy. By the early 2000s it still lacked a clear economic rationale and was seen as a mere aggregation of Member States' conventional spheres of influence.

The subsequent phase in the EU's PTA strategy coincided with the "third wave regionalism" and the end of the "US unipolar moment." In 2006, the "Global Europe" communication would decry the fact that existing "bilateral agreements support[ed] the EU's neighborhood and development objectives well, [whereas its] main trade interests, including in Asia, [were] less well served" (European Commission 2006). In response, the EU sought to establish clear and formal economic criteria for the selection of new FTA partners. This new approach was to increase both the objectivity of counterpart selection and the size of the contribution to the EU's economic growth. As a result, market potential—i.e. economic size, potential growth, and existing levels of protection—became the key measures for any PTA. Any successful negotiations were to enhance growth by opening new export-markets through either enforced regulatory reform (Meunier and Nicolaidis 2006) or the fight against "exporter discrimination" (Elsig and Dupont 2012: 501).

Despite the continued path-dependencies associated with the political origins of the internal market-building agenda which prompted the CCP, the PTA agenda of the EU's global trade strategy has increasingly embraced neoliberal trade options (Hanson 1998, Young 2004, De Ville and Orbie 2014). Preferential trade negotiations have come to "epitomize the EU's contradictions caught between the willingness to protect its social [and regulatory] model and the [aggressive] search for profitable ... markets abroad for its competitive firms" (Crespy 2014). TTIP and to a lesser extent JEUFTA mark the first time these two historically embedded readings of trade liberalizations—i.e. a market building tool on the one hand and a liberalizing one on the other—have been directly confronted, thereby challenging the EU's capacity to continue to use regulatory market-building measures to pursue its goal of ever greater continental cohesion.

Accordingly, as the outlier case of regionalism uniquely committed to customs, economic, and monetary union (Hoekman and Kosteck 2013: 474–512), mega-PTAs carry with them the inherent risk of fundamentally challenging the long-term policy paths the EU has set itself with regard to both the process of European integration as well as the ecology of the various cohabitating models of European capitalisms (Schmidt 2006). A distinctly European concern is therefore whether the possible new interactions or trade deviations created by a given mega-PTA would weaken existing regional integration and intra-regional trade patterns (Heydon and Woolcock 2009: 233).

Japan

The last member of the Triad to develop a distinct PTA policy was Japan. Following World War II, Japan was singularly committed to fully rejoining the international community under Washington's stewardship (Akaneya 1992). GATT accession in 1955 would see Japan subscribe for the first time to the twin principles of tariff reductions and the application of MFN treatment (Forsberg 1998: 190). Japan's accession was also the first test of the GATT's policy of open membership as the country posed a real challenge to established members. As a result, Tokyo pioneered "acceding without full reciprocity [as] Japan's high industrial capacity to produce and export created immediate import competition for existing member states while the lack of Japanese import liberalization added limited export market increases for existing members" (Wilf and Davis 2011: 9).

Initially, "Japan's [GATT] membership was in reality only partial since nearly half of the existing members [including the major European States] chose to exercise their right under GATT Article XXXV to refuse MFN treatment" (Wilf and Davis 2011: 38). Till the late 1970s, Japanese trade policy revolved around the process of sequential liberalization, which would see remaining tariff obstacles to trade phased out over time. Once Tokyo had reasserted its territorial sovereignty with the return of the Ryukyu Islands, and had become an equal member of the GATT, Japan turned its foreign policy gaze towards developing a distinct regional/ bilateral policy set. Japan's return to Asia was facilitated by two exogenous factors: the so-called "Nixon Shokku" at the start of the 1970s, which saw Washington unilaterally reorient its monetary and China policies, and the end of the Vietnam War by the end of that same decade.

The 1977 Fukuda doctrine proved a crucial turning point as it would frame future ASEAN-Japan relations (Sudo 2005). If the Fukuda doctrine marked the start of a Japanese regional policy, Prime Minster Obuchi's 1999 declaration entrenched its free trade dimension. By endorsing an Asian Free Trade Area, the Obuchi government saw Japan fully join the "third wave regionalism." All of METI's annual white papers since have included a dedicated section on promoting intra-Asian trade. Eventually these intra-Asian ties would see the establishment of a tight web of PTAs geared towards supporting Japanese Regional Production Networks. Ultimately, under PM Hatoyama, this Asia-centric PTA strategy would hit a ceiling when dedicated efforts and significant political capital proved unable to surmount domestic divisions and exogenous resistance preventing said web of Japan-centric agreements from developing into deeper political and economic integration (Nakamura 2015).

The DPJ (Democratic Party of Japan) government revised its PTA strategy following the failure to see a comprehensive regional political project take root. Building on the previous LDP (Liberal Democratic Party) government's "2008 Basic Policies for Economic and Fiscal Reform," which set out objective criteria measuring the relative economic benefits of potential PTAs, the Noda cabinet adopted the "Basic Policy on Comprehensive Economic Partnership," which is the basis for both JEUFTA and TPP/US-JAP (Ponjaert 2015). Over time, a Japanese FTA Strategy emerged geared towards seeing Japan "take a stance linking FTAs to economic reforms in Japan [because otherwise the country would] not succeed in making them a means of improving the international competitiveness of Japan as a whole" (MOFA 2002). Akin to earlier evolutions in Europe we see a shift in PTA-bound considerations away from regional/neighborly political considerations in favor of growth and structural reform. As a result, PTAs are to enhance Japanese competitiveness by shrinking costs either through more streamlined (regional) production networks (Oyane 2004: 58) or, more recently, by gradually removing burdensome protective barriers in investment, services, standards, and certifications (Munakata 2004).

What Drives Them?

Although they came to PTAs at different times and from different angles, it is striking that each of these three major advanced economies concomitantly opted to start PTA negotiations with the other two partners. If the stalling of talks at the WTO provided a shared context, the similarity in policy reactions is nonetheless remarkable and raises the question whether said apparent policy convergence is deeply rooted in overlapping domestic agendas or merely a by-product of correlating reactions to a common challenge.

Building on Aggarwal's seminal work on the interregional dimension of the EU trade policy (Aggarwal and Fogarty 2004), one can extrapolate a possible hypothesis on the endogenous drivers of any given PTA strategy and check whether Tokyo, Washington, and Brussels are on parallel or competing tracks. The choice to engage in a given PTA negotiation can be driven by: (1) identity building, (2) domestic interest constellations, (3) bureaucratic attempts at influence maximization, and (4) reactions to systemic constraints, be they either external threats or nested institutions. If identity building through negotiations with third parties is a distinctly European concern, how the remaining drivers have played out in each of the three actors' body politic is a further indicator of whether these mega-PTAs are inherently mutually reinforcing or necessarily set on a collision course.

Interest groups
Interest groups' impact on trade agreements is determined by their: institutional environment, resources, coherence, and preferences (Aggarwal and Fogarty 2004: 13). In this respect we see all three polities confronted with comparable dynamics. As mature open democracies Japan, the US, and the EU have diverse and engaged civil societies. On the one hand, large-scale employer associations contributed significantly to the initial outlines of each mega-PTA thus helping to shape the contours of all three negotiation agendas.[2] On the other hand, those sectors traditionally more skeptical of liberalization—such as representatives of the rural economy, consumer organizations, and trade unions—have shown their usual reserve.

In all three polities societal groups hoping to curb the human and environmental cost of intensified economic activity have come to condition their support on the retention and promotion of existing safeguards. Considering it can be particularly tough to embed such protections into global multilateral agreements, because of the strength of the plurality of vested private interests and the diversity of regulatory systems, the bilateral/interregional level often appears better suited to the diffusion of regulatory norms and the leveraging of market power.

---

2   In the run-up to the negotiations Keidanren for Japan, the Chamber of Commerce for the US, and Business Europe in the EU all provided foundational policy papers and lobbying work in favor of these mega-PTAS.

Consequently, standard setting and regulatory harmonization are the main mobilizing issues in all three of these negotiations. However, in said policy areas the quest for regulatory simplification clashes with the call to preserve existing rules and standards. This foray into behind the borders issues has led to trade policies facing unprecedented levels of societal mobilization. However, if Tokyo, Brussels, and Washington have all come to experience conflicting societal pressures, their relative intensities are incomparable. JEUFTA's low political and societal salience is obvious when compared to TTIP or TPP/JAP-US. Invariably, trade talks involving the US become a defining political issue reflecting wider geo-strategic stakes while also serving as shorthand for politicians' positions along the political spectrum. This point was dramatically illustrated as the European Commission's consolidated public consultation on JEUFTA garnered 89 formal contributions whereas the TTIP consultation numbered over 150,000 responses before consolidation. Legislative chambers also echo these differences in mobilization as illustrated for example by the relative number of votes in the European Parliament (Figure 11.3).

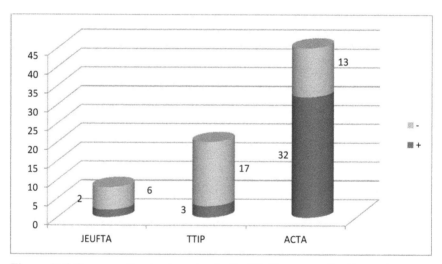

Figure 11.3 Comparative trade votes in the 7th European Parliament

Bureaucratic resources
Comparably, trends affecting bureaucratic resources in all three partners have evolved in similar directions but with profoundly different results. As trade became an increasingly visible component in contentious political debates surrounding preferred macroeconomic growth strategies, trade policy technocrats have been confronted with increased polarization. This has led to little change in the US, where a lean trade authority is functionally incorporated into the wider presidential office and serves as an extension of the president's comprehensive foreign policy

goals. Conversely, Japan and the EU have witnessed a series of administrative reforms encouraging greater political acumen and a more comprehensive approach to trade (Ponjaert 2015).

In Europe, the autonomy of DG Trade was checked by the Amsterdam Treaty's strengthening of the Member States' oversight (Meunier and Nicolaïdis 1999: 499) and the Lisbon Treaty's increase of the European Parliament's sway in matters of oversight and consent (Kleimann 2011: 13–15). Concurrently, greater coherence was sought by consolidating bureaucratic resources through the creation of the EEAS (Mayer 2013, Carta 2013). In Japan, more pro-active and less fragmented foreign policy-making was to be fostered by way of a more presidential style of policy-formation (Shinoda 2004, Ponjaert 2015), but without creating an independent administrative trade authority.

As a result, political intent and strategic considerations have come to weigh more heavily in all three polities' appreciation of trade negotiations. However, the resulting increase in number and complexity of negotiations launched at the behest of political imperatives has not always been met by an equivalent increase in resources. TTIP, TPP/US-JAP, and JEUFTA are therefore clearly competing for scarce bureaucratic resources (Figure 11.4). Compounded by dwindling autonomy from the political sphere, civil servants who are stretched too thinly are ill equipped to take on the socializations and networking mechanisms which habitually contribute towards greater trust among negotiating technocrats, thus increasingly leaving only political arbitration as a possible means of fostering agreement.

	🇺🇸	🔴	🇪🇺
AGENCY	USTR	METI - Trade Policy Bureau	DG Trade
STAFF	+/- 600	+/- 250	+/- 700
CRITICAL JUNCTURE	"Competitive Liberalization Agenda" (2002 -)	METI White Paper on Asian Trade (2000 -)	"Global Europe" (2006 -)
PARL. REVIEW	High *Ex Ante & Ex Post*	Low *Ex Post*	High *Ex Ante & Ex Post*
OVERSIGHT	Political	Bureaucratic	Hybrid
LAUNCH	Presidential & Congressional Politics	PMO	Council on Commission Proposal
NEGOTIAT.	Cabinet-lead under Presidential Direction	Bureaucratic (METI/MOFA) driven by PMO	Autonomous Bureaucracy

Figure 11.4 Comparative bureaucratic resources in Japan, Europe and the US

Reactions to systemic constraints

Finally, stipulating these mega-PTAs are the product of knock-on effects born of shared exogenous factors invites reflection on the international systemic constraints and opportunities facing Japanese, American, and European trade policy. Again we see commonalities when considering the trends shaping the broader institutions within which these mega-PTAs are nested. Their continued commitment to the WTO as an overarching trade organization sees all three espouse PTAs in the hope of changing the overall multilateral environment to a sufficient extent such that WTO talks might come unstuck.

Mega-PTAs also reflect the challenge posed by the rise of multipolarity (Gamble 2014), which sees these longstanding partners repeatedly attempt to revive their cooperation and its associated institutions because since "the end of the Cold War, ... absent of the concern of Soviet aggression, the traditional alliance among the United States, Western Europe and Japan [has] shown patent signs of strain" (Baker 1995). While broader institutional trends see Japan, Europe, and the US largely of one mind, the external threat perceptions which might prompt joint responses are increasingly different. As a result, these three actors remain without a clear unifying exogenous factor able to generate any trilateral political momentum. If negotiations in the Pacific are clearly marked by competitive balancing effects related to the rise of China and its promotion of a Regional Comprehensive Economic Partnership (RCEP) devoid of US influence (Capling and Ravenhill 2011), the negotiations across the Atlantic or Eurasia (Shu 2015) are lacking such a geostrategic edge as concerns focus on domestic growth, continued reciprocal engagement, and shifts in the GVC.

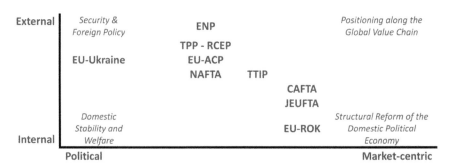

Figure 11.5 Competitiveness-driven trade agreements compared

Overall, even though these mega-PTAs reflect shared trends, their preceding negotiations and eventual implementation will necessarily be very dissimilar as the domestic mix of catalysts in Tokyo, Brussels, and Washington reflect distinct endogenous environments. Beyond the competition in material interests inherent to any trade negotiation, the initial political arbitrations made within each of the three considered polities and the specific internal contradictions these mega-PTAs must bridge are radically different in each case. This has resulted in three mega-PTA negotiations which at face value seem rather similar but have quite different set-ups and agendas (Figure 11.5).

Mega-PTAs: Their Divergent Set-Ups and Agendas

Varying domestic incentive structures and calculations have led Tokyo, Washington, and Brussels to institutionalize three distinct negotiation environments which run largely parallel to each other. If a general awareness of the relative progress made in each negotiation track obviously informs all three negotiations, TTIP, JEUFTA, and TPP/US-JAP present separate and self-propelling institutional environments. Strategic interactions or domino effects are therefore likely to remain fairly limited. Each mega-PTA is negotiated in light of a given set-up and agenda defined by its founding choices. At best one can expect tactical knock-on effects as negotiators use successes in one track to pressure another, yet considering the clout of the actors involved, such scare tactics have but limited scope. Above all, overriding endogenous concerns drive these three systemically significant and contemporaneous mega-PTA negotiations.

JEUFTA is the least politically salient of the mega-PTAs because of limited growth prospects, the relationship's historical "expectation deficit" (Tsuruoka, 2008), the fact most trade disputes have been resolved (Ponjaert 2015), the comparable levels of regulation they enjoy, and the often very loose networks linking societal groups on either side (Scheurs 2015, Fukuda 2015). Launched on 25 March 2013, these institutionalized negotiations have resulted in a near textbook case of indirect compound polities engaged in coordinative politics (Schmidt 2010) where mobilization and direct dialogue with the citizenry takes a backseat to technocratic politics. The agenda was clearly spelled out from the onset following a dedicated scoping exercise mandated by the Europeans. Negotiations are consequently dominated by technocratic issues focused on lightening the regulatory and tariff burdens on either side. The resulting agenda is deep and very focused, it is set to cover "Trade in Goods (including Market Access, General Rules, Trade Remedies), Technical Barriers to Trade and Non-Tariff Measures, Rules of Origin, Customs and Trade Facilitation, Sanitary and Phytosanitary Measures, Trade in Services, Investment, Procurement, Intellectual Property, Competition Policy, Trade and Sustainable Development, Other issues (General and Regulatory Cooperation, Corporate Governance and Business Environment, Electronic Commerce, Animal Welfare) and Dispute Settlement" (European Commission 2013f). Traditional bargaining and inter-sectoral trade-offs dominate the process with the car sector and public procurement as particularly sensitive issues. Institutionally, negotiations are organized along principles set out by the EU combining third-generation FTAs with a PCA (Börzel and Risse 2004: 26). Finally, if subject to interference from other agreements, other than possible reallocations of bureaucratic resources, these are most likely not to come from either TTIP or TPP/US-JAP. Only precedents set by agreements concluded under a similar EU-centric FTA/PCA mold could constrain JEUFTA's options (e.g. CEFTA, EU-South Korea FTA, etc.), whereas only concluded agreements covering similar trade flows would drive the negotiations forward (e.g. the EU-South Korea FTA). Both wider geo-economic and geo-strategic calculations are fairly limited in JEUFTA's case, where negotiations are dominated on either side by endogenous institutional and political considerations (Ponjaert 2015).

Kick-started by PM Abe on 23 July 2013, TPP/US-JAP is the product of a very different set of policy paths and catalysts. The TPP process itself emerged in 2008 as an Asian response to the insufficiencies of APEC's Free Trade Agenda. The G.W. Bush administration would quickly join the process to ensure its compatibility with Washington's "competitive liberalization" agenda, whereas Tokyo would take a further five years to join, at which stage both the format and the agenda of the negotiations were largely set (Terada 2012). As a result, Tokyo opted to join a complex series of negotiations which had come to be dominated by the US and were largely molded following the NAFTA precedent. TPP's multi-level negotiations combine a plurilateral umbrella agreement geared toward enhancing the regulatory coherence needed for regional production networks to thrive, alongside a set of bilateral agreements which delve into the more sensitive issues related to market access. As a result, those issues related to the regulatory-investment-IP-services nexus underpinning Asian supply chains are essentially covered by the plurilateral agreement, whereas (American) offensive interests lie in the bilateral ones. Key concerns for all Asian parties including Japan are regulatory coherence, simplified rules of origin, and facilitated professional mobility, as well as reliable investment and IP protection. The US for its part seeks greater market access, improved investment facilities, and streamlined dispute settlement mechanisms, as well as higher competition in (financial) services and a diffusion of its preferred norms and standards. The resulting multi-party, multi-tiered, and multi-dimensional negotiations are uniquely voracious in terms of bureaucratic resources leaving only the largest players with room for other negotiations. Just as this complexity isolates engaged parties from exogenous pressures, this same negotiation pattern created a two-level playing field with clear set of internal domino effects, be it between the various negotiating parties or the multilateral and bilateral levels. Moreover, although functioning as a compound polity overall, the inclusion of clearly identifiable bilateral tracks involving the US and its offensive interests has seen the need for communicative politics become ever more manifest in light of mounting protest. As a result, despite the negotiations' dogged focus on technical trade issues such as rules of origin, regulatory simplification and tariff reduction, negotiators must increasingly call upon domestic political capital to maintain the necessary momentum in both components of TPP/US-JAP—i.e. the plurilateral and bilateral ones.

TTIP, as the most contested of the three mega-deals, caught EU negotiators accustomed to expert-driven coordinative trade negotiations relatively off guard. In contrast to past bilateral negotiations with the US, TTIP impressed on European officials the need for third-generation trade negotiations to engage more directly with societal groups through direct communication with the body politic. Accordingly, for the first time DG Trade opted to invest heavily in greater transparency by: creating a dedicated website, making sections of the negotiation mandate publically available, and launching several topical online consultations. Conversely, US negotiators both more accustomed to political polarization and covered by the presidential mandate have been less concerned with direct communication with the wider public but rather more focused on securing a compact with a hostile US Congress. The shriller politics of these negotiations are a consequence of TTIP's fluid agenda and the tight web of networks linking societal groups on both sides of the Atlantic. This has allowed for powerful domestic forces to mobilize and directly influence the negotiations by ratcheting up the political cost of any deal. This has opened up the agenda to intrusion from several domestic, transatlantic, and global agendas which reach well beyond mere regulatory simplification and tariff reduction. The exact coverage and political significance of TTIP was not outlined at the time of its launch but was to be determined by the level of convergence achieved through open-ended negotiations.

In the absence of a comparable precedent and without a prior scoping exercise, the EU and the US are to a large extent making up the agenda as they go along. Negotiators have no clear parameters other than the Commission's unusually elusive negotiation mandate identifying three broad chapters[3] while only allowing for specific provisions in a single case: the audio-visual sector. As a result, TTIP's agenda is quite unique, both in relation to other mega-PTAs as well as in comparison to any previous reciprocal trade negotiations either of the partners has been engaged in so far. It set itself up as an unprecedented exercise in market-building through "living" regulatory harmonization—i.e. progressive and continued convergence. This fluid and unparalleled set-up reflects both the absence of a hegemon or lead able to provide a frame of reference. Furthermore, European and American negotiators have come to the table on slightly differing bases as the CCP saw DG Trade necessarily engage negotiations with a defined negotiation mandate, whereas USTR has emphasized the fact it was entering negotiations with a strong presidential political mandate, a set of ambitious goals, and no taboos. The lion's share of energies has therefore gone into bridging this relative mismatch between a European semi-autonomous trade authority with vast experience in multilateral market-building and regulatory reform but relatively constrained by a closed mandate, on the one hand; and a politically empowered

---

3 (1) Market Access—including Tariffs, Rules of Origin, Trade Defence Measures, Services, Investment, and Public Procurement, (2) a "Living Agreement" on Regulatory Issues—including sanitary and phyto-sanitary standards, regulatory compatibility in key sectors, regulatory convergence in services, and common dispute settlement mechanisms, and (3) Joint Responses to Common Global Challenges—including IP Protection, Sustainable Development, and adjusting to changes in the GVC.

Table 11.2 Relative implication of various forms of regulatory convergence

	Regulatory Harmonization	Mutual Recognition		Common Conformity Testing	Agreement's Possible Impact	
		Ergo Omnes	Reciprocal		On Existing Standards	On Global Standards
Within TTIP	**Politically Determined** Uncertain and Limited to certain sectors	**Politically Impractical** Low Salience	**Technocratic in outlook** Feasible in most sectors but no 3rd party implications	**Technocratic in outlook** High likelihood but no 3rd party implications	Potential race-to-the top in those harmonized sectors, otherwise moderate risk for a race-to-bottom	Low except for those harmonized sectors
Within TPP/ US-JAP	**Politically Impractical** Low Salience	Not on the agenda	**Technocratic in outlook** yet still Limited to certain sectors with no 3rd party implications	**Technocratic in outlook** Feasible in most sectors but no 3rd party implications	Potential risk for a race-to-bottom	Low beyond the institutional context of the TPP
Within JEUFTA	**Politically Impractical** Low Salience	**Politically Impractical** Low Salience	**Politically Impractical** Low Salience	**Technocratic in outlook** High likelihood but no 3rd party implications	Neutral	None

branch of the American executive with little experience of give-and-take in behind the border issues acting on the basis of an open-ended and untested mandate, on the other. This leaves little space for interference from third parties as both negotiating actors are engaged in a complex and endogenously determined harmonization exercise. Ultimately, the central stake of TTIP is whether, and to what extent, the parties can bring their regulatory systems in line. No other mega-PTA comes close to the same potential level of regulatory convergence (Table 11.2), but it remains an unproven and highly risky political gambit which could for domestic reasons easily be downgraded to a simple exercise in conformity testing or even a simple business dialogue. Only the highest levels of convergence would have any impact on third parties and in the absence of a hegemon, domestic factors will singularly determine the scope and feasibility of the regulatory convergence and correlated market-building agendas.

In conclusion, besides the multiplication in acronyms and increased political chatter they have brought about, the three mega-PTAs negotiated since 2013 are not to be seen as a coherent whole. They are at best a concomitant set of policy-responses to the differentiated challenges facing each actor's domestic political economy. They are neither a concerted geo-strategic re-balancing effort by established powers seeking to safeguard their shared interests in the face of new rising powers, nor a concerted geo-economic push towards reshaping the Global Value Chain in their shared interests. These are three very different negotiations, which, from their respective vantage points, offer a conservative perspective seeking to both preserve the multilateral system as well as maintain the GVC and its three constituent poles (Table 11.3). JEUFTA is of little concern to third parties as its knock-on effects are expected to remain fairly limited since it is essentially an exercise in institutional consolidation and trade facilitation with a set agenda. TPP/US-JAP is of greater global significance as it would have wider implications for both the GVC and regional balancing within East Asia. By way of its sheer scale TPP/US-JAP would transform a TPP/excl. Japan exclusively geared towards the region's consumer of last resort—i.e. the US—into a deepened and widened transpacific production hub. This potential geo-economic shift is magnified by the geo-political balancing effect of TPP with regards to the rise of China and its competing RCEP project. Accordingly, TPP has wide geo-political and geo-economic implications but ones that are mainly endogenously determined on either side of the Pacific, and are but indirectly correlated to the Atlantic or Eurasian spheres. Lastly, TTIP has the potential for the most widespread impact on third parties but only where the highest levels of regulatory convergence is secured. The negotiation's unprecedented format and agenda as well as its ambitious and fluid scope maintain a shroud of uncertainty over its broader implications. In response, third parties and other negotiations (e.g. JEUFTA or TPP) have kept a close eye on TTIP's progress but have also moved ahead their own policy paths regardless of TTIP's progress or intent.

Table 11.3 Varied set of giants: the largest PTAs compared

	JEUFTA	TPP	TTIP	RCEP
Negotiating Parties	Japan + the EU *i.e. 29 States*	12 States	The US + the EU *i.e. 29 States*	16 States
Driving Force	Joint leadership within a framework set by the EU	Pulled forward by the US	Joint leadership with an open-ended mandate	Pushed by ASEAN
Most Referenced Precedent	EU-Korea FTA	NAFTA	N/A *Unprecedented*	ASEAN+1 FTAs
Quality and Size	Deep and focused	Deep but narrow *90% is covered by the sole TPP/ US-JAP*	Deep and open-ended	Shallow but wide
Key Purpose	Support structural reform	Rule-making in support of regional production networks	Build a transatlantic market	Export market expansion
Flexibility	Low in terms of both format and scope	Low in terms of format, high in terms of scope	High in terms of both format and scope	High in terms of both format and scope
Covered Areas	19	21	Under negotiation but the EU mandate foresees 3 chapters – *i.e. Market access, regulatory issues and shared global challenges*	8
Approach to Services	Positive list	Negative list	Positive list	Limited positive list
Format of Standards in Labor and Environment	Adherence to global standards *(e.g. ILO, WHO ...)* and joint protocols	Direct applicability of existing US standards	Under negotiation	Specific clauses included in the agreement

	JEUFTA	TPP	TTIP	RCEP
Scope of Standards in Labor and Environment	Under negotiation, ranging from reciprocal to *erga omnes*	Strictly within the scope of the agreement	Under negotiation, ranging from reciprocal to *erga omnes*	Limited and strictly within the scope of the agreement
Political Dialogue	Comprehensive and formalized	Isolated from the trade talks	Comprehensive and informally associated	Isolated from the trade talks
Negotiation Style	A single bilateral undertaking between an autonomous European and self-directing Japanese trade authority	A set of sequentially negotiated parallel bilateral agreements in a multilateral framework involving a series of self-directing *(e.g. Japan)* and politically steered *(e.g. Malaysia, Australia, US, ...)* trade authorities	A single bilateral undertaking between an autonomous European and a politically steered US trade authority	A sequential multilateral undertaking involving a series of autonomous *(e.g. Korea)*, self-directing *(e.g. Japan)*, and politically steered *(e.g. Malaysia, China, ...)* trade authorities

PART IV
Impact on Multilateral Institutions and Regime Complexes

Chapter 12
Let's Stick Together:
The TTIP, the WTO and WTO 2.0

Petros C. Mavroidis[1]

The WTO: Victim of Its Own Success

The number of preferential trade agreements (PTAs) has exploded in the post-Uruguay Round era. And this is *prima facie* counter-intuitive, since we observe more and more PTAs at the moment when tariffs are at an all time low. Why is this the case?

Inquiring into what drives PTAs is like searching for clues in Pandora's box. PTAs have been concluded for heterogeneous reasons over the years, a scenario that, in today's world, will most likely continue.

There is, nevertheless, one explanatory factor that cuts across PTAs, at least across those PTAs designed by WTO Members that want to 'deepen' their integration process. There is only so much the GATT/WTO regime can do, and some solutions for enhanced integration have to be searched within 'smaller' groups of countries, i.e. within 'clubs'.

The GATT/WTO regime's recipe for addressing non-tariff barriers (NTBs) is non-discrimination, an instrument that helps but does not guarantee market access. We will explain.

The GATT/WTO regime has managed, absent a few peaks, to reduce tariffs to (almost) redundancy, as Irwin (1998) has shown. Consequently, markets are largely segmented through NTBs.

Semantics first: in this chapter, no negative connotation is attached to the term 'NTB'. Yes, say, a demanding public health policy thwarts imports of cheese infected with salmonella. But only a fool would understand trade liberalization as synonymous with trade liberalization at all costs.[2]

Negotiations regarding trade liberalization with respect to NTBs take place both multilaterally as well as bilaterally (regionally). At the multilateral level, the dominant method of integration, as briefly stated above, is non-discrimination.

---

1 For helpful discussions I am indebted to Jagdish Bhagwati, André Sapir and Alan Sykes.

2 Even if societies are on occasion prepared to live with some minimal risk as long as the gains from the activities that are pursued can be used to finance research that aims at reducing the level of accepted risk, if not at eliminating it altogether.

Ever since the inception of the GATT, regulation of NTBs was meant to be a sort of 'supporting act' to tariff commitments so that the value of the latter would not be eroded through subsequent unilateral actions. It was then agreed, and continues to be the case today, that trading nations would be allowed to unilaterally define domestic policies (i.e. NTBs) as long as they would abide by the principle to apply them in a non-discriminatory manner across domestic and imported goods.[3]

The problem with non-discrimination, as in the game of American football, is that it takes you a few yards down the pitch but is no touchdown. Yes, the Home Team cannot impose consumption taxes on the Away Team's widgets higher than what it imposes on its own widgets, but if the Home Team requires that widgets sold in its market are produced with renewable energy, the Away Team will never be in a position to sell to the Home Team's market its widgets which are produced using fossil fuels, even if the Home Team's import duties on widgets have been bound at 0 per cent.

Can we realistically go further at the multilateral level? This is a tough question, but one thing is clear. Unlike tariffs, where reduction of their level entails loss of income, reduction of NTBs makes the Home Team vulnerable to 'importing' health, environmental etc. hazards. In the case of tariffs reduction, income loss can be compensated through reciprocal commitments by the Away Team to reduce its level of tariffs. In the case of NTBs, it does not work this way.

The Home and Away Teams can, of course, move beyond non-discrimination. They can harmonize their standards. However, producing widgets with renewable energy adds to the fixed cost of production and, maybe, the Away Team cannot afford to do this for a variety of reasons. Let's assume, for example, that the Away Team is a developing country like three quarters of the WTO Members. The Away Team will have a different hierarchy of social preferences to satisfy than the Home Team, a developed country: environmental protection might rank below food security in its hierarchy of targets to pursue. Or, to be more nuanced, even if environmental protection is an objective the Away Team wants to pursue, it could be that because of budgetary constraints it is prepared to impose, say, border tax adjustments, but unprepared to subsidize clean energy.

The two countries can also sign a recognition agreement, but why would the Home Team sign a similar instrument with a country that does not share the same objective, e.g. to reduce CO_2 emissions? Even in our 'nuanced' scenario, there is no point, no reason at all indeed to sign a recognition agreement.

What can we do then? What if the Home Team wants to promote market integration without giving up on its environmental aspirations? Let's recall that non-discrimination is no guarantee of market access even if two countries share

---

3   With respect to a sub-set of NTBs, those coming under the aegis of the WTO Agreement on Technical Barriers to Trade (TBT) and the Agreement on Sanitary and Phyto-Sanitary Measures (SPS), e.g. labelling schemes or measures aiming at protecting public health and/or environment, trading nations must further observe additional obligations which, nevertheless, do not extend beyond 'negative integration'.

the same objective but use different means to achieve it. What's worse: even in cases where they use the same means, market access could be hampered because, for instance, the measurement of a nefarious substance in the exporting country is not recognized as satisfying the criteria for measurement in the importing country.

As a result, what happens in similar cases is that the Home Team looks for like-minded partners to promote its market integration agenda without eviscerating the bite of its social policies. The Away Team will do the same.

By the 'like-minded' partners, we want to capture other countries which share the same goals with the Home (or the Away Team, as the case may be) and have symmetric capacity with the Home (or the Away Team, as the case may be) to pursue them. They move beyond non-discrimination in 'clubs', as opposed to moving all together. Recognition agreements are signed between the Home and the Home-like Teams, trading nations that the Home Team can 'trust'. The same is true for the Away Team.

The Home and Away Teams will continue to be bound by non-discrimination as far as the relations between them are concerned, whereas the Home Team and its like-minded partners will move to 'deeper' integration.[4]

Why did we not observe similar deals in the early years of world trade integration? Baldwin (1970) was probably right when he stated that the swamp was full of invisible snags when GATT entered into the realm of international relations. Through a series of successful trade rounds focusing essentially on tariff protection, the GATT managed to drain the swamp. As a result, the snags are now visible. Alas, they cannot be taken care of in the same way as tariffs. The GATT/WTO, through multilateral action, helped bring about a problem that is hard to resolve in a multilateral manner.

Did the GATT prepare its own demise? 'No' is the short answer. It still has a large role to play, a quintessential role in the realm of international trade relations in the years to come. It is just that some adjustments are in order, as explained in the following section.

Negotiating the NTBs in Clubs

TTIP is No Outlier

Against this background, the negotiation of TTIP should not come as a surprise. To the extent that TTIP is concerned with 'deep' integration, it will then, of course, be negotiation within a 'club' between a few like-minded entities.

Indeed, from what we have seen so far (since a lot of information regarding the TTIP agenda remains confidential at the time of writing), TTIP looks like an ambitious project. The EU, for instance, has put on the table proposals regarding

---

4   Costinot (2008) offers a formal explanation of this point. Marchetti and Mavroidis (2012) provide some empirical proof in the context of trade in services.

mutual recognition of conformity assessment, the ultimate barrier in ensuring market access for goods that are undergoing scientific risk assessment (whose number is large and rising). The partners are prepared to negotiate a novel investor-to-state dispute settlement system. They might also end up writing standards for probably the entire world. The list is long and might get longer as negotiations progress over the next few months.

When it comes to the choice of the subject-matter, TTIP follows a pattern that has been shaping up since the successful conclusion of the Uruguay Round. Horn et al. (2010) examine all PTAs signed by the EU and the US between 1992–2008. They inquire into the subject-matter of PTAs signed by the two major hubs and conclude that, in part, it covers areas coming under the current mandate of the WTO but at a quicker pace of integration (what they term WTO+) and, in part, it extends to areas that are not covered by the WTO mandate (WTOx).[5]

In their work, they identify dozens of areas which qualify as NTBs and feature in various PTAs. All of the WTOx (which constitutes the majority of the subject-matter in all PTAs reviewed) concerns NTBs. A sizeable percentage of WTO+ concerns NTBs as well.

PTAs Are Not the Only Game in Town Anymore

NTBs can also be negotiated in the context of plurilateral agreements across like-minded countries, which is the only concession to the 'variable geometry' made during the Uruguay Round.

The Uruguay Round was negotiated following the so-called 'single undertaking' approach. The idea was to do away with the GATT's 'à la carte' approach that had been followed during the Tokyo Round. All trading nations would from now on be parties to all the signed agreements. Thus we move from GATT's 'à la carte' to a WTO menu.

A concession was made for four agreements only, two of which are still in force: the Agreement on Civil Aviation (largely subsumed by the WTO Agreement on Subsidies and Countervailing Measures) and the Government Procurement Agreement.

Plurilaterals are Pareto-sanctioned in the sense that they will not enter into force unless the WTO Members have by consensus approved their content: it is thus to be expected that no one will feel worse off as a result and some may even be better off following the entry into force of a plurilateral. Plurilaterals have not flourished yet, but they provide a promising avenue to negotiate deals across like-minded countries.

In fact, as Hoekman and Mavroidis (2014) point out, they are more WTO-friendly options than PTAs. PTAs are not 'cleared' through the multilateral review before they can be consumed. Those who believe that they have been negatively

---

5   The WTO World Trade Report for 2011 endorsed this classification of the subject-matter (WTO 2011b).

affected by the entry into force of a PTA can, of course, litigate. For reasons ranging from a collective action to strategic behaviour, litigation happens very scarcely, if at all. As a result, PTAs are tolerated but not necessarily acquiesced to.

Plurilaterals, on the other hand, must be approved by the WTO Members, otherwise they cannot be consumed at all. The 'umbilical chord' to the WTO is thus kept tight.

Clubs Exist Elsewhere As Well (in More Homogeneous Corners)

Inside the EU, following endless discussions to what extent the monetary union was or was not the first form of a 'variable geometry', the possibility of clubs has entered the centre stage in the form of 'enhanced cooperation': a sub-set of EU Members can go ahead and integrate in the areas where others are not prepared to move in.

To avoid (minimize) the negative external effects stemming from enhanced cooperation, a voting mechanism has been introduced in the Council of the EU: a threshold value (minimum) must be in favour, otherwise the suggested scheme cannot be introduced.

Now, the EU is, of course, a group of countries sharing a much higher homogeneity-index (no matter whether measured in terms of GDP per capita, cultural affinity, public order proximity etc.) than the WTO. Still, it was felt that it was simply not the case that everyone was willing to move equally fast and equally far. If true for the EU, it should *a fortiori* be true for the WTO with its very diverse members.

TTIP Message (in a Bottle) to Geneva

The preceding discussion underscores that clubs are inevitable in today's world. Indeed, they are an almost natural consequence of the WTO's success to exhaust the multilateral agenda by driving tariffs (almost) out of the trading nations' arsenal.

There is nearly inevitability in seeing the clubs picking up from where the GATT/WTO has left it off. The question that needs to be asked is: what should the WTO do about it? Before we can suggest some sketchy thoughts on this issue, we should first have a look at what the WTO does about the situation as it now stands.

WTO

A Tale of Two Cities

The PTA- and the WTO-agenda leaves us with the impression that the latter is still dealing with yesterday's world. This statement is a factual observation which is void of any value judgment and which is not meant as criticism of the WTO. In the view of this author, there is only a certain limit that the WTO can do if it continues to keep the same integration-pace for the totality of its increasing number of members (160 and counting).

The question is what should the WTO's attitude be in light of the inevitability that some members will integrate faster and some slower? The suggestion of this chapter is that the WTO should not stop the frontrunners.

From the Bali Package to the Bali Mandate: A New Beginning

The outcome of the Bali Ministerial Conference (December 2013) was rightly hailed as a major success on the way to re-establishing the traumatized relevance of the WTO. The Doha Round has been going on for almost a decade and a half, now outlasting any trade round that was negotiated before. Before the Bali meeting, in terms of success, the Doha Round had only the Aid for Trade initiative to show.

Then, probably against any expectations, the WTO Members managed to pull off a deal that comprised the Agreement on Trade Facilitation.

A rather obscure decision which is equally, if not more, important was adopted during the Ministerial Conference. The Director-General of the WTO has been mandated by its Members to come up with a proposal on what to do with the remaining items that featured in the agenda of the Doha Round.

The agenda can be designed by using different benchmarks. The discussion so far suggests that it must be designed so as to ensure that it bridges the clusters of deep integration, i.e. the clubs discussed above.

WTO 2.0

Guardian of the Liberalizing Past

The GATT/WTO has so far achieved a lot. The accomplished liberalization is locked within the 'WTO safe' and there is no way back without renegotiation, a daunting prospect by any reasonable benchmark. For this reason, the WTO has always been relevant when it comes to trade commitments, no matter whether any additional commitments are entered in PTAs or plurilaterals.

Moreover, any disputes which might arise regarding the precise ambit of the commitments made can only be adjudicated before the WTO. Article 23.2, Dispute Settlement Understanding (DSU), leaves no doubt on this score.

Building Bridges to TTIP and to Today's Trade Agenda

The WTO needs to build bridges, or revamp the existing ones, over to the clusters of deep integration.

The chord with plurilaterals, as suggested above, is quite tight. It is the link to PTAs that must be rethought. The Transparency Mechanism asks some of the right questions: what matters for the multilateral regime is to know what exactly is happening behind the closed doors where PTA partners meet. However, it stops when things start getting interesting.

PTAs are rarely a one-off issue: they have a life of their own. They create secondary law. They often provide for adjudication of disputes under their own dispute settlement system. This is precious information that does not necessarily reach Geneva. It might affect non-participants. It might also provide them with inspiration as to what to do next.

The WTO should develop into a sort of 'Transparency Exchange' mechanism, a comprehensive database where trade liberalization efforts at various levels will be stored and made accessible to the interested parties.

A Genuine World Court

Commentators have by now run out of names describing the WTO dispute settlement system: the 'crown jewel of the system', a 'unique achievement' etc. The process for resolving disputes much more than its effectiveness (which is essentially a function of the identities of the disputing parties) has a lot to be proud of: disputes are resolved by dis-interested judges in a peaceful manner, a rarity or, indeed, a unique feature in the realm of international relations.

An idea that could, and probably should, be explored in the near future is whether it could develop into a genuine 'World Trade Court'. This idea would be that disputes, even if taking place in bilateral or regional fora (in PTAs), could be appealed before the WTO. This would make the WTO a relevant forum (even if partially) for trade integrations worldwide.

An enhanced transparency and adjudication-relevance are the ways forward for the WTO. Investing in these two areas while remaining the guardian of a liberalizing past will make the WTO the unifying cornerstone of all future trade integrations, which, unavoidably, as stated in this chapter, will occur in clubs. In short, the argument here is that instead of demonizing what it cannot fight for, the WTO should adopt a different attitude and look at co-existing along the various emerging liberalization schemes at the bilateral or plurilateral level.

Chapter 13

WTO Oversight over Bilateral Agreements: From a Notification to an Examination Process?

Jens L. Mortensen

Introduction

The TTIP will – like other free trade agreements (FTAs) – violate one of the cornerstones of the WTO, i.e. the Most-Favoured-Nation (MFN) principle. However, the multilateral trading system has since 1947 permitted the formation of trading blocs and preferential bilateral trading partnerships. GATT Article XXIV, which was later supplemented by GATS Article V concerning trade in services and the Enabling Clause concerning trade between developing countries, exempts customs unions (CUs) and FTAs from the MFN principle provided that such arrangements are notified to the WTO, detailed information is made transparent and they qualify as trade liberalizing and not as trade discriminatory arrangements. This 'permissibility test' embedded in the WTO oversight mechanism appears to be a straightforward matter: FTAs must, on balance, further – and not obstruct – trade liberalization. Yet, prior to their approval, the WTO itself is not permitted to openly criticize or take action against any failure to comply with these provisions. Only WTO Members are entitled to react against any possible discrimination that results from the TTIP by filing a formal WTO complaint to the Dispute Settlement system.

Article XXIV remains one of the most criticized WTO provisions. Bhagwati called it 'full of holes' (1993: 44), whereas Devuyst and Serdarevic (2008: 5) called it '... practically non-functional'. Already back in 1985, the Leutwiler Group stated that '... the exceptions and ambiguities which have thus been permitted have seriously weakened the trade rules' (quoted in Chase 2006: 2). Their warning is as relevant today as it was back then. FTAs set the dangerous precedent for selectivity in modern trade diplomacy which threatens to fragment the trading system and damage the trade interests of non-participants. It is telling that their calls for reexamination of ambiguity in GATT Article XXIV's and its inconsistent application have been ignored for more than 30 years. Even the WTO itself concluded that '... [o]f all the GATT articles, this is one of the most abused, and those abuses are among the least noted ...' (WTO 1995: 63). In 2013, The Panel on Defining the Future of Trade came to an almost identical conclusion:

'... [t]he multilateral system will remain deficient until a real set of disciplines is established to facilitate the convergence of PTAs [preferential trade agreements] with the multilateral trading system' (WTO 2013a: 28).

This chapter asks how the WTO can fulfil its task of ensuring that FTAs do not systematically undermine the multilateral trading order. It focuses on the issue of transparency in the current oversight process and discusses whether the WTO Secretariat should be granted a stronger mandate to investigate proactively the economic effects of the notified FTAs.

GATT Article XXVI has long been depicted as a dangerous design flaw in the WTO that is responsible for the systemic erosion of the multilateral trading order. Indeed, the oversight mechanism endangers the centrality of the WTO in the global economy and its credibility as an institution. It is not easy to fix the flaw, however. The 'permissibility test' in GATT Article XXIV: 5 is rooted in ambiguities of the GATT/WTO institution itself. Still, the principle is that FTAs should be considered WTO-compatible only if it is demonstrated that duties and other regulations on the whole are no higher or no more restrictive than the existing ones. Yet, it is not clear who, how or according to what criteria this should be established. Even though the introduction of the Transparency Mechanism (TM) in 2006 improved the FTAs oversight process, the permissibility test is plagued by chronic unresolved tensions between the WTO trade policy surveillance and the WTO dispute settlement. The non-functionality of GATT Article XXIV exposes the deep-rooted cracks of the WTO.

The tensions created by the multipolarization of the trading order are amplified by the 'dispute settlement awareness' that transcends much of what is actually happening within the WTO. Even a remote potential of future WTO litigation against the criticized aspects of an FTA has had a chilling effect on the political demand for effective oversight. With the only often-mentioned exception of Mongolia, each WTO member is a party to at least one kind of a preferential trade agreement. On average, each WTO member is a party to 13 agreements. The solution of equipping the WTO Secretariat with a stronger mandate to initiate factual investigations of the notified FTAs is a potential threat to every WTO member. This is the untold truth about the flawed Article XXIV process: nobody is interested in the effective WTO FTAs oversight.

In addition, it is difficult to determine 'who gets what' – and, in particular, 'who gets worse-off' – in the new generation of twenty-first-century FTAs. The effects of TTIP will be felt globally; it will be difficult to isolate and thus analyse these independently. TTIP is essentially about liberalizing regulatory trade barriers. Yet the estimated impact of the TTIP-led liberalization of the 'behind-the-border' barriers is largely analytically unchartered waters (Baldwin 2011). Under such circumstances, even if the WTO Secretariat were to be mandated to examine independently the economic and systemic impact of the new twenty-first-century FTAs, the analytical framework and applied methodology could be easily contested and the impartiality of the WTO Secretariat could be subsequently called into question.

Bearing this in mind, a completed TTIP will pass the existing 'permissibility test' of GATT Article XXIV. After all, TTIP will be the most ambitious *free* trade agreement ever to be concluded. The problem is that 'the permissibility test' of FTAs, as currently established by the WTO treaty, is overly complicated, arguably ambiguous, methodologically underspecified and conceptually imprecise. As this chapter demonstrates, its legal definitions have been left unclear, there is no consensual understanding of its purpose and what methodology should be applied. The outcome (or, more precisely, the lack thereof) has been dictated by politics and not by an independent economic analysis.

GATT Article XXIV

From its humble beginnings in 1947, the GATT was designed as a pragmatic and flexible arrangement. It is not just about unconditional trade liberalization. Exceptions to the unconditional MFN treatment are scattered throughout the various WTO agreements, such as the permissibility of antidumping and countervailing duties (GATT Article VI) and temporary quantitative restrictions for balance-of-payment reasons (GATT Articles XII, XVIII). GATT Article XXIV is amongst the most important of these exceptions, allowing for an exception to FTAs and CUs. Therefore, the TTIP is permissible, provided that it fulfils certain provisions laid out in the GATT Article XXIV provisions and its later modifications.

Technically, the GATT Article XXIV permits the establishment of CUs (i.e. common tariff barriers) and FTAs (i.e. preferences or privileges between parties). The GATT Article XXVI: 4 states that the '... contracting parties recognize the desirability of increasing freedom of trade by the development, through voluntary agreements, of closer integration between the economies of the countries parties to such agreements'. However, the GATT Article XXIV conditions its endorsement of FTAs by emphasizing that the purpose '... should be to facilitate trade between the constituent territories and not to raise barriers to the trade of other contracting parties with such territories'.

Accordingly, the GATT Article XXIV formulates the both *substantive* and *procedural* conditions under which FTAs are permissible. The substantive requirement is that 'the duties and other regulations of commerce maintained in each of the constituent territories' of an FTA '... shall not be higher or more restrictive than the corresponding duties and other regulations of commerce existing in the same constituent territories prior to the formation of the free-trade area ...' (GATT Article XXIV: 5 (a)).

Article XXIV is not a textbook example of legal precision. The text frequently refers to the key concept 'substantially'. For instance, it defines the product coverage by stating that restrictive regulations of commerce should be 'eliminated' with respect to 'substantially all the trade' between the parties 'or at least ... substantially all the trade' in the originating products (GATT Article XXI: 8(a)(i), 8(b)). A similar requirement is included in paragraph (b) on FTAs where it is stated that such elimination shall be made on 'substantially all the trade' in the originating products. The intent is to maximize the product coverage; yet the precise meaning has always been unclear. The preamble to *Understanding on the Interpretation of Article XXIV* (WTO 1994) tried to clarify this. However, the interpretation has remained contentious.[1] All in all, the intention of GATT Article XXIV is clear: FTAs must be about *free* trade. However, the legal clarity of the substantive requirements in GATT Article XXIV leaves a number of questions unanswered. The text is open to interpretation: what is meant by the elimination of restrictions on 'substantially all trade' between the parties to a preferential trade arrangement? Does this allow for exclusion of sectors that enjoyed protection prior to the particular agreement? Moreover, GATT Article XXIV is imprecise in stipulating how to measure the elimination of restrictions on 'substantially all trade' between the signatories.

The FTA Oversight Process in the WTO: From GATT 1947 to the 2006 Transparency Mechanism

GATT Article XXIV is – perhaps most importantly – about procedural legitimization of FTAs. The original GATT 1947 provision did not establish a proper 'examination' or 'review' of the notified FTAs. However, a practice of mandating a working party to 'examine in the light of the relevant provisions of the GATT' each FTA which was notified under GATT Article XXIV and to 'report thereon' emerged (WTO 2002: 8). Article XXIV was not fully included in the otherwise impressive reforms of the Uruguay Round 1986–1993, i.e. in the establishment of the Trade Policy Review Mechanism (TPRM) and the WTO Dispute Settlement system, including the Appellate Body. Instead, the Uruguay Round Agreement created a fragmented review system. The WTO Committee on Regional Trade Agreements (CRTA) was given the task of verifying compliance with WTO rules in both trade in goods and services and that were notified under the GATT Article XXIV and GATS Article V, respectively.

However, it is the WTO Committee on Trade and Development which has the authority to examine and discuss FTAs between developing countries. An institutionalized divide between North-North, North-South and South-South FTAs was created. This fragmentation continues today. Although frequently challenged in the Rules Negotiation Group, it has developed into a principled debate between the developing and developed WTO Members in the Group discussions (WTO 2011a).

---

1 Two interpretative approaches have been suggested: a quantitative interpretation which relies on statistical benchmarks, such as percentage of trade, and a more ambitious qualitative interpretation whereby all sectors are included in the product coverage, not only in terms of trade flows but also in terms of tariff lines that are used in the Harmonized System classification scheme (see WTO 2002: 8–9).

The pre-2006 review mechanism had a troubled existence, as illustrated by Figure 13.1. The original mechanism of *ad hoc* working parties was workable. For much of the period until the 1980s, it was also a relatively manageable task. The system was nevertheless put under stress as the number of FTAs exploded. The original process envisioned a factual investigation by the WTO Secretariat for the notified agreements. Thereafter, the reports were adopted by the Council. After 1995, as indicated, the number of unadopted reports but completed investigations multiplied until 2002. After that, the system stopped functioning. The Doha Mandate reflected this development and the CRTA was mandated with the task of improving the oversight of FTAs.

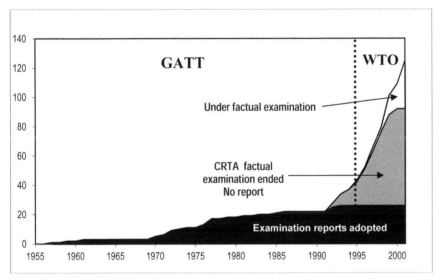

Figure 13.1 Examination process: CUs and FTAs notified to the GATT/ WTO under the GATT Article XXIV, 1948–2002

Source: WTO 2002: 9.

Only one of the examination reports which was adopted in the old review system found that the agreement in question was completely compatible with the relevant rules (Chase 2006: 1). By 2002, as Figure 13.1 illustrates, the review process had fallen into complete disuse. Despite the increasing number of notifications (the white area) and completed factual investigations (grey area), no formal examination report was produced from 1995 to 2002 (the black area).

The current system remains fragmented. There is no single forum for the WTO oversight of the notified FTAs. Provisions exist for trade in goods (GATT Article XXIV), for trade in services (GATS Article V) and for trade with developing countries (the Enabling Clause). Table 13.1 summarizes some of the key provisions regarding what information WTO Members are required to submit and what review process any notification is subject to.

Table 13.1 Notification and surveillance provisions

	GATT	The Enabling Clause	GATS
Provision of information	Article XXIV: 7(a) Any contracting party deciding to enter into a customs union or free-trade area, or an interim agreement leading to the formation of such a union or area, shall promptly notify the CONTRACTING PARTIES and shall make available to them such information regarding the proposed union or area as will enable them to make such reports and recommendations to contracting parties as they may deem appropriate.	Para. 4. Any contracting party taking action to introduce an arrangement ... shall: a) notify the CONTRACTING PARTIES and furnish them with all the information they may deem appropriate relating to such action; b) afford adequate opportunity for prompt consultations at the request of any interested contracting party with respect to any difficulty or matter that may arise. The CONTRACTING PARTIES shall, if requested to do so by such contracting party, consult with all contracting parties concerned with respect to the matter with a view to reaching solutions satisfactory to all such contracting parties.	Article V: 7(a) Members which are parties to any agreement ... shall promptly notify any such agreement and any enlargement or any significant modification of that agreement to the Council for Trade in Services. They shall also make available to the Council such relevant information as may be requested by it. The Council may establish a working party to examine such an agreement or enlargement or modification of that agreement and to report to the Council on its consistency with this Article.

Firstly, none of the three provisions *specify* what information is required. The wording is unclear. It is up to the relevant committee or council to ask for that information. Secondly, none of the provisions specifies the consequences of non-notification. Nor are there any specific time-limits established. The Enabling Clause on FTAs between developing countries in particular has been criticized. It does not call for any examination: it merely suggests bilateral consultations. In contrast, GATS Article V states that the Committee can decide whether an FTA is to be examined. As mentioned previously, proposals tabled in the Rules Group have tried to unify the notification system by requiring that all FTAs and CUs, irrespective of whether they are notified under Article XXIV, the Enabling Clause or GATS Article V, are notified to a single body, i.e. the reformed CRTA. There has been no consensus in the Rules Group on this issue.

The 2006 Transparency Mechanism: From Factual 'Investigations' to Factual 'Presentations'

After years of inconclusive negotiations, a minor breakthrough occurred in December 2006 when the Rules Group received an approval – on a provisional basis – from the General Council to establish a TM system (WTO 2006). It is currently under review. In essence, the TM provides for an early announcement, stricter notification to the WTO and improved procedures enhancing the transparency of FTAs in operation (Table 13.2, p. 166). It must be noted, however, that the Secretariat's factual investigations and subsequent policy discussions among WTO Members still take place in the three different venues mentioned above.

The TM is arguably an improvement: time-limits and required information are specified. Information about any change in or implementation of the completed agreements is also included. Since 2009, all information required by the TM has been made public on the WTO website.

The reformed mechanism is far more explicit about what is required by WTO Members. It is, however, telling that the term 'factual investigations' has been replaced with 'factual presentations'. The Annex to the Decision (WTO 2006) specifies more precisely what information WTO Members are required to make available to the WTO Secretariat. It mandates the WTO Secretariat, 'on its own responsibility and in full consultation with the parties', to prepare a factual presentation of the FTA (para. 7(a)). The TM does not allow for an independent fact-finding examination. Rather, the Secretariat's presentation '... shall be primarily based on the information provided by the parties; if necessary, the WTO Secretariat may also use data available from other sources, taking into account the views of the parties in furtherance of factual accuracy' (para. 8). Moreover, the Decision states that '... in preparing the factual presentation, the WTO Secretariat shall refrain from any value judgement' (para. 8). It restates what was also the case prior to the Decision, namely that the Secretariat's factual presentation '... shall not be used as a basis for dispute settlement procedures or to create new rights and obligations for Members' (para. 9).

It has been a fairly successful reform. In the period January–October 2013, the CRTA received 31 notifications of RTAs, 19 in goods and 12 in services (CRTA 2013). During 2013, 13 factual presentations were distributed reflecting 23 notifications (CRTA 2013), which is an improvement in comparison to the pre-2006 situation. Yet, reports of absent FTA notifications are frequent, especially those concerning the Enabling Clause.

Table 13.2 Key features of the 2006 Transparency Mechanism

Process	Requirements
Early Announcement	WTO Members participating in negotiations should inform the WTO Secretariat. Parties to a newly signed FTA should transmit information, including its official name, scope, date of signature, any foreseen timetable for its entry into force or provisional application, relevant contact points and/or website addresses and any other relevant unrestricted information.
Notification	The notification should take place as early as possible, in general no later than the parties' ratification of the FTA. Parties should specify under which provision(s) of the WTO agreements the FTA is notified and provide the full text and any related schedules, annexes and protocols.
Procedures to Enhance Transparency	The consideration by Members of a notified FTA shall be normally concluded within one year after the date of notification. Parties shall make data available to the Secretariat as soon as possible, but normally within a period of 10 weeks (or 20 weeks in the case of developing countries) after the date of notification. A formal meeting will be devoted to the consideration of each notified FTA. The factual presentation, additional information, written questions, replies or comments must be transmitted in advance.
Subsequent Notification and Reporting	Any changes affecting the implementation of an FTA, or the operation of an already implemented FTA, should be notified to the WTO as soon as possible. After implementation, the parties shall submit to the WTO a short written report on the realization of liberalization commitments as originally notified.

Source: WTO website: http://www.wto.org/english/tratop_e/region_e/trans_mecha_e.htm [accessed 13 August 2014].

What is the WTO Secretariat entitled to do in the TM? No mandate is given for independent fact-finding examinations by the WTO Secretariat. The terms of reference for the CRTA include: 'examinations of agreements … and thereafter present its report to the relevant body for appropriate action' and '… to consider the systemic implications of such agreements and regional initiatives for the multilateral trading system and the relationship between them, and make appropriate recommendations to the General Council' (WTO 2013c). It remains unclear what is understood by 'systemic'. The WTO Secretariat is required to assist Members, especially those from developing countries, with these tasks. The WTO oversight process of FTAs remains member-driven, fragmented and loosely defined. The role of the Secretariat is limited to presenting a descriptive and factual overview of the FTA in question. Its primary role is limited to facilitation of discussions rather than to criticizing the FTA under review.

Should the WTO Be Given Any Independent Powers to Examine FTAs?

Transparency and enforcement is a 'problematic tandem' since WTO Members themselves have such divergent understandings of the rules. The WTO Secretariat is explicitly prevented from presenting any 'value judgments': its role is limited to factual presentations. The reports on the WTO website are highly informative, descriptive and detailed listings of what each FTA contains, trading relationship between the parties and so forth, but any analysis is largely absent. This is no coincidence. The Secretariat is simply not allowed to analyse the impact of the FTAs.

The Secretariat's presentations are required to be neutral. Any effective transparency is thus made difficult by the reluctance of WTO Members to engage wholeheartedly in the review. The process is hampered by what has been termed a 'dispute-settlement awareness': a 'reluctance to provide information or agree to conclusions that could later be used or interpreted by a dispute settlement panel' (WTO 2002: 8). Even a remote prospect of any future WTO litigation against the criticized aspects of an FTA has had a chilling effect on Members' willingness to demand improved transparency.

Yet this is not an accidental 'design flaw' of the WTO. GATT Article XXIV was a political choice (see Chase 2006). The TPRM is plagued by similar problems. Neither of them can be seen as potential inputs in the WTO dispute settlement system. This limits the scope of any effective WTO transparency. The rationale is to reduce political pressures for protection by asking Members to voluntarily notify the WTO about their laws and decisions, share information and discuss sensitive issues. The intent is to create peer pressure. However, the WTO is caught in the dilemma of 'transparency without enforcement': if the WTO transparency requirements are not enforceable, no one will have any incentive to provide information, but everybody will have an incentive to hide the truth. The political reluctance to demand more effective transparency is thus not a new issue.

The fear of any potential WTO litigation prevents a more active role by the Secretariat in the oversight mechanism. Any criticism of FTAs must come from outside, e.g. from think tanks, the OECD or NGOs. However, if independent FTA assessments are to be commissioned from outside the WTO by autonomous trade policy experts, these assessments may easily be ignored as they lack the legitimacy of the WTO. Independent assessments can contribute to the debate about the FTAs, but what is needed is more frequent WTO oversight of the new FTAs that is accepted as legitimate, fair and reliable by the entire trade policy community. Commissioning the FTA studies by the WTO solves only a part of the problem.

Can the WTO Secretariat Investigate the Effects of the New FTAs at All?

At present, uncertainties about the precise economic impact of the TTIP may also accentuate the risks of a politicized FTA oversight mechanism. Little is known about how FTA-led regulatory liberalization affects the outside exporters. Even if the WTO acquires any investigatory powers, it is difficult to determine the economic effects of the new FTAs. For decades, economists have discussed whether trade diversion is more significant than trade creation. Recently, it has been pointed out that the unprecedented regulatory ambitions of a TTIP-led liberalization make it incomparable with other FTAs (Baldwin 2011, Baldwin 2014a). It is a qualitatively different FTA, reflecting the twenty-first-century world economy. Consequently, there is a need for rethinking the underlying economic models.

The bulk of the promised gains of TTIP stems from regulatory harmonization. Yet, how will the outside producers and exporters be affected? The standard argument is that a more simplified market access and product approval process will benefit everyone. As argued by Pauwelyn in this volume, the new generation of FTAs can no longer be considered private club goods with exclusive benefits but public goods with system-wide effects. This challenges the *ex-ante* calculation of estimated effects of FTAs. How do we know whether the trade flows created by a proposed FTA will outweigh the trade diversion effects? Given the complexities of the regulatory agenda of the new FTAs, and the globalization of world trade, *ex-ante* predictions of their effects are increasingly uncertain. In contrast, an *ex-post* analysis of the existing FTAs would be much less complicated.

Products created by the global production networks are 'global products'. The complicated definitions of rules of origin obscure the identification of any tangible benefits (or losses) of the new generation of trade agreements with the TTIP becoming their centrepiece. The economic reality escapes the political logic and legal fiction of any territorial discriminatory trade arrangements. The traditional trade policy instruments are ineffective, multilateral trade diplomacy is futile and the existing institutions have lost support from business. Critics fear a drift towards structural empowerment of the competitive trading powers at the expense of permanently de-globalized and uncompetitive economies.[2]

Projections of the external impact of the TTIP do not reach identical results. For instance, the independent but European Commission-sponsored CEPR study concluded that about 30 per cent of the economic gains from the TTIP lie outside the EU and the US (CEPR 2013). The study uses direct spill-overs off-setting

---

2   For instance, UNCTAD emphasizes: '… the RTAs of the future should be careful to avoid the pitfalls of distorting firms' choices and losing the connection with the rest of the value chain' (OECD, WTO and UNCTAD 2013: 17).

the negative trade diversion effects, i.e. the shift of trade from effective 'outside' producers to ineffective 'inside' producers in the US and EU. Furthermore, it assumes that the rest of the world will adopt the common EU-US standards, certification procedures and so on.[3] On the one hand, the TTIP will reduce the product approval and market access costs for outside exporters. On the other hand, the rest of the world must accept the transatlantic-led harmonization of international standards and regulatory procedures and secure its access to the envisioned common TTIP certification process.

Other projections substantially differ from the CEPR forecasts. Felbermayr et al. (2013) estimated that the effects of comprehensive reduction of non-tariff barriers (NTBs) would *increase* the *net*-costs of exports and would not reduce the net-costs of trade. Whereas tariffs redistribute the income from consumers to producers, so the argument goes, NTBs inflict direct costs to the producers. To gain access to the transatlantic market, products must be approved by the relevant regulatory bodies. This increases the costs and risks associated with exports to the EU and US for outsiders. The winners are the US, the EU and primarily the Asian economies which are tied into the global production network, plus a few resource-rich countries (such as Brazil). The losers seem to be the African countries (Felbermayr et al. 2013: 27).

The two contrasting projections illustrate well the uncertainty surrounding the *ex-ante* estimated effects of the TTIP. However, the WTO process hinges on the calculation of the economic effects of tariff-reductions, i.e. trade diversion/creation, but fails to recognize that NTB liberalization creates more diffuse effects. Critics claim that weaker outside exporters (who are marginally positioned in the global production chain) gain less from reduction of administrative costs for exports into the single TTIP market than from the increase in costs of acquiring approved regulatory access to the single TTIP market.

The transnationalized economic reality escapes the political logic of territorially-defined FTAs. However, the WTO remains firmly rooted in a territorially-defined political reality. FTAs have to come up with a way to define who is preferred and who is not, i.e. the rules of origin, in order to determine 'the identity' of a product.[4] This is a complicated task. The effects of the TTIP will be felt throughout the entire global production network. It is difficult to estimate exactly in advance who

---

3   The report bases its conclusions on the scenario that '… the rest-of-world impact hinges critically on the assumed potential for streamlining of EU and US regulations in the process of negotiations and convergence of EU-US standards, linked to scope for some resulting convergence on global standards and cross-recognition as well. These effects imply some improvement of market access for third countries, helping to offset trade diversion' (CEPR 2013: 81).

4   For instance, the EU's FTAs require that a product must be either (1) manufactured from the raw materials or components of the beneficiary country or (2) undergo a specified amount of working or processing as set out in 'the list rules' in order to have 'originating' status in order for a product to qualify for the privileged market access (Woolcock 2007: 6).

benefits and who loses. The real significance of the TTIP lies in the regulatory effects *outside* the transatlantic partnership, i.e. its regulatory spillover effects on the global standards. These are extremely difficult to quantify at present. Any discussions within the CRTA will inevitably reflect this uncertainty.

Conclusion

Any future of the WTO hinges on its ability to reform the current mechanisms of overseeing, scrutinizing and permitting the formation and continued operation of FTAs, particularly the deeper liberalizing FTAs, such as the TTIP. Baldwin recently issued this warning:

> Thinking ahead ... it is clear that global trade governance faces a historical turning point. The current trajectory seems certain to undermine the WTO's centricity, with the mega-regionals taking over as the main loci of global trade governance. Without reforms that bring existing deep RTA disciplines under the WTO's aegis and facilitate development of new disciplines inside the WTO, the trend will continue. ... WTO centricity could erode beyond the tipping point where nations ignore WTO rules, since everyone else does. ... The GATT/WTO would go down in history as a 70-year experiment where world trade was rules-based instead of power-based. (Baldwin 2014a: 39)

Therefore, the issue of boosting the WTO's mandate and capacity to conduct self-initiated and independent policy examinations of every notified FTA goes beyond the debate whether FTAs constitute 'stumbling' or 'building' blocks for trade liberalization. It is also about the distinctiveness of the TTIP as a prototype for the new type of FTAs that reflect an age of genuinely globalized trade and production where investment flows are just as important as trade flows for economic growth, where trade barriers are almost undetectable 'behind the border' regulation, where knowledge is traded just as much as products and where export competiveness is the political obsession across the globe.

The limited oversight capacity of the WTO is a reflection of the fundamental purpose of the GATT/WTO as a member-driven institution with its distinctive multilateral qualities: a sovereignty-sensitive compromise between trade liberalization and economic statecraft. In addition, the tension between enforceability and transparency cuts across numerous spheres within the WTO governance. The WTO transparency cannot be made effective as it clashes with WTO Members' 'dispute settlement awareness', that is, the fear of potential WTO litigation. Any reform is therefore not as straightforward as it appears. WTO Members are reluctant to give the WTO the means and the mandate to act independently. Even so, it is difficult to understand the continued debate in the Rules Group about even less ambitious reform proposals, such as unifying the review process in a single committee.

The greatest systemic threat to the multilateral trade system is perhaps not new and more ambitious FTAs like the TTIP, but ossification of the WTO institution itself in a sense that WTO discussions have become meaningless exchanges of fixed and predetermined positions. As Depledge (2006: 3) points out, an ossified institution fails '... to develop new concepts and ideas, or even to substantively debate and discuss new proposals, remaining in the grip of old, perhaps outdated, paradigms that do not allow the regime to advance'. Today, the WTO exhibits clear signs of ossification through being plagued by entrenched political alliances, mutual mistrust, the member-driven nature of the WTO institution and the 'dispute settlement awareness' amongst WTO Members.

The persistent failure to reform the WTO oversight mechanism symbolizes everything that has gone wrong in the trading system. Despite a near-universal agreement on the current system's inadequacies, the actual political will to reform the system is minimal. The issue has become a battleground for a principled North-South debate. The ossification of the WTO has clearly become evident through the inconclusive talks in the Rules Group on reviewing the TM initiative. It has even proven to be impossible to create a single venue for the notification and subsequent discussions on the notified FTAs. It is unlikely that the WTO will ever be equipped with an effective and autonomous capacity to conduct self-initiated reviews of the notified FTAs. The WTO remains a member-driven organization with a minimal mandate to act on its own for a foreseeable future.

Chapter 14

No Agreement is an Island: Negotiating TTIP in a Dense Regime Complex[1]

Sophie Meunier and Jean-Frédéric Morin

Introduction: Changing the Metaphor

Bilateral trade and investment negotiations, including the Transatlantic Trade and Investment Partnership (TTIP), are often analysed with metaphors borrowed from mechanics, like 'building blocks', 'stumbling stones', 'parallel tracks', 'hub and spoke', 'gravity models', 'ratchet effect', 'domino theory', 'bicycle theory' etc. These mechanical metaphors are not just nice figures of speech. As heuristic devices, they powerfully – and perhaps insidiously – structure our thinking. They imply that trade and investment agreements are created independently from one another and that their internal composition remains stable until they fall apart under exogenous pressure. These assumptions are useful if one is aiming to isolate variables, attribute causality and predict impacts. But are these mechanical metaphors at all accurate in the first place?

The ongoing TTIP negotiations can hardly be conceived of in isolation. They are taking place parallel to other major ongoing negotiations and in an environment of already dense, complicated and overlapping existing agreements. In this context, it may be more suitable to borrow an alternative metaphor to conceptualize trade and investment agreements from ecology (Haas 1982).

An ecosystem is a network of several interacting living organisms, evolving in conjunction with their environment in different niches, at different scales and at different paces. Trade and investment agreements can be seen as such 'living organisms' – some negotiators themselves refer to TTIP as a 'living agreement' (De Gucht 2013b). They are 'living' because they are the direct result of earlier generations of agreements, and they evolve constantly over their life span as they interact with other institutions. Far from being autonomous and rigid, they are full of ambiguities and open to constant (re)production. They evolve formally through ministerial decisions and interpretations (Brower 2005), amendments and renegotiations (Pauwelyn and Alschner 2014), increasing delegation of

1 Many thanks to Jean-François Brakeland, Robert Keohane, Simon Lacey and Neysun Mahboubi for comments on an earlier version of this chapter.

authority to regulatory bodies (Büthe 2008), and dispute resolutions (Alter and Meunier 2006), but also informally through changing practices and discourses (Wolfe 2005). These 'living' agreements, with partly overlapping mandate and membership, constitute an intertwined ecology, otherwise known as the 'trade and investment regime complex' (Davis 2009, Orsini, Morin and Young 2013).

However, the ecosystemic metaphor also has its limits: institutions do not adapt to their environment through natural selection – as they rarely die – but through learning (Haas and Haas 1995). Yet, as genetic diversity favours biological adaptation, institutional diversity enables trial and error and learning from experimentations. Under pressure from institutional competition, thriving institutions are those that learn from and adapt to their changing environment (Abbott, Green and Keohane 2013).

To what extent does the imbrication of TTIP in the existing trade and investment complex shape the negotiations? In turn, does TTIP have the potential to shape the rest of the complex moving forward? Our central argument is that TTIP negotiators face both learning constraints and learning opportunities as a result of the trade and investment complex, which will not only influence the current negotiation process but also the potential outcome of negotiations. The first section of this chapter portrays the ever growing trade and investment complex in which TTIP is being negotiated. The second section analyses the constraints and opportunities faced by TTIP negotiators. The third section explores some of the negotiators' strategic calculations as they internalize the impact of the dense regime complex. The conclusion suggests implications of TTIP on the rest of the trade and investment complex.

The Ever-Growing Trade and Investment Complex

Even though there is no prior transatlantic free trade or investment agreement to act as template, the TTIP negotiations are not starting from a blank slate. Instead, they are taking place in a dense and ever growing complex of trade and investment institutions, as well as in parallel to trade and investment negotiations involving the US or the EU as negotiating parties.

The trade and investment complex is expanding in three dimensions. It is first expanding institutionally. Until the early 2000s, the elemental components of the complex were primarily intergovernmental organizations, regional customs unions and bilateral agreements. Recently, other institutional forms have mushroomed, including plurilateral sectoral agreements (e.g. the Anti-Counterfeiting Trade Agreement), trade summits (e.g. the India-Brazil-South Africa Summits), venues for regulatory agencies (e.g. the International Competition Network), collaborations among intergovernmental organizations (e.g. the Standards and Trade Development Facility), private organizations (e.g. the International Accounting Standards Board) and 'mega-regionals' (e.g. the Trans-Pacific

Partnership). These alternative institutions are on the rise and contribute towards making the trade and investment complex even more multiscalar and multiform.

Secondly, the trade and investment complex is expanding thematically. Rather than simply building on the WTO legacy with 'WTO-plus' commitments, it covers an increasing number of 'WTO-extra' issues such as anti-corruption, data protection, money laundering, statistic harmonization and tax evasion (Horn et al. 2010, Baldwin 2014b). These issues were not initially on the WTO agenda, but are now addressed by various trade initiatives and broadening the thematic frontiers of the trade and investment complex.

The third expanding dimension of the trade and investment complex is geographical. Until recently, only a handful of countries were aggressively promoting trade and investment agreements. Today, the number of countries negotiating simultaneously on several fronts is such that former hubs are progressively losing their strategic position. Figure 14.1, for example, illustrates that several countries that have signed free trade agreements with the US have also signed similar agreements with one another. Likewise, Figure 14.2 shows that several countries that are negotiating comprehensive trade agreements with the EU, including the US, are also negotiating together in parallel. Both figures reveal the high density and intricacy of the trade and investment regime complex.

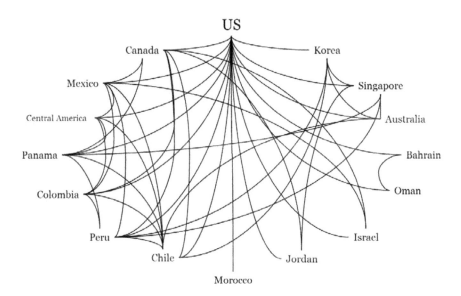

Figure 14.1 Trade agreements in force with the US and among US partners

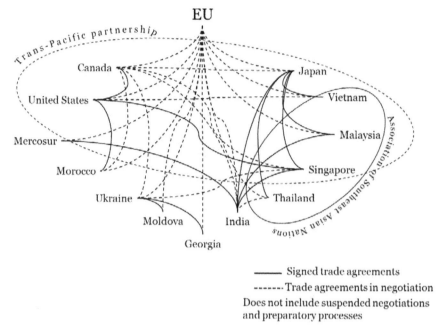

Figure 14.2 Parallel trade negotiations with the EU and among EU partners

Institutions in this trade and investment ecosystem are not clinically isolated but rather in constant interaction. They are informally – if not formally – connected to each other. Innovations emerging in one setting are often replicated elsewhere. For example, Chile, having negotiated bilaterally with the US the liberalization of public procurement, has subsequently included similar provisions in bilateral agreements with third countries (Woolcock 2013). The rapid multiplication of trade initiatives is a vehicle for norm diffusion. As a result, the characteristics of recent agreements are strong predictors – apparently even better than power asymmetry and countries' economic properties – of the characteristics of agreements to follow (Chen and Joshi 2010, Kinne 2013).

There are also 'systemic reverberations' between the different scales of the complex. Several bilateral and regional agreements strengthen multilateral institutions. Countless free trade agreements, for example, require the ratification of the multilateral agreements of the World Intellectual Property Organization and refer to the International Centre for Settlement of Investment Disputes. In this context, changes at the multilateral level are rapidly reverberated at the bilateral level. When in 2005 WTO members adopted an amendment to facilitate the export of generic drugs, it was soon reproduced at the bilateral level: for example in the 2008 agreement between Colombia and the European Free Trade Association. Importantly, the flow of influence between the different layers of governance is not only top-down, but multidirectional. Bilateral agreements orient multilateral negotiations as much as the other way around. For instance, novel approaches for the liberalization of services were first experimented with bilaterally before being promoted regionally and plurilaterally, notably in the context of the Trade in Services Agreement (Mattoo and Sauvé 2011).

While new norms orient subsequent institutions, they can also transform older institutions. These iterative interactions are particularly perceptible in the interpretation, implementation and adjudication of trade and investment agreements. Despite fear of incompatible rulings and strategic forum shopping between dispute settlement mechanisms, blatant inconsistencies have not been observed. The various dispute settlement mechanisms do not operate in isolation from each other. They are part of the same social and normative soup (Alter and Meunier 2006, Gomez-Mera and Molinari 2014, Wolfe 2005).

Some agreements even explicitly promote coherence within the existing complex. The EU-Korea free trade agreement provides that a 'party shall not seek redress of an obligation which is identical under this Agreement and under the WTO Agreement in the two forums' (Art. 14.19) and that an arbitration panel set up under this bilateral agreement 'shall adopt an interpretation which is consistent with any relevant interpretation established in rulings of the WTO Dispute Settlement Body' (Art. 14.16). This same agreement also obliges its parties to revise its provisions at the end of the Doha Round to integrate the outcomes of these WTO negotiations, notably on intellectual property, services, trade facilitation and trade remedy.

The trade and investment complex is thus a system that can be analysed as a whole (Pauwelyn and Alschner 2014). Its density and intricacy make it greater than the sum of its parts. In the 1980s, some analysts used to question whether the GATT was truly multilateral since negotiation practices for tariff reduction were essentially bilateral and commitments were based on reciprocity. Today, the bilateral, regional, plurilateral and transnational initiatives are so profoundly embedded in a global ecology, negotiated and implemented in the shadow of each other, that one could wonder whether they constitute a new of form of multilateralism (Muzaka and Bishop 2014): a polycentric multilateralism that is not centralized in one organization, but held together by a plurality of connected institutions.

A complex comprising a plurality of institutions provides significant opportunities (Abbott, Green and Keohane 2013). It enables trial and error and could favour incremental adaptation to a changing economic environment (Pauwelyn 2014). It also comes with drawbacks, such as redundancies and duplication, some confusion and the need for constant management of institutional interactions. But these could be a fair price to pay to have a governance structure that is flexible, adaptive, creative and less vulnerable to crisis, provided that participants in the trade and investment complex have the capacity to learn from small-scale institutional experimentations. These learning constraints and opportunities are further discussed in the next section.

**Constraints and Opportunities Provided by the Trade and
Investment Complex**

While learning is essential for innovation and adaptation, the growth of the trade
regime complex raises challenges for European and American negotiators. How
does the architecture of existing agreements and concurrent negotiations shape
the TTIP negotiations? This section examines both the learning constraints and
learning opportunities faced by TTIP negotiators.

The existence of prior agreements, both between the negotiating parties as
well as between them and third countries, significantly informs the substantive
provisions that can be included in the new agreement under negotiation. Bilaterally,
while the EU and the US are not united by a prior agreement, they are joint parties
to many pre-existing transatlantic dialogues, such as the Transatlantic Economic
Council and the US-EU High Level Regulatory Cooperation Forum. Nevertheless,
American TTIP negotiators may well find themselves bound by the existence of
prior agreements with some of the EU Member States. For instance, when it comes
to investment, the US signed BITs with nine individual Member States before they
joined the European Union (Bulgaria, 1992; Croatia, 1996; Czech Republic, 1991;
Estonia, 1994; Latvia, 1995; Lithuania, 1998; Poland, 1990; Romania, 1992;
Slovak Republic, 1991). These prior agreements create certain minima and basic
levels of provisions that the TTIP agreement will need to meet. However, they are
older generation BITs; in the meantime the US has significantly revised its own
BIT model, and the EU aims to replace the nine BITs with new provisions. So
while they do not provide a template directly applicable in the current negotiations,
they do establish a reference point for what the new agreement needs to achieve.

The existence of prior agreements between the negotiating partners and
third countries also serves as useful information to learn and gauge what might
be feasible in the current negotiations. For instance, American negotiators at
USTR have been actively studying the practices of EU Member States regarding
investment treaties (AmCham EU 2013), and the European Commission seems to
have drawn lessons from NAFTA case law on investment protection, particularly
with regard to the contentious notions of 'indirect expropriation' and 'fair and
equitable treatment' (European Commission 2013d) (see Figure 14.3). American
negotiators are also dissecting the many FTAs in which the EU has been involved
in the past decade, while the EU negotiators are closely studying American FTAs.
Their respective templates vary significantly, as US FTAs tend to provide more
'WTO-plus commitments', building on issues already addressed at the WTO,
while EU FTAs favour 'WTO-extra commitments', dealing with issues that
are not currently on the WTO agenda (Horn et al. 2010, Baldwin 2014b). The
assumption is that the negotiating partner will be willing to do at least as much
in the current negotiations. Following this logic, TTIP will likely provide for an
economic integration that is equally deep (WTO-plus) and broad (WTO-extra).

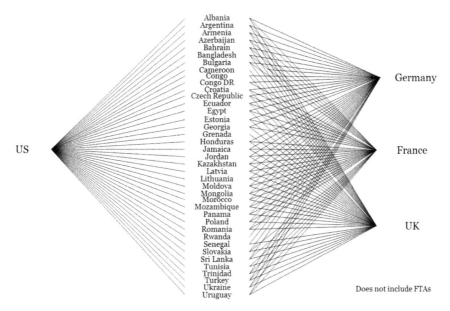

Figure 14.3 US BITs partners and their BITs with Germany, France and the UK

While building on previous practice may speed up the negotiating process, at least in the beginning, it may, however, create a sense of inertia and hamper creativity and out-of-the-box thinking. Previous agreements may be seen as templates to be replicated instead of experimentations to be improved upon. With its 14 FTAs, the US has developed a particular approach and architecture to its trade and investment agreements. As the basic framework has been relatively constant since NAFTA, in part because of Congressional pressures, this may turn into an intransigent way of approaching new agreements which are not allowed to deviate from that framework. As for investment, American negotiators insist on the fact that their template has been the subject of intensive discussion with stakeholders, and they are therefore not particularly amenable to revising that template (Froman 2014).

The constraint of past agreements as templates is less true in the case of the EU because the subsequent shifts in competence have made the agreements more varied and less 'cookie-cutter' over the years. Initially the EU had competence only over trade in goods; Member States negotiated other aspects of trade agreements, including trade in services. After the institutional reforms included in the Treaty of Nice (2000), the EU negotiated most aspects of international agreements relating to trade in services as well, such as the EU-Chile Association Agreement and the EU-Korea Free Trade Agreement. The Treaty of Lisbon (2009) transferred the competence for international investment policy to the supranational level as well, so the EU has been negotiating investment-related provisions on behalf of its

Member States since then, such as the EU-Canada Comprehensive Economic and Trade Agreement (CETA).

These template constraints may play out in a particular way in the transatlantic case. The EU and the US have been used to negotiating comprehensive agreements with developing countries, and more recently with advanced industrialized economies, but not with each other. Presumably, past practices have created negotiating habits and framed negotiators' mindsets in a way that might not be appropriate for a transatlantic agreement. For example, it is likely that TTIP will include investment and IP provisions initially designed for countries that offer different levels of FDI and IP protection and, in some cases, have lax legal systems and weak enforcement mechanisms. However, duplicating these norms in TTIP might be sub-optimal, if not quite inappropriate. An upward harmonization of IP law could reassure foreign investors in developing countries, but hardly in the transatlantic relation. Likewise, an investor-state dispute settlement mechanism could be justified in agreements signed with developing countries, but serves no clear purpose when an agreement is signed among countries with domestic legal systems developed and impartial enough to comfort foreign investors. Conversely, it could be argued that several trade-related issues that could have been relevant for the transatlantic context (such as tax evasion and economic sanctions targeting third countries) were not put on the agenda because they did not figure out in templates developed from previous negotiations.

In addition to past agreements, the existence of simultaneous negotiations in which the US or the EU may currently be involved also creates learning constraints and opportunities for TTIP. Negotiating several agreements at once may put a severe constraint on the resources available to carry out effectively another set of international negotiations. Parallel negotiations may create in principle manpower issues and personnel shortage, leading to a slowdown or stop-and-go process of negotiations, though in practice this has happened neither in the US nor in the EU case (in the EU, DG Trade personnel have been redeployed to TTIP from the anti-dumping unit). The limited size of the negotiating personnel pool to draw from can, however, also be an opportunity. On the American side, the office of the USTR is rather small, with about 200 employees. As a result, the USTR is well positioned to learn from past agreements and parallel negotiations. This small size fosters a highly collaborative environment where information flows back and forth between negotiators and technical experts involved in all simultaneous negotiations through both institutionalized and *ad hoc* informal meetings. On the EU side, the situation is similar. Sectoral experts monitor several negotiations simultaneously. The EU chief negotiator actually negotiated the recent EU-South Korea Free Trade Agreement and has been involved in the FTA negotiations with India, which facilitates the flow of ideas from one agreement to the other.

We therefore see that the imbrication of TTIP in the trade and investment regime complex creates both learning constraints as well as opportunities for the negotiators. On the one hand, norm diffusion and isomorphism from past and simultaneous negotiations reduce opportunities for experimentation and out-of-the-box thinking. A complex calls for specialized technical expertise (Alter and Meunier 2009), and negotiators naturally turn to the other elements of the complex for guidance. On the other hand, the expansion of issues and scale creates ambiguity, which can be turned into creativity. The existence of prior and concurrent agreements can also accelerate the negotiating process and lift up the substance of the negotiation.

Strategic Implications of the Dense Regime Complex

Students of international relations often discuss negotiations as part of a 'two-level game', involving both inter-state and domestic politics (Putnam 1988). The TTIP negotiations suggest that the two-level game vision may be outdated. To borrow from a baking metaphor, instead of a layered cake with the domestic and international layers neatly stacked on top of each other, trade and investment negotiations today resemble more a marble cake, whose dense layers have been swirled around. In other words, the dense regime complex in which the TTIP is negotiated creates a *multidimensional and multi-level game*, in which each level is more intertwined than the traditional two-level game view presumes.

Consider first the intergovernmental level of this game. Negotiating several agreements simultaneously implies careful legal and political coordination of what is happening in all these negotiations. Negotiators working on one agreement have to be very vigilant about what their peers are doing in other negotiations. Such an instance of simultaneous negotiations creates a certain framework and may give rise to issues of interpretation that are expected to carry over across negotiations. Therefore, agreements negotiated simultaneously have to be consistent.

Negotiators need to assess not just the costs and benefits of particular agreements and strategies to improve prospects for a favourable outcome; they need to devise strategies that take into account other negotiations, either those occurring simultaneously with different partners, those regarding the implementation of existing agreements, or those on possible future negotiations. The existence of a dense regime complex therefore enormously complicates the strategic calculations of negotiators.

Furthermore, the negotiators, who are well aware that they operate within a complex and dense institutional environment, may try to craft the current agreement with an eye to future negotiations. They may include provisions in TTIP which would set a precedent for forthcoming negotiations. Although this is not based on evidence, one might argue that the insistence on including an investor-to-state dispute settlement (ISDS) mechanism in TTIP may be to create a precedent, for instance for negotiations with China (Sapir 2014). Other examples of this forward-looking approach may include the inclusion of provisions on energy and raw materials as well as on state-owned enterprises.

The need both to be consistent and to anticipate effects on future and past agreements can help move the negotiation forward and faster. If negotiations get stuck because of a sticky problem, the answer to the pressing policy question may be found in the other negotiation context. For instance, the 'negative list approach' that the EU is using in the CETA negotiations for service liberalization might greatly facilitate the incorporation of a negative list approach in TTIP. The EU had never used a negative list before CETA, and it took the Commission considerable time to list all the exclusions, but the work is already cut out for TTIP. Another CETA innovation that can easily be transplanted into TTIP is the implication of sub-federal units such as provinces and cities in public procurement, since both Canada and the US are federal systems. As for the European public consultation regarding the ISDS in TTIP, it refers directly to the CETA text (European Commission 2014a).

Alternatively, strategically anticipating the effect of the current negotiations on future agreements may also have the opposite effect and slow down the negotiating process. The provisions that negotiators may want to include in agreements currently negotiated in order to ensure that they are part of the template for later use are, by nature, controversial. So instead of delaying the fight until later, negotiators with this strategic, forward-looking outlook are provoking the public debate at an earlier time, which may slow down or even stall the negotiations.

This need to anticipate effects on future negotiations also has the potential to result in the highest, not the lowest, common denominator. Every new agreement lifts the standards higher. Especially if the EU and the US tend to favour higher standards, their calculations about future negotiations with other states provide incentives for them to raise standards in TTIP, in order to set a favourable benchmark for such future negotiations. Contrary to what many critics of TTIP suggest, therefore, the embeddedness of TTIP in the trade and investment complex leads instead to an expectation that there will not be any race to the bottom.

For instance, TTIP tries to make opportunities for small and medium-size enterprises (SMEs) the focus of the agreement. According to a joint transatlantic document, 'US and EU negotiators are working to ensure that SMEs are in a position to take full advantage of the opportunities that an agreement would provide. As part of this effort, negotiators are discussing the inclusion of a chapter dedicated to SME issues' (EU Publications Office 2014). One of the implicit intentions of American policymakers may be to have these provisions specially designed for SMEs travel over to TPP (Hamilton 2014a). In that way, TTIP may impact the substance of agreements subsequently negotiated with third countries.

Now turn to the domestic side of this multidimensional two-level game. Negotiators have to be aware of the arguments to be used to 'sell' the agreement at home. If they are crafting the agreement with an eye to simultaneous or future negotiations, it may be difficult to explain the provisions – especially if their strategies towards other states depend on a certain amount of guile. Furthermore, if the case is made that a new agreement is worth ratifying because it includes several provisions and innovations that will be useful in other negotiations, then it will be a hard sell politically if the next agreement to come along for ratification does not include the same provisions.

While we can expect the negotiators themselves to capitalize on the learning opportunities from past and simultaneous negotiations, the emergence of new actors on the scene – actors that often operate transnationally and blur the international-domestic divide – may make the process even more complex. Several 'novice' actors recently empowered by new competences or attracted by new issue-areas might integrate the trade and investment complex differently than seasoned actors in their analysis of the situation. On the one hand, they may rely even more than others on existing templates, since they first have to learn the tools of their trade and can be co-opted by those who teach them how things are done, leading to more conformism. On the other hand, they may engage in turf wars and try to assert their newfound power, resulting in negotiations that are both procedurally and substantially different from past negotiations.

Such new actors may include, on the American side, states and cities on issues of public procurement, as well as health and safety regulatory authorities such as the Consumer Product Safety Commission and the National Highway Traffic Safety Administration. On the European side, new actors include the European External Action Service (EEAS), which is now sharing the overall geopolitical strategy underlying TTIP with the Commission's DG Trade. Also new on the scene is the European Parliament, whose role on trade matters was greatly enhanced by the 2009 Lisbon Treaty, mostly at the expense of the relative autonomy of the Commission (Woolcock 2012). Moreover, many non-governmental actors have been empowered in these negotiations, both because of public consultation and because of social media, and many of the TTIP issues are particularly sensitive in some domestic contexts (GMOs, geographical indications and audio-visual in France, data protection in Germany etc.) and are getting a lot of media attention, including front-page coverage. How these new actors or newly empowered actors take their cues from or against the precedent of existing agreements will have a major impact on the substantive TTIP negotiations.

From a strategic perspective, TTIP illustrates how negotiators' calculations are immensely complicated by the combination of new actors entering the scene and the embeddedness of negotiations in a dense existing regime complex. Negotiators' strategies not only impact the strategies of negotiating partners and are constrained by domestic politics, as in the two-level games framework; they also influence the strategies of other states and of transnational actors, which both complicates negotiations and makes the domestic politics of ratification more difficult.

Conclusion

The negotiation of TTIP is an implicit recognition that, given the complexity of the unresolved issues in the trade and investment sphere, the WTO is not the appropriate forum to tackle such issues with any chance of success – at least in the foreseeable future. The EU and the US being 'like' economies, it may be easier to tackle non-trade barriers and thorny regulatory issues which would stand no chance if negotiated at the multilateral level. But this raises the question of whether any agreement today can be an 'island'. Can there still be a purely transatlantic agreement, both in its origin and in its impact?

As this chapter has shown, TTIP is shaped by the trade and investment complex. It cannot refer purely and exclusively to transatlantic economic relations. What the US and the EU have concluded in prior agreements with third countries, in addition to those with each other, and what they are currently negotiating simultaneously are important determinants of the substance of TTIP, and their strategies in TTIP are profoundly impacted by the other actual and anticipated negotiations that they are considering.

Given the economic weight of the two parties, their frequent trade disputes, their numerous trade agreements with third countries and their significant normative influence in world politics, TTIP will have a strong systemic impact on the entire trade complex, including on past and on future agreements. However, these impacts are hardly predictable. Years of research on building blocks vs stumbling blocks does not support clear-cut and universalistic claims. One needs to acknowledge that results of empirical research are mixed, uncertain and often case-specific (Kono 2007, Mansfield and Solingen 2010).

Amplifying this uncertainty is the fact that TTIP will focus on non-tariff barriers and regulations. This form of liberalization is significantly more difficult to model than tariff reductions, especially due to measurement problems and lack of available data. We can only speculate on the impact on third countries, as no other agreement of this systemic magnitude has ever been concluded. It is difficult to tell, for instance, whether third countries will face greater anti-dumping scrutiny if the EU and the US agree to reduce anti-dumping actions between themselves (Prusa and Teh 2010). Worsening further uncertainty, the impact on third countries will likely vary depending on a long list of factors, including whether these countries are already FTA partners of the US and the EU, whether they are currently negotiating an FTA with them, whether they benefit from most-favoured nation or preferential status, or whether a customs union agreement is already in place.

Regardless of the uncertainty about particular provisions and whether a comprehensive deal will be struck, TTIP will itself have an impact on the shape of the trade and investment complex, especially when it comes to non-tariff barriers and regulations. The potential for the transatlantic deal to have a meaningful impact beyond the transatlantic borders is not an afterthought; rather, it is internalized by the negotiators as they consider strategically what to include in the present deal. As the USTR Mike Froman states,

> we see TTIP as providing an opportunity for the US and the EU to not only deepen the transatlantic space that reflects our shared interests and values, but to work together to strengthen those values beyond our borders. TTIP is an opportunity to articulate and promote globally our shared values on the rule of

law, transparency, public participation, and accountability. ... It's about shaping a global system – one with our shared values at the core. (Froman 2014)

In more academic terms, the implication of Froman's remark is that the whole regime complex is path-dependent: the *status quo* influences what can be negotiated, and what is negotiated helps to create a new *status quo*. Since the past foretells the future, smart negotiators who are concerned about the future seek to shape what will soon become the past.

Chapter 15

Taking the Preferences Out of Preferential Trade Agreements: TTIP as a Provider of Public Goods?

Joost Pauwelyn

Preferential trade agreements (PTAs), of which TTIP is but a recent incarnation, are not as 'preferential' as they used to be. Traditional PTAs mainly exchanged 'club goods', that is goods or tariff concessions that are 'non-rivalrous' (use by one does not diminish their availability to others) but 'excludable' (some can be excluded from use). Modern PTAs are increasingly providing 'public goods', i.e. goods or concessions that are 'non-rivalrous' *and* 'non-excludable': they are available to everyone irrespective of whether one contributed to producing the good (Olson 1965, Bodansky 2012: 652). More precisely, whereas most commitments in traditional PTAs (tariff concessions) were exclusive to PTA partners, many commitments in twenty-first-century PTAs are either *de facto* or *de jure* extended on a most-favoured nation (MFN) basis to outsiders too, often unconditionally, sometimes conditionally. This chapter explains why this is the case with reference to recent US and EU PTAs, especially those with South Korea. It also offers some thoughts on what this means for the global trading system and the WTO moving forward.

Twentieth-Century versus Twenty-first-Century PTAs

Traditional (or shallow) PTAs used to focus on reciprocal exchanges of *tariff* reductions, i.e. reductions that were granted exclusively to PTA partners and not to other countries. Rules of origin made such tariff preferences possible: if a good is not found to be 'made in' the PTA partner, the tariff preference is denied. Economic discussions on the impact of such traditional PTAs have focused on the 'trade creation' versus 'trade diversion' effect of PTA tariff preferences: more trade within PTA partners means possibly less trade for those countries excluded from the PTA (Bhagwati and Panagariya 1996; Freund and Ornelas 2010). In this era, PTAs were very much a matter of 'you're-in-or-you're-out'. The expected end point was reduced tariffs for all, bound at the WTO on an MFN basis; PTA tariff preferences were (hoped to be) just a temporary stepping stone towards this end point (Baldwin 2010).

More recent (or deep) PTAs – such as the TTIP – continue to reduce tariffs on a preferential or discriminatory basis. Yet MFN tariff rates have fallen so low that PTA tariff preferences are hard to get. Although (in 2008) 34.5 per cent of world merchandise exports occurred between PTA partners (and this number *excludes* intra-EU trade), only 16 per cent of world merchandise exports benefited from preferential tariffs even if we assume full preference utilization rates (WTO 2011b: 64). This can be explained because, in many cases, PTAs do not improve on MFN rates: the MFN rate may, for example, already be zero or the PTA may leave intact sensitive tariff peaks. In 2007, the trade weighted average tariff rate for EU-US manufacturing trade was approximately 2.8 per cent (Felbermayr et al. 2013: 3). It is somewhat higher for agricultural trade, and important tariff peaks in specific sectors remain (such as motor vehicles, processed foods and textiles). The expected tariff benefits of TTIP are therefore limited. Moreover, since WTO rules on PTAs (GATT Article XXIV) allow for certain tariffs to stay in place (internal PTA trade needs only to be liberalized for 'substantially all trade'), some tariffs and tariff peaks can be expected to remain in place even after TTIP.

As a result, TTIP, like other recent deep PTAs, goes well beyond tariffs. Its core aim is to reduce trade costs by limiting or coordinating non-tariff barriers, in particular behind-the-border regulations and standards on goods and services (e.g. financial and telecom services, e-commerce) as well as government procurement, competition, intellectual property rights, capital flows and investment (both establishment and post-entry protection). Deep PTAs also impose good governance-type obligations in the fields of transparency, customs administration, trade facilitation, investment protection and the making and enforcement of labour and environmental laws and regulations (in EU PTA parlance, the chapter on Trade and Sustainable Development).

As Richard Baldwin put it, twentieth-century PTAs were helping to 'sell things' by reducing barriers for *goods* to cross borders; twenty-first-century PTAs are there to help 'make things' by enabling *factories* to cross borders and to set up or insert themselves into global value chains that are facilitated by access and assurances in terms of border and domestic regulations, investment and capital flows, transport and infrastructure, IP protection and overall good governance (Baldwin 2014a). One of the fundamental consequences of this shift from tariffs and (selective) market access for goods to (general) standards and regulations for goods, services, capital and IP is that many of the concessions exchanged in deep PTAs can no longer be made on a securely selective or preferential basis: once a commitment is made *vis-à-vis* one PTA partner, the commitment tends to leak to or benefit also third countries.

Economic studies have accounted for the positive spillover effects of modern PTA concessions to non-PTA parties. Instead of trade diversion or losses to third parties (predicted in standard economics on PTAs), an increasing number of studies find or predict gains from deep PTAs for both parties and non-parties. One recent study estimating the economic effects of concluding TTIP, commissioned by the European Commission, took account of direct and indirect spillovers for third parties on the following assumptions (CEPR 2013). Firstly, bilateral streamlining of regulations and standards between the EU and the US should also reduce the trade costs for third country exports to the EU and the US through e.g. economies of scale or having to meet only EU or US requirements to get into both markets (direct spillover estimated at 20 per cent of the bilateral fall in trade costs).

Secondly, because of the combined market size of the EU and the US, some third countries can be expected to adopt the common standards agreed between the EU and the US, making these standards *de facto* common global standards which in turn would create efficiency gains (indirect spillover estimated at 10 per cent of the bilateral fall in trade costs). Another recent study (WTI 2014), gauging the impact of TTIP on the Swiss economy, assumes the same 'regulatory spillovers' in the scenario of an ambitious TTIP (50 per cent reduction in actionable non-tariff barriers) especially for a country like Switzerland that is already streamlining its technical regulations with those of the EU and all the more so in case Switzerland (through EFTA) were to conclude its own PTA with the US. The study predicts a Swiss GDP gain of 0.96 per cent from a deep TTIP integration with Switzerland as a passive agent, and as much as 2.87 per cent in case TTIP were flanked by an EFTA-US PTA. Other studies predict negative (trade diversion) effects of TTIP for third countries, by leaving out the two spillover assumptions above (Felbermayr et al. 2013), or warn against the risk that harmonizing standards upwards may reduce the exports of excluded countries, especially developing countries, and that mutual recognition agreements (open to third countries) are more uniformly trade promoting (Chen and Mattoo 2008).

There are at least five reasons why TTIP concessions may leak to or benefit also third countries and, in one way or another, become 'public goods':

- public goods *by necessity* (pure public goods: non-rivalrous and non-excludable)
- public goods *by volition* (excludable but, in effect, voluntarily made available to all countries)
- public goods *through MFN* (excludable and exclusive but, by law, to be extended to at least some third countries)
- public goods *by circumvention* (excludable but where exclusion is difficult to enforce)
- public goods *by emulation* (PTA standards that become global standards)

Public Goods by Necessity

Firstly, by their very nature, certain commitments in modern PTAs benefit everyone and cannot be limited to nationals or companies of PTA partners. Publication or transparency commitments, for example (to which an entire chapter is devoted in both recent EU and US PTAs), benefit everyone: it is practically impossible to publish a proposed law or regulation for the eyes of PTA partners only. The same is true for commitments in respect of subsidies, anticompetitive business conduct or corruption (for example, Korea-US PTA Articles 16.1 and 21.6): limiting subsidization or fighting anticompetitive behaviour or local corruption or bribery practices cannot be done on a 'bilateral basis'; such commitments benefit all competitors in the market place, including those from non-PTA partners. Similarly, when a country commits to privatize a particular services sector or to set up and run its regulatory authority in, for example, the postal and courier or telecommunications services sectors in line with certain principles (for example, Korea-EU PTA Articles 7.26 and 7.27–36), it cannot do so for PTA partners only: it necessarily happens across the board. Other examples are PTA commitments to accede to or comply with pre-existing IP, environmental or labour conventions.

In the Korea-US FTA, for example, Korea commits to ratify or accede to no less than 10 IP conventions and to make 'all reasonable efforts' to ratify or accede to another three IP treaties (Korea-US PTA Articles 18.3 and 18.4). In the Korea-EU PTA (Article 13.4(3)), the parties 'commit to respecting, promoting and realizing' specific fundamental labour rights and 'reaffirm the commitment to effectively implementing the ILO Conventions that Korea and the Member States of the European Union have ratified respectively'. The same is done for certain environmental treaties (Article 13.5) and internationally agreed financial standards (Article 7.24). A country cannot 'accede' to a multilateral IP, labour or environmental treaty and limit its accession only with respect to the PTA partner. If a PTA partner complies with or implements treaty obligations of a collective nature (e.g. respects human or labour rights of its people or reduces carbon emissions), it does so, by necessity, for the collective benefit of all treaty partners, if not all countries.

Public Goods by Volition

Secondly, even where PTA commitments could technically be limited to benefit only PTA partners, in practice, they have sometimes been committed to, or implemented domestically, so as to benefit all countries. When a country commits to notice and comments procedures or minimum delays for the preparation and implementation of technical regulations, in most cases, such procedures, as implemented in domestic law, allow not only PTA partners to comment or get informed, but also nationals or affected firms from other countries (see Korea-US PTA Article 21.2(b) committing to provide 'interested persons', not just 'interested persons of the other Party', a reasonable opportunity to comment on proposed measures). The same is true in respect of advanced rulings or domestic appeals procedures for customs matters (see Korea-EU PTA Articles 6.6 and 6.7) or commitments in the Korea-US PTA in respect of 'fair, reasonable and non-discriminatory' procedures for the listing of pharmaceutical products, medical devices and their reimbursement at 'competitive market-derived prices' (Article 5.2), principles in respect of electronic authentication or signatures (Article 15.4) or the authority to resolve competition law cases by mutual agreement (Article 16.5).

Although they could technically be designed as 'club goods', they are promised and implemented for the benefit of all traders, not just PTA partners. Similarly, when Korea and the EU commit in their PTA to detailed rules on liability of online service providers and intermediaries (Articles 10.62–66), they do so in general terms and not just *vis-à-vis* service providers or intermediaries of the other party only. In US PTAs and bilateral investment treaties (BITs), performance requirements in respect of the establishment or operation of investments (e.g. requirements to export or use domestic content or transfer technology) are prohibited not just for the benefit of investors of BIT/PTA partners but 'investors of a Party *or of a non-Party*'. In other situations, the domestic *status quo* in terms of, for example, services liberalization is simply legally bound in a PTA (without *de facto* enhancing market access): everyone already benefits from the *status quo* and the *status quo* is simply bound in a PTA with one or more countries. All of these concessions could have been extended as club goods. Yet the parties chose to extend them to all countries as *de facto* 'public goods'.

Public Goods through MFN

In other situations, PTA commitments may be exchanged as club goods, that is, exclusively to PTA partners. Yet, through the operation of an MFN clause in another treaty, these club goods are *de jure* transformed into 'public goods' or, more precisely, they must be extended on an MFN basis to at least some countries. Where a country fails to do so, it would violate its MFN obligation in the other treaty (be it the WTO, another PTA or a BIT). At least four such scenarios can be envisaged.

Firstly, the WTO treaty imposes MFN in respect of trade in goods, trade in services and the protection of IP rights. For trade in goods and trade in services, it allows for MFN exceptions and thus discrimination or club goods in, respectively, GATT Article XXIV (and the Enabling Clause) and GATS Article V. The Trade-Related Aspects of Intellectual Property Rights (TRIPS) Agreement, in contrast, does not include a general exception for free trade agreements or customs unions: where WTO members agree to TRIPS-plus commitments, be it in a treaty like the Anti-Counterfeiting Trade Agreement (ACTA) or deep PTAs such as TTIP, these TRIPS-plus commitments must be extended to all WTO members by virtue of TRIPS Article 4 (MFN), subject to limited exceptions in TRIPS Articles 4(a) to (d) and 5 (e.g. in respect of TRIPS-plus copyright protection which may be conditioned on reciprocity). This means that generally speaking, concessions in the IP chapters of PTAs – even where, in the PTA, those concessions are explicitly limited to 'nationals' of PTA partners – must be extended on an MFN basis to nationals of *all* WTO members and, to that extent, become public goods. The Korea-US PTA, for example, extends the scope of trademark protection to signs that are not visually perceptible such as sounds or scents (Article 18.2.1). Korea must and did implement this TRIPS-plus commitment on an MFN basis (Korea Trademark Act Article 2(1) as amended in December 2011).

Secondly, WTO agreements on sanitary and phytosanitary (SPS) or technical barriers to trade (TBT) and services matters include explicit provisions on mutual recognition or equivalence. A PTA may include mutual recognition of technical regulations, standards or licensing criteria. Third countries can rely on this recognition to seek approval also of their regulations, standards or service suppliers. MFN and recognition/equivalence clauses in the WTO's GATT, GATS, SPS or TBT agreements (GATS Article VII, SPS Article 4 and TBT Article 6) may force PTA parties to accept another country's standards if those meet the PTA country's 'appropriate level of protection' (SPS Article 4.1), a type of conditional MFN, or oblige them to 'afford adequate opportunity for other interested Members' to negotiate a comparable recognition agreement or allow other countries to 'demonstrate that education, experience, licenses, or certifications obtained or requirements met in that other Member's territory should be recognized' (GATS Article VII: 2). In other words, if a PTA country previously accepted one country's standards in a PTA, such acceptance – through the operation of the conditional MFN clauses listed above – can facilitate recognition also of third country standards.

The Korea-EU PTA, for example, commits Korea to gradually open its legal services sector to EU law firms (Annex 7-A-4, CPC 861), thereby recognizing the qualifications of EU lawyers. The PTA provisions are limited to law firms of Member States of the EU. In its implementing legislation, however, Korea extends benefits to all law firms whose head office is established in a country with whom Korea has a PTA that includes the practice of foreign legal services (e.g. Foreign Legal Consultant Act 2011 Article 34–2). In other words, Korea extends benefits on a conditional MFN basis, the condition being that of having concluded a PTA with Korea (benefits are currently extended not only to the EU and the US but also to ASEAN and Peru). A similar approach was followed for certified public accountants.

Thirdly, exclusively worded PTA commitments in the field of establishment, commercial presence or (post-entry) investment protection may have to be extended to third countries on the ground of MFN clauses that these third countries negotiated in a BIT with one of the PTA partners. US BITs, for example, include an MFN provision, obliging the US to extend to its BIT partners 'treatment no less favorable than it accords, in like circumstances, to investors of any non-Party' (2012 US Model BIT Article 4). Most US BITs do so without an exception for free trade agreements (like TTIP) or customs unions (many BITs concluded by EU nations, in contrast, do have such an exception; see Article 3(3) of the 2008 German Model BIT). This means that investment-related concessions the US grants to the EU in TTIP must also be extended to third countries that have a BIT with the US. This, in effect, means that such US concessions in TTIP would be made on an MFN basis and benefit also third countries that have a BIT with the US.

Fourthly, some PTAs themselves include limited MFN clauses. To the extent TTIP concessions would fall within the scope of such MFN clauses concluded by the EU or the US with other countries, TTIP concessions would need to be extended also to third countries. The CARIFORUM-EC Economic Partnership Agreement (EPA Article 19), for example, obliges the EU, in respect of customs duties on goods, to 'accord to the CARIFORUM States any more favorable treatment applicable as a result of the EC Party becoming party to a free trade agreement with third parties after the signature of this Agreement' (Oettli and Hovius 2009). This means that any EPA-plus tariff concessions the EU may concede to the US in TTIP must also be extended to CARIFORUM States. The same MFN clause is included in Articles 70 and 79 of the CARIFORUM-EC EPA in respect of post-EPA concessions by the EU in the field of cross-border supply of services and establishment. Similarly, the Korea-EU PTA (Articles 7.8 and 7.14) includes a limited MFN clause in respect of additional cross-border services or establishment commitments that either party may concede to in subsequent PTAs. As a result, if the EU were to give more in this respect to the US under TTIP, certain additional TTIP concessions may have to be extended also to Korea.

The Korea-EU PTA also includes an MFN clause in respect of internal taxes and emission regulations on motor vehicles 'including as provided in any free trade agreement' with a third country (Annex 2-C, Article 5). Although GATT Article I MFN would already achieve this result (GATT Article XXIV is unlikely to allow for discriminatory internal taxation as between PTA partners), this clause was included primarily to make sure that any tax concessions granted by Korea in the Korea-US PTA (Article 2.12) would also be extended to the EU. However, if the EU were now to make tax or emission regulations concessions on motor vehicles to the US in TTIP, such extra concessions would also have to be extended to Korea pursuant to this MFN clause in the Korea-EU PTA.

Public Goods by Circumvention

Even where PTA parties may want to exchange concessions on an exclusive basis, in matters concerning trade in services, flows of capital or the protection of IP rights, doing so may be difficult or easily circumvented by entities outside of the PTA states. This is the case because rules of origin for services, capital and IP rights are hard to pin down and can be more easily circumvented than those on goods. To get the label 'made in X' for goods, one generally needs to shift at least some important stages in the production process to X. To be seen as a service of country X, it is generally enough to be supplied 'from or in the territory of' X without further specification of what that entails (see GATS Article XXVIII(f), Korea-US PTA Article 12.13, Korea-EU PTA Article 7.4(3)(a)). GATS and most PTAs do not have rules of origin for services. To qualify as a service supplier (investor or IP right holder) of X, it is generally enough to incorporate a legal entity in X.[1] This makes it more difficult to reserve many deep PTA commitments exclusively for PTA partners. When it comes to TTIP, for example, a Japanese or Swiss company may benefit from TTIP concessions by having or setting up an EU or US subsidiary or branch or by shifting assets to such EU or US-based entity.

Public Goods by Emulation

Finally, standards agreed upon in a PTA may be adopted (either unilaterally or by treaty) also by other countries and thereby become global standards. As noted earlier, converging standards in two major markets like the EU and the US already benefit, for example, Mexican exporters (even without Mexico adopting the same standard) as Mexican exporters can now produce to one standard and get access to both markets. Global standards have positive scale, network and efficiency effects that stand to increase welfare beyond the PTA partners and as the number of standard-adopters increases. The transition from PTA to global standards may occur for several reasons such as (i) persuasion (the PTA standard is simply the state-of-the-art industry or scientific benchmark), (ii) market forces (if the EU and the US agree on a standard, market forces may push producers and/or regulators to adopt the standard also outside these countries) or (iii) coercion (future PTA partners of the EU or the US may be 'convinced' to adopt TTIP standards in return for access to the EU or US market on a PTA basis).

Crucially, however, not all standards adopted in modern PTAs must become global standards. Depending on the issue, harmonization may be best at the local, national, regional or global level (compare zoning, ground water standards and education with, for example, technical standards for cars, fundamental human or labour rights and climate change). Whereas tariff concessions in twentieth-century PTAs were (hoped to be) just a temporary steppingstone towards multilateral binding agreement at the GATT/WTO, commitments in twenty-first-century PTAs should not necessarily be multilateralized and may be optimally coordinated in smaller groups of like-minded countries.

---

1   See GATS Article XXVIII(m)(i); Korea-US PTA Articles 1.4 and 12.13; and Korea-EU PTA Article 7.2(f)(1), adding the requirement of having 'its registered office, central administration or principal place of business' in the EU or Korea, the latter can even be sufficient, without local legal incorporation, if the entity 'engages in substantive business operations' in the territory concerned. See also the same two-prong definition of 'enterprise of a Party' in Article 11.28 (Chapter on Investment), qualified by the Denial of Benefits provision in Article 11.11. TRIPS protects IP of 'nationals' of WTO members and TRIPS footnote 1 defines nationals as 'persons, natural or legal, who are domiciled or who have a real and effective industrial or commercial establishment in that customs territory'.

Consequences for the Global Trading System

That twenty-first century PTAs provide benefits beyond PTA partners – be it in the form of 'public goods' by necessity, volition, MFN, circumvention or emulation – has several consequences for thinking ahead about the global trading system and the WTO in particular.

Firstly, when discussing the pros and cons of modern PTAs we should be less worried about discrimination or trade diversion. The WTO's focus on discrimination in GATT Article XXIV and, especially, GATS Article V (whose requirements of 'substantial' liberalization only applies to national treatment) may, therefore, be increasingly misplaced.

Secondly, the fact that many PTA concessions are *de jure* or *de facto* benefitting also third countries may partly explain the move to mega-regionals: if a country can give away something only once, it is better to give it away in a broader PTA so as to obtain a reciprocal commitment from as many other countries as possible (and, preferably, countries that are as large as possible). Conversely, what the WTO has proven to be good at is enabling reciprocal exchanges of market access openings, following a largely mercantilist, zero-sum ('what I give to you I lose myself') mindset. If the WTO wants to enter into the business of binding deep PTA-type concessions, especially those offering public goods (whereby a commitment on e.g. good governance, transparency or liberalization benefits all parties, including the party making the commitment and third countries), the WTO will need to drastically change its operating system and culture (see Pauwelyn 2008).

Thirdly, the public goods effects of modern PTAs mean that also the conclusion of PTAs poses increasing risks of free-riders: countries staying out of PTAs may still reap the benefits of PTAs concluded by others without committing themselves. To provide incentives to such free-riders, club goods or the possibility for cross-issue bargaining continue to be important. Japan, Brazil or China may benefit from public goods exchanged in TTIP; to convince these countries to conclude a PTA with the EU or the US and/or to also adopt TTIP standards or liberalization (in a PTA, plurilateral or at the WTO), Japan, Brazil or China will need to be provided certain club goods of which they currently remain deprived (e.g. exclusive tariff or services/government procurement concessions) and/or be offered benefits in other fields (e.g. cuts in EU/US agricultural subsidies). Since the EU and the US can only 'give once' the public goods exchanged in the TTIP (or may already have offered these public goods in prior PTAs), the promise of these goods (which other countries already got, either *de jure* or *de facto*) will not be enough.

Fourthly, to the extent TTIP standards may become global standards (and, as noted above, this is certainly not a necessity for all standards), it is crucially important to take account already at the TTIP negotiations stage of interests of third countries. Once large markets like the EU and the US agree on a standard, the scale and network effects may be such that adapting the standard *ex post* is extremely difficult. Giving voice to outsiders at an early stage will also facilitate the subsequent multilateralization of TTIP standards, be it at the WTO or elsewhere.

Fifthly, if PTAs are less discriminatory and may actually benefit rather than hurt outsiders, the strict rules in the WTO treaty on plurilaterals may need to be softened: for a plurilateral agreement (that is, an agreement between a sub-set but not all WTO members) to be included in the WTO treaty's annex 4, consensus of *all* WTO members is currently required (WTO Agreement, Article X: 9), even those that are not bound by the plurilateral. Housing a plurilateral within the WTO may benefit outsiders not only through the public goods effects described above. In addition, negotiating and monitoring the plurilateral within the WTO is likely to enhance transparency and openness of the plurilateral to the views and concerns of third countries that are not party to the plurilateral but members of the WTO. The launch of plurilateral environmental goods negotiations within the WTO by 14 WTO members in July 2014 is a positive development in this direction (WTO 2014b).

Finally, and more as a caveat, the fact that PTA commitments may extend beyond the parties does not say anything about the extent to which these commitments are really deep or go substantially beyond, for example, GATS or TBT/SPS commitments at the WTO. In other words, one should not equate the public goods effects of PTAs with the fact that PTAs effectively address twenty-first-century trade problems. Reducing agricultural subsidies, for example, is not happening even in deep PTAs and remains a topic that only multilateral or at least critical mass negotiations will be able to address.

What TTIP and other negotiators of twenty-first-century PTAs should realize is the distinction between (i) what they will (or realistically can) offer exclusively ('club goods'), e.g. tariff or government procurement concessions, certain services liberalizations, and (ii) what they will either expressly, *de facto* or through MFN clauses in other treaties extend or will have to extend also to third countries ('public goods'). Public goods benefit more people. But you can only give them once. And only once you can get something for them in return.

Theory tells us that since people can free ride on the efforts of the others, public goods (as they are non-excludable) tend to be under-provided (Bodansky 2012: 653). The recent practice of deep PTAs, and the many public goods they provide even in agreements between two or among a limited number of countries, therefore leads to a puzzle: why do, for example, the EU/US and Korea commit themselves to provide public goods in their PTAs, knowing that other countries can benefit from them without having to give anything in return? An explanation is that the public goods provided this way also (or even predominantly) benefit the country making the commitment (e.g. transparency, good governance, liberalization). PTAs then work as instruments to lock-in or enable domestic reforms that governments see as desirable even unilaterally but for which they need international pressure to convince opposing domestic interests. Another explanation is that PTAs, as much as they offer public goods, do not cover liberalization that currently blocks WTO negotiations, be it cuts in agricultural subsidies or services liberalization, beyond a mere lock-in of current laws. Here deep PTAs, including TTIP, have a hard time to deliver and, as a result, a crucial role remains for the multilateral WTO or at least plurilateral critical mass negotiations.

Bibliography

2014. Klare Sicht auf TTIP. *Neue Gesellschaft/Frankfurter Hefte*, 10.

Abbott, K.W., Green, J.F. and Keohane, R.O. 2013. *Organizational Ecology and Organizational Strategies in World Politics*. Discussion Paper No. 2013–57, Cambridge, MA: Harvard Project on Climate Agreements.

Abbott, K.W., Keohane, R.O., Moravcsik, A., Slaughter, A.M. and Snidal, D. 2000. The concept of legalization. *International Organization*, 54 (3), 401–419.

Abbott, K.W. and Snidal, D. 2001. Hard and soft law in international governance. *International Organization*, 54, 421–456.

Aggarwal, V.K. 1985. *Liberal Protectionism: The International Politics of Organized Textile Trade*. Berkeley, CA: University of California Press.

———. 1993. Building international institutions in Asia-Pacific. *Asian Survey*, 33(11), 1029–1042.

———. 2001. Economics: international trade, in *Managing a Globalizing World: Lessons Learned*, edited by P.J. Simmons and C. Oudraat. Washington, DC: The Carnegie Endowment for International Peace, 234–280.

Aggarwal, V.K. and Evenett, S.J. 2013. A fragmenting global economy: a weakened WTO, mega FTAs, and murky protectionism. *Swiss Political Science Review*, 19(4), 550–557.

Aggarwal, V.K. and Fogarty, E. 2004. *EU Trade Strategies: Between Globalism and Regionalism*. London: Palgrave.

Aggarwal, V.K. and Lee, S. 2011. *Trade Policy in the Asia-Pacific: The Role of Ideas, Interests, and Domestic Institutions*. New York, NY: Springer.

Aggarwal, V.K. and Ravenhill, J. 2001. *Undermining the WTO: The Case Against 'Open Sectoralism'*. Asia-Pacific Issues No. 50, Honolulu: East West Center.

Akaneya, T. 1992. *Nihon no GATTO kanyu mondai: 'rejimu riron' no bunseki shikaku ni yoru jirei kenkyu* [A Regime Theory Perspective on Japan Joining the GATT]. Tōkyō: Tōkyō Daigaku Shuppankai.

Allen, F.L. 1953. *Le grand changement de l'Amérique*. Paris: Amiot-Dumont.

Allison, G. and Zelikow, P. 1999. *The Essence of Decision*. New York, NY: Longman.

Alter, K.J. and Meunier, S. 2006. Nested and overlapping regimes in the transatlantic banana trade dispute. *Journal of European Public Policy*, 13(3), 362–382.

———. 2009. The politics of international regime complexity. *Perspectives on Politics*, 7(1), 13–24.

AmCham EU. 2013. *Second Round of TTIP Negotiations: Summaries of Meetings* [Online: American Chamber of Commerce to the European Union]. Available at: http://www.amcham.it/detail.asp?c=1&p=0&id=6863 [accessed: 30 April 2014].

Atlantic Community. 2014. *TTIP: Top 5 Concerns and Criticism* [Online: 26 February]. Available at: http://www.atlantic-community.org/-/ttip-top-5-concerns-and-criticism [accessed: 17 July 2014].

Baker, J.A. 1995. *The Politics of Diplomacy: Revolution, War, and Peace, 1989–1992*. New York: G.P. Putnam's Sons.

Baldwin, R.E. 1970. *Non-Tariff Distortions in International Trade*. Washington, DC: Brookings Institution Press.

——. 1993. *A Domino Theory of Regionalism*. Working Paper No. 4465, Cambridge, MA: National Bureau of Economic Research.

——. 2006. Failure of the WTO Ministerial Conference at Cancun: reasons and remedies. *The World Economy*, 29, 677–696.

——. 2008. Managing the noodle bowl: the fragility of East Asian regionalism, *The Singapore Economic Review*, 53(3), 449–478.

——. 2010. *21st Century Regionalism: Filling the Gap Between 21st Century Trade and 20th Century Trade Rules*. Working Paper No. 2010–31, Geneva: Geneva Graduate Institute.

——. 2011. *21st Century Regionalism: Filling the Gap Between 21st Century Trade and 20th Century Trade Rules*. Staff Working Paper No. ERSD-2011–08, Geneva: World Trade Organization, Economic Research and Statistics Division.

——. 2012. *WTO 2.0.: Global Governance of Supply Chain Trade*. Policy Insight No. 64, London: Centre for Economic Policy Research.

——. 2014a. *Multilateralising 21st Century Regionalism*. Global Forum on Trade: Reconciling Regionalism and Multilateralism in a Post-Bali World, Paris, 11–12 February, Organization for Economic Cooperation and Development.

——. 2014b. WTO 2.0: Governance of the 21st century trade. *Review of International Organizations*, 9(2), 261–283.

Bandow, D. 2010. State capitalism versus free markets. *The Washington Times* [Online: Cato Institute, 28 June]. Available at: http://www.cato.org/publications/commentary/state-capitalism-versus-free-markets [accessed: 9 September 2014].

Bandy, J. 2000. Bordering the future: resisting neoliberalism in the borderlands. *Critical Sociology*, 26(3), 232–267.

Barroso, M. 2013. *Statement on the Transatlantic Trade and Investment Partnership*, 13 February.

Bátora, J. 2013. The 'mitrailleuse effect': the EEAS as an interstitial organization and the dynamics of innovation in diplomacy. *Journal of Common Market Studies*, 51(4), 598–613.

Baum, G. 2014. Ich bin stolz auf die German Angst. *Frankfurter Allgemeine Zeitung*, 15 July, 15.

BDI. 2014a. *Grosse Chance für Europa* [Online: Bundesverband der Deutschen Industrie, 1 April]. Available at: http:www.bdi.eu/Aktuelles_zu_TTIP_18775.htm [accessed: 28 August 2014].

——. 2014b. *TTIP bietet Chance für Europa* [Online: Bundesverband der Deutschen Industrie, 15 April]. Available at: http:www.bdi.eu/Aktuelles_zu_ TTIP_18928.htm [accessed: 28 August 2014].

——. 2014c. *Wir wollen ein umfassendes Freihandelsabkommen abschliessen* [Online: Bundesverband der Deutschen Industrie, 12 May]. Available at: http:www.bdi.eu/Aktuelles_zu_TTIP_19064.htm [accessed: 28 August 2014].

——. 2014d. *BDI-Präsident Grillo in TTIP-Beirat berufen* [Online: Bundesverband der Deutschen Industrie, 26 May]. Available at: http:www.bdi.eu/Aktuelles_ zu_TTIP_19106.htm [accessed: 28 August 2014].

Belloc, H. 1987. *Cautionary Verses*. London: Duckworth.

Bergsten, C.F. 1994. APEC and the world economy, in *Asia Pacific Regionalism*, edited by R. Garnaut and P. Drysdale. Sydney: Harper, 199–224.

——. 1996. *Competitive Liberalization and Global Free Trade: A Vision for the Early 21st Century*. Working Papers Series, No. 96-15, Washington, DC: Institute for International Economics.

——. 1997. *Whither APEC?: The Progress to Date and Agenda for the Future*. Washington, DC: Institute for International Economics.

Betts, A. 2009. Institutional proliferation and the global refugee regime. *Perspectives on Politics*, 7(1), 53–58.

Bhagwati, J. 1993. Regionalism and multilateralism: an overview, in *New Dimensions in Regional Integration*, edited by J. Melo and A. Panagariya. New York, NY: Cambridge University Press.

——. 2008. *Termites in the Trading System: How Preferential Agreements Undermine Free Trade*. Oxford: Oxford University Press.

Bhagwati, J. and Panagariya, A. 1996. *The Economics of Preferential Trade Agreements*. Washington, DC: AEI Press.

Bhandari, S. and Klaphake, J. 2011. U.S. trade policy and the Doha Round negotiations. *Ritsumeikan Annual Review of International Studies*, 10, 71–93.

Blyth, M. 2013. *Austerity: The History of a Dangerous Idea*. Oxford: Oxford University Press.

Bodansky, D. 2012. What's in a concept? Global public goods, international law and legitimacy. *European Journal of International Law*, 23(3), 651–668.

Börzel, T. and Risse, T. 2004. One size fits all? EU policies for the promotion of human rights, democracy and the rule of law. Paper prepared for the Workshop on Democracy Promotion, 4–5 October 2004, Center for Development, Democracy and the Rule of Law, Stanford University.

Brower, C.H. 2005. Why the FTC notes of interpretation constitute a partial amendment of NAFTA article 1105. *Virginia Journal of International Law*, 46(1), 347–364.

Buchter, H., Pinzler, P. and Uchatius, W. 2014. TTIP: Was handeln wir uns da ein? *Die Zeit*, 26 June, 13–15.

Bull, H. 1977. *The Anarchical Society: A Study of Order in World Politics*. London: Macmillan.

Bündnis 90/Die Grünen. 2013. *TTIP im Fokus: kein Freihandelsabkommen zwischen Europa und den USA im Fokus ohne hohe Standards für Ökologie und Verbrauxherschutz.* Beschluss Bundesdelegiertenkonferenz, Berlin, 18–20 October.

Businessweek. 1995. Remember Nafta? Well, here comes Tafta. *Businessweek* [Online: 7 May]. Available at: http://www.businessweek.com/ stories/1995-05-07/remember-nafta-well-here-comes-tafta-intl-edition [accessed: 28 August 2014].

Büthe, T. 2008. The globalization of health and safety standards: delegation of regulatory authority in the SPS Agreement of the 1994 Agreement establishing the World Trade Organization. *Law and Contemporary Problems*, 71(1), 219–254.

Cafruny, A. and Ryner, M. 2007. *Europe at Bay: In the Shadow of US Hegemony.* London: Lynne Rienner.

Campact. 2014. *Transatlantic Trade and Investment Partnership (TTIP)* [Online]. Available at: https://www.campact.de/ttip/appell/english-version/ [accessed: 15 August 2014].

Capling, A. and Ravenhill, J. 2011. Multilateralising regionalism: what role for the Trans-Pacific Partnership Agreement? *The Pacific Review*, 24(5), 553–575.

Carta, C. 2013. The EEAS and EU executive actors within the foreign policy-cycle, in *The EU's Foreign Policy: What Kind of Power and Diplomatic Action?*, edited by M. Telò and F. Ponjaert. Farnham: Ashgate, 87–104.

Castells, M. 2008. The new public sphere: global civil society, communication networks, and global governance. *The ANNALS of the American Academy of Political and Social Science*, 616, 78–93.

CDU. 2014. *Transatlantisches Freihandelsabkommen. Der größte Markt der Welt mit Chancen für Arbeit, Beschäftigung und Wachstum in Deutschland und Europa* [Online: Christlich Demokratische Union Deutschlands, 8 May]. Available at: https://www.cdu.de/sites/default/files/media/dokumente/140508-transatlantisches-freihandelsabkommen.pdf [accessed: 28 August 2014].

CEPR. 2013. *Reducing Transatlantic Barriers to Trade and Investment: An Economic Assessment* [Online: Centre for Economic Policy Research]. Available at: http://trade.ec.europa.eu/doclib/docs/2013/march/tradoc_150737. pdf [accessed: 13 August 2014].

Chase, K.A. 2005. *Trading Blocs: States, Firms, and Regions in the World Economy.* Ann Arbor, MI: University of Michigan Press.

———. 2006. Multilateralism compromised: the mysterious origins of GATT Article XXIV. *World Trade Review*, 5(1), 1–30.

Chen, J. 2013. Mei Ou Zi Mao Qu Jiu Meng Neng Fou Cheng Zhen [Will the 'old dream' of the US-EU free trade area come true?]. *Nan Fang Ri Bao* [South Daily], 1 March.

Chen, M.X. and Joshi, S. 2010. Third-country effects on the formation of free trade agreements. *Journal of International Economics*, 82(2), 238–248.

Chen, M.X. and Mattoo, A. 2008. Regionalism in standards: good or bad for trade? *Canadian Journal of Economics/Revue canadienne d'économique*, 41(3), 838–863.

China Daily. 2013. Fourth annual US-China CEO and former senior officials' dialogue concludes in Beijing [Online: 5 June]. Available at: http://www.chinadaily.com.cn/china/2013–06/05/content_16571993.htm [accessed: 17 August 2013].

Chinese Ministry of Commerce. 2013. *MOFCOM Spokesman Shen Danyang Answers Questions from the Press* [Online: 25 June]. Available at: http://www.mofcom.gov.cn/article/ae/ag/201306/20130600174593.shtml [accessed: 9 September 2014].

Cho, S. 2010. The demise of development in the Doha Round negotiations. *Texas International Law Journal*, 45, 573–601.

Clark, I. 1999. *Globalization and International Relations Theory*. Oxford: Oxford University Press.

———. 2007. Legitimacy in international society or world society?, in *Legitimacy in an Age of Global Politics*, edited by A. Hurrelman, S. Schneider and J. Steffek. Basingstoke: Palgrave, 193–210.

———. 2011. *Hegemony in International Society*. Cambridge: Cambridge University Press.

Coen, D. and Grant, W. 2005. Business and government in international policymaking: the transatlantic business dialogue as an emerging business style?, in *The Politics of International Trade in the Twenty-First Century: Actors, Issues and Regional Dynamics*, edited by D. Kelly and W. Grant. Basingstoke: Palgrave Macmillan, 47–67.

Cook, M. 1995. Mexican state-labor relations and the political implications of free trade. *Latin American Perspectives*, 22(1), 77–94.

Costinot, A. 2008. A comparative institutional analysis of agreements on product standards. *Journal of International Economics*, 75, 197–213.

Council of the European Union. 2013. *Council Approves Launch of Trade and Investment Negotiations with the United States* [Online: 14 June]. Available at: http://www.consilium.europa.eu/uedocs/cms_data/docs/pressdata/EN/foraff/137485.pdf [accessed: 28 September 2014].

———. 2014. *Council Conclusions on the EU's Comprehensive Approach* [Online: 12 May]. Available at: http://www.consilium.europa.eu/uedocs/cms_Data/docs/pressdata/EN/foraff/142552.pdf [accessed: 28 September 2014].

Crespy, A. 2014. Studying European discourses, in *Research Methods in European Union Studies*, edited by K. Lynggaard, I. Manners and K. Löfgren. Basingstoke: Palgrave Macmillan.

Croome, J. 1995. *Reshaping the World Trading System: A History of the Uruguay Round*. Geneva: World Trade Organization.

CRTA (Committee on Regional Trade Agreements). 2013. Report of the Committee on Regional Trade Agreements to the General Council, WT/REG/23, Doc #: 13-5806. Accessible through WTO search website: https://docs.wto.org/dol2fe/

Pages/FE_Search/FE_S_S009-DP.aspx?language=E&CatalogueIdList=1285
26,120284,87333,95403,102021,71794,81286,58320,53335,85109&Current
CatalogueIdIndex=1&FullTextSearch= [accessed: 13 August 2014]. The link
can be generated from the Annual Report search engine at: http://www.wto.org/
english/tratop_e/region_e/region_e.htm [accessed: 13 August 2014].

Damro, C. 2012. Market power Europe. *Journal of European Public Policy*,
19(5), 682–699.

Danaher, K. and Mark, J. 2003. *Insurrection: Citizen Challenges to Corporate Power*. London: Routledge.

Davis, C.L. 2009. Overlapping institutions in trade policy. *Perspectives on Politics*, 7(1), 25–31.

Davis, C. and Wilf, M. 2011. *Joining the Club: Accession to the GATT/WTO*, APSA 2011 Annual Meeting.

De Burca, G., Keohane, R.O. and Sabel, C. 2013. New modes of pluralist global governance. *NYU Journal of International Law and Politics*, 45(3), 723–786.

De Gucht, K. 2010. *Open Trade, Open Minds*, Civil Society Trade Seminar 2010, Prague, March 24.

———. 2013a. *A European Perspective on Transatlantic Trade* [Online: European Commission, 2 March]. Available at: http://europa.eu/rapid/press-release_SPEECH-13–178_en.htm [accessed: 9 September 2014].

———. 2013b. *Transatlantic Trade and Investment Partnership: Solving the Regulatory Puzzle* [Online: European Commission, 10 October]. Available at: http://europa.eu/rapid/press-release_SPEECH-13–801_en.htm [accessed: 9 September 2014].

———. 2013c. *TTIP: The New EU-US Commercial Relationship and the Future of the EU-Swiss Trade* [Online: European Commission, 15 November]. Available at: http://europa.eu/rapid/press-release_SPEECH-13–933_en.htm [accessed: 16 July 2014].

———. 2014. *Fresh Momentum for a Transatlantic Economic Partnership* [Online: European Commission, 3 July]. Available at: http://europa.eu/rapid/press-release_Speech-14–529_en.htm [accessed: 22 August 2014].

De Gucht, K. and Lambsdorff, A.G. 2014. *Eine noch stärkere Brücke über den Atlantik*. Band No. 03, Berlin: Atlantik-Brücke.

De Man, H. 1919. *Au pays du taylorisme*. Bruxelles: Le Peuple.

De Ville, F. and Orbie, J. 2014. The European Commission's neoliberal trade discourse since the crisis: legitimizing continuity through subtle discursive change. *British Journal of Politics and International Relations*, 16(1), 149–167.

Depledge, J. 2006. The opposite of learning: ossification in the climate change regime. *Global Environmental Politics*, 6(1), 1–22.

Destler, I.M. 1986. Protecting congress or protecting trade? *Foreign Policy*, 62(Spring), 96–107.

Deutsch, K., Burrell, S.A., Kann, R.A., Lee, M., Lichterman, M., Lindgren, R.E., Loewenheim, F.L. and Van Wagenen, R.W. 1957. *Political Community and the North Atlantic Area*. Princeton, NJ: Princeton University Press.

Deutscher Bundestag. 2014. *Antwort der Bundesregierung: Soziale, ökologische, ökonomische und politische Effekte des EU-USA Freihandelsabkommrens.* BT-Drucksache 18/432, Berlin.

Devuyst, Y. and Serdarevic, A. 2008. The WTO and regional trade agreements: bridging the constitutional credibility gap. *Duke Journal of Comparative and International Law*, 18(1), 1–75.

DGB. 2013. *Statement of the German Trade Union Confederation (DGB) Concerning the Planned Negotiations for a Transatlantic Trade and Investment Partnership Between the EU and the US (TTIP)* [Online: Deutscher Gewerkschaftsbund, 29 April]. Available at: http://www.dgb.de/ themen/++co++b803bbb0–9a17–11e3-a1f3–52540023ef1a/@@dossier.html [accessed: 23 September 2014].

———. 2014a. *Freihandelsverhandlungen mit den USA aussetzen. Kein Abkommen zu Lasten von Beschäftigten, Verbrauchern oder der Umwelt* [Online: Deutscher Gewerkschaftsbund, 15 May]. Available at: http://www.dgb.de/ themen/++co++0643b170–08d3–11e4-b547–52540023ef1a [accessed: 23 September 2014].

———. 2014b. *DGB Position: Suspend the Negotiations for a Free Trade Agreement with the USA. No Agreement at the Expenses of Workers, Consumers or the Environment* [Online: Deutscher Gewerkschaftsbund, June]. Available at: http://www.dgb.de/themen/++co++39c1026e-0d92–11e4–906b-52540023ef1a [accessed: 23 September 2014].

Dieter, H. 2014. *The Structural Weakness of TTIP: Transatlantic Partnership Threatens More than Just Consumer Protection.* SWP Comments No. 32, Berlin: German Institute for International and Security Affairs.

Ding, C. 2013. Mei Ou Zi Mao Qu Tan Pan Dui Xin Xing Jing Ji Ti Qian Zai Ying Xiang Bu Rong Hu Shi [The potential effects of the TTIP on emerging economies should not be underestimated]. *Wenhui*, 25 February.

Donfried, K. 2014. *Will U.S.-Germany Relations Recover?* [Online: Council on Foreign Relations, 17 July]. Available at: www.cfr.org/germany/us-germany-relations/p33256 [accessed: 18 July 2014].

Downs, G.W., Rocke, D.M. and Barsoom, P. 1998. Managing the evolution of multilateralism. *International Organization*, 52(2), 397–417.

Dreiling, M. and Wolf, B. 2001. Environmental movement organizations and political strategy tactical conflicts over NAFTA. *Organization and Environment*, 14(1), 34–54.

Dür, A. 2008. Bringing economic interests back into the study of EU trade policy-making. *British Journal of Politics and International Relations*, 10(1), 27–45.

———. 2010. *Protection for Exporters: Power and Discrimination in Transatlantic Trade Relations, 1930–2010.* Ithaca, NY: Cornell University Press.

Dür, A. and De Bièvre, D. 2007. Inclusion without influence? NGOs in European trade policy. *Journal of Public Policy*, 27(1), 79–101.

Dür, A. and Mateo, G. 2013. Gaining access or going public? Interest group strategies in five European countries. *European Journal of Political Research*, 52(5), 660–686.

——. 2014. Public opinion and interest group influence: how citizen groups derailed the Anti-Counterfeiting Trade Agreement. *Journal of European Public Policy*, 21(8), 1199–1217.

Egan, D. 2001. The limits of internationalization: a neo-Gramscian analysis of the multilateral agreement on investment. *Critical Sociology*, 27(3), 74–97.

Ehrlich, S.D. 2008. The tariff and the lobbyist: political institutions, interest group politics, and U.S. trade policy. *International Studies Quarterly*, 52(2), 427–445.

Eichengreen, G. 2012. *Exorbitant Privilege*. Oxford: Oxford University Press.

Elsig, M. 2007. The World Trade Organization's legitimacy crisis: what does the beast look like? *Journal of World Trade*, 41(1), 75–98.

Elsig, M. and Dupont, C. 2012. The European Union meets South Korea: bureaucratic interests, exporter discrimination and the negotiations of trade agreements. *Journal of Common Market Studies*, 50(3), 492–507.

EU Publications Office. 2014. *Transatlantic Trade and Investment Partnership: The Opportunities for Small and Medium-Sized Enterprises*. Brussels.

EurActiv. 2014. MEPs call for freezing EU-US trade talks over spying allegations. *Euractiv* [Online: 2 July]. Available at: http://www.euractiv.com/global-europe/meps-call-freezing-eu-us-trade-t-news-529020 [accessed: 28 September 2014].

European Commission. 2006. *Global Europe: A Strong Partnership to Deliver Market Access for EU Exporters*. Brussels: European Commission DG Trade.

——. 2013a. *European Commission Adopts Price Undertaking in EU-China Solar Panels Case* [Online: 2 August]. Available at: http://trade.ec.europa.eu/doclib/press/index.cfm?id=957 [accessed: 17 August 2013].

——. 2013b. *Initial EU Position Paper on Public Procurement for the EU-US Transatlantic Trade and Investment Agreement* [Online: 16 July]. Available at: http://trade.ec.europa.eu/doclib/docs/2013/july/tradoc_151623.pdf [accessed: 9 September 2014].

——. 2013c. *Initial EU Position Papers on the EU-US Transatlantic Trade and Investment Agreement* [Online: Institute for Agriculture and Trade Policy, 2 July]. Available at: http://www.iatp.org/documents/european-commissions-initial-position-papers-on-ttip [accessed: 9 September 2014].

——. 2013d. *Investment Protection and Investor-to-State Dispute Settlement in EU agreements* [Online: November]. Available at: http://trade.ec.europa.eu/doclib/docs/2013/november/tradoc_151916.pdf [accessed: 25 August 2014].

——. 2013e. *Transatlantic Trade and Investment Partnership: The Economic Analysis Explained* [Online: September]. Available at: http://trade.ec.europa.eu/doclib/docs/2013/september/tradoc_151787.pdf [accessed: 16 July 2014].

——. 2013f. Progress reached at the 3rd round of EU-Japan trade talks. [Online: 23 March]. Available at: http://europa.eu/rapid/press-release_IP-13-998_en.htm [accessed: 15 November 2014].

———. 2014a. *Public Consultation on Modalities for Investment Protection and ISDS in TTIP* [Online: March]. Available at: http://trade.ec.europa.eu/doclib/docs/2014/march/tradoc_152280.pdf [accessed: 25 August 2014].

———. 2014b. *The Juncker Commission: A Strong and Experienced Team Standing for Change* [Online: 10 September]. Available at: http://europa.eu/rapid/press-release_IP-14–984_en.htm [accessed: 28 September 2014].

European Commission and High Representative of the European Union for Foreign Affairs and Security Policy. 2013. *Joint Communication by the High Representative and the European Commission to the European Parliament and the Council on the EU's Comprehensive Approach to External Conflict and Crises* [Online: 11 December]. Available at: http://www.eeas.europa.eu/statements/docs/2013/131211_03_en.pdf [accessed: 28 September 2014].

European Parliament. 2013. *EU Trade and Investment Negotiations with the United States of America.* European Parliament Resolution, P7_TA(2013)0227, Strasbourg, 23 May.

Eurostat. 2013. [Online]. Available at: http://epp.eurostat.ec.europa.eu/portal/page/portal/statistics/search_database [accessed: 5 April 2013].

Evenett, S.J. 2004. The sequencing of regional integration. *Aussenwirtschaft*, 59(4), 351–378.

———. 2007. EU commercial policy in a multipolar trading system. *Review of European Economic Policy/Intereconomics*, 42(3), 143–155.

Evenett, S.J. and Meier, M. 2008. An interim assessment of the US trade policy of 'competitive liberalization'. *The World Economy*, 31(1), 31–65.

Fan, G. 2013. Interview with Mr Fan Gang, Director of the National Economic Research Institute, China Reform Foundation. *Yicai* [Online: 2 April]. Available at: http://www.yicai.com/news/2013/04/2599428.html [accessed: 9 September 2014].

Feinberg, R.E. (2003) The political economy of United States' free trade arrangements. *World Economy*, 26(7), 1019–1040.

Felbermayr, G., Heid, B. and Lehwald, S. 2013. *Transatlantic Trade and Investment Partnership: Who Benefits from a Free Trade Deal?* [Online: Bertelsmann Stiftung, 17 June]. Available at: http://www.bfna.org/sites/default/files/TTIP-GED%20study%2017June%202013.pdf [accessed: 13 August 2014].

Felbermayr, G., Larch, M., Flach, L., Yalcin, E. and Benz, E. 2013. *Dimensions and Effects of a Transatlantic Free Trade Agreement between the EU and the US*. Munich: IFO Institut.

Fleisher, R., Bond, J.R., Krutz, G.S. and Hanna, S. 2000. The demise of the two presidencies. *American Politics Research*, 28(1), 3–25.

Flockhart, T. 2013. *Can TTIP Be an Economic NATO?* [Online: German Marshall Fund of the United States Blog, 14 October]. Available at: http://blog.gmfus.org/2013/10/14/can-ttip-be-an-economic-nato/ [accessed: 16 September 2014].

FoEE. 2013. *Trading Away Our Future?* [Online: October]. Available at: foeeurope.org [accessed: 25 August 2014].

Fordham, B.O. and McKeown, T.J. 2003. Selection and influence: interest groups and congressional voting on trade policy. *International Organization*, 57(3), 519–549.

Forsberg, A. 1998. The politics of GATT expansion: Japanese accession and the domestic political context in Japan and the United States, 1948–1955. *Business and Economic History*, 27(1), 185–195.

Freund, C. and Ornelas, E. 2010. Regional trade agreements. *Annual Review of Economics*, 2, 136–167.

Froman, M. 2014. *Remarks by Ambassador Michael Froman at the German Federal Ministry for Economic Affairs and Energy* [Online: Office of the United States Trade Representative, 5 May]. Available at: http://www.ustr.gov/about-us/press-office/press-releases/2014/May/Remarks-by-Ambassador-Froman-at-German-Federal-Ministry-Economic-Affairs-Energy [accessed: 16 July 2014].

Fukuda, K. 2015. Accountability and the governance of food safety policy in the EU and Japan, in *The European Union and Japan: A New Chapter in Civilian Power Cooperation?*, P. Bacon, H. Mayer and H. Nakamura. Farnham: Ashgate.

Gais, T.L. and Walker, J.L. 1991. Pathways to influence in American politics, in *Mobilizing Interest Groups in America*, edited by J.L. Walker. Ann Arbor, MI: University of Michigan Press, 103–122.

Gamble, A. 2012. The changing world order: from the opening of the Berlin Wall to the financial crash, in *State, Globalization and Multilateralism*, edited by M. Telò. Den Haag: Springer, 45–60.

——. 2014. *Crisis without End: The Unravelling of Western Prosperity*. London: Palgrave Macmillan.

Gammelin, C. 2014. Berlin lehnt Freihandelsabkommen mit Kanada vorest ab [Online: Sueddeutsche.de, 26 July]. Available at: http://www.sueddeutsche.de/wirtschaft/streit-ueber-investorenschutz-berlin-lehnt-freihandelsabkommen-mit-kanada-vorerst-ab-1.2063763 [accessed: 26 July 2014].

Garside, J. 2014. Europe takes on digital giants. *The Guardian Weekly*, 11–17 July, 1.

Gaycken, S. 2014. Mehr Staat fürs Netz. *Internationale Politik*, 69(4), 100–105.

Giegold, S. 2014. *Stop TTIP: EU-Commission Shuts Out Citizens from TTIP Decision* [Online: Sven Giegold Website, 11 September]. Available at: http//www.sven-giegold.de/2014/free-ttip-eci [accessed: 16 September 2014].

Gilpin, R. 2000. *Global Political Economy*. Princeton, NJ: Princeton University Press.

GMF and ECIPE. 2012. *A New Era for Transatlantic Trade Leadership: A Report from the Transatlantic Task Force on Trade and Investment*, Washington, DC and Brussels: German Marshall Fund of the United States and European Centre for International Political Economy.

Gomez-Mera, L. and Molinari, A. 2014. Overlapping institutions, learning, and dispute initiation in regional trade agreements: evidence from South America. *International Studies Quarterly*, 58(2), 269–281.

Gramsci, A. 1978. *Americanismo e fordismo*. Turin: Einaudi.

Greenwood, J. 2007. *Interest Representation in the European Union*. Basingstoke: Palgrave Macmillan.

Greive, M. 2014. Freihandelsabkommen ist Gabriels Verliererthema. *Die Welt* [Online: 10 March]. Available at: http://www.welt.de/politik/article125632514/Freihandelsabkommen-ist-Gabriels-Verliererthema.html [accessed: 28 August 2014].

Grevi, G. 2013. The EU strategic partnerships: process and purposes, in *The EU's Foreign Policy: What Kind of Power and Diplomatic Action?*, edited by M. Telò and F. Ponjaert. Farnham: Ashgate, 159–174.

Guo Ji Shang Bao [International Business Daily]. 2013. Ying Dui Mei Ou Mao Yi Lian Shou Tiao Zhan Zhong Guo Xu Zuo Liang Shou Zhun Bei [China must stand prepared in response to the challenges of the US-EU trade alliance]. 27 February.

Haas, E.B. 1982. Words can hurt you: or, who said what to whom about regimes. *International Organization*, 36(2), 207–243.

Haas, P.M and Haas, E.B. 1995. Learning to learn: improving international governance. *Global Governance*, 1(3), 225–280.

Habermas, J. 2006. *The Divided West*. London: Polity.

Haendel, T. 2014. Wirtschafts-NATO kontra Beschäftigte. *Neues Deutschland* [Online: 2 April]. Available at: http://www.neues-deutschland.de/artikel/928914.wirtschafts-nato-kontra-beschaeftigte.html [accessed: 16 September 2014].

Hakim, D. 2013. European officials consulted business leaders on trade pact. *The New York Times* [Online: 8 October]. Available at: http://www.nytimes.com/2013/10/09/business/international/european-officials-consulted-business-leaders-on-trade-pact-with-us.html [accessed: 26 April 2014].

Hall, R.L. and Deardorff, A.V. 2006. Lobbying as legislative subsidy. *American Political Science Review*, 100(1), 69–84.

Hamilton, D.S. 2014a. America's mega-regional trade diplomacy: comparing TTP and TTIP. *International Spectator*, 48(1), 81–97.

———. 2014b. Transatlantic challenges: Ukraine, TTIP and struggle to be strategic. *Journal of Common Market Studies Annual Review*, 52(1), 25–39.

———. 2014c. *TTIP's Geostrategic Implications*. Transatlantic Partnership Forum Working Paper Series, Washington, DC: Johns Hopkins SAIS Center for Transatlantic Relations.

Hanson B.T. 1998. What happened to fortress Europe? External trade policy liberalization in the European Union. *International Organization*, 52(2), 55–85.

Harman, S. 2012. *Global Health Governance: Global Institutions*. New York: Routledge.

Haughton, T. 2007. When does the EU make a difference? Conditionality and the accession process in Central and Eastern Europe. *Political Studies Review*, 5(2), 233–246.

Hawley, C. and Warner M.B. 2013. World from Berlin: Obama visit highlights 'genuine trans-atlantic dissonance'. *Spiegel International* [Online: 20 June]. Available at: http://www.spiegel.de/international/world/german-press-reactions-to-us-president-obama-berlin-visit-a-906894.html [accessed: 16 September 2014].

He, W. 2013. Mei Ou Tan Zi Mao, Zhong Guo Zao Ying Dui [China should give early response to the TTIP]. *Huan Qiu*, 26 February.

Helfer, L.R. 2009. Regime shifting in the international intellectual property system. *Perspectives on Politics*, 7(1), 39–44.

Hettne, B. 2007. Interregionalism and world order: the diverging EU and US models, in *European Union and New Regionalism*, edited by M. Telò. Second edition. Aldershot: Ashgate, 107–126.

Hettne, B. and Ponjaert, F. 2014. Interregionalism and world order: the diverging EU and US models, in *New Regionalsim and the European Union*, edited by M. Telò. Farnham: Ashgate, 115–141.

Heydon, K. and Woolcock, S. 2009. *The Rise of Bilateralism: Comparing American, European and Asian Approaches to Preferential Trade Agreements*. Tokyo: United Nations University Press.

High Level Working Group on Jobs and Growth. 2012. *Interim Report to Leaders from the Co-Chairs* [Online: European Commission, 14 June]. Available at: http://trade.ec.europa.eu/doclib/docs/2012/june/tradoc_149557.pdf [accessed: 28 September 2014].

——. 2013. *Final Report* [Online: European Commission]. Available at: http://trade.ec.europa.eu/doclib/docs/2013/february/tradoc_150519.pdf [accessed: 16 July 2014].

Hilary, J. 2013. *The Transatlantic Trade and Investment Partnership: A Charter for Deregulation, an Attack on Jobs, an End to Democracy* [Online: War on Want]. Available at: http://waronwant.org/about-us/publications/doc_download/123-the-transatlantic-trade-investment-partnership/ [accessed: 25 August 2014].

Hocking, B. and McGuire, S. 2004. *Trade Politics*. London: Routledge.

Hoeckman, B.M. and Kosteck, M.M. 2013. *The Political Economy of the World Trading System*. Third Edition. Oxford: Oxford University Press.

Hoekman, B., Martin, W. and Mattoo, A. 2009. *Conclude Doha: It matters!* Policy Research Working Paper No. 5135, Washington, DC: World Bank.

Hoekman, B.M. and Mavroidis, P.C. 2015. WTO menu or WTO à la carte? *World Trade Review*, forthcoming.

Hogenboom, B. 1996. Cooperation and polarisation beyond borders: the transnationalisation of Mexican environmental issues during the NAFTA negotiations. *Third World Quarterly*, 17(5), 989–1005.

Horn, H., Mavroidis, P.C. and Sapir, A. 2010. Beyond the WTO? An anatomy of EU and US preferential trade agreements. *The World Economy*, 33(11), 1565–1588.

Hornbeck, J.F. and Irace, M.A. 2013. *International Trade and Finance: Key Policy Issues for the 113th Congress*. CRS R41553, Washington, DC: Congressional Research Service.

Howorth, J. 2011. The 'new faces' of Lisbon: assessing the performance of Catherine Ashton and Herman van Rompuy on the global stage. *European Foreign Affairs Review*, 16(3), 303–323.

——. 2013. The Lisbon Treaty, CSDP and the EU as a security actor, in *The EU's Foreign Policy*, edited by F. Ponjaert and M. Telò. Farnham: Ashgate, 65–77.

Hugues, V. 2012. *Why is the WTO Dispute Settlement System so Successful?*. 20th Annual ANZSIL Conference, Victoria University of Wellington, New Zealand, 6 July.

Huyer, S. 2004. Challenging relations: a labour-NGO coalition to oppose the Canada-US and North American Free Trade Agreements 1985–1993. *Development in Practice*, 14(1–2), 48–60.

Ikenberry, J. 2012. *Liberal Leviathan: The Origins, Crisis and Transformation of the American World Order*. Princeton, NJ: Princeton University Press.

Irwin, D.A. 1998. Changes in US tariffs: the role of import prices and commercial policies. *American Economic Review*, 88, 1015–1026.

Jing Ji Can Kao Bao [Economic Reference Newspaper]. 2013. Da Guo Yu Chong Gou Shi Jie Mao Yi Ge Ju [The great powers are going to rebuild the world trade pattern]. 7 February.

Joffe, J. 2014. Selbst Erwischt. *Die Zeit*, 21 August, 1.

Johnston, J. and Laxer, G. 2003. Solidarity in the age of globalization: lessons from the anti-MAI and Zapatista struggles. *Theory and Society*, 32, 39–91.

Journal of European Public Policy. 2006. *The European Union and the New Trade Politics*, Special Issue 13(6).

Jupille, J., Mattli, W. and Snidal, D. 2013. *Institutional Choice and Global Commerce*. Cambridge: Cambridge University Press.

Kagan, R. 2004. *Paradise and Power: America and Europe in the New World Order*. London: Atlantic Books.

——. 2012. *The World America Made*. New York: Alfred A. Knopf.

Katzenstein, P.J. 1997. Introduction: Asian regionalism in contemporary perspective, in *Network Power: Japan and Asia*, edited by P.J. Katzenstein and T. Shiraishi. Ithaca, NY: Cornell University Press, 1–44.

Kay, T.K. 2011. *NAFTA and the Politics of Labor Transnationalism*. Cambridge: Cambridge University Press.

Kelley, J. 2010. *The Role of Membership Rules in Regional Organizations*. Working Paper Series on Regional Economic Integration No. 53, Mandaluyong City: Asian Development Bank.

Keohane, R.O. 1984. *After Hegemony*. Princeton, NJ: Princeton University Press.

——. 2006. *The Contingent Legitimacy of Multilateralism*. Garnet Working Paper No. 09/06, Coventry: GARNET Network of Excellence.

Kerremans, B. 2004. What went wrong in Cancun? A principal-agent view on the EU's rationale towards the Doha Development Round. *European Foreign Affairs Review*, 9(3), 363–393.

King, T. 2014. Juncker deals out the pack. *European Voice*, 10 September.

Kinne, B.J. 2013. Network dynamics and the evolution of international cooperation. *American Political Science Review*, 107(4), 766–785.

Kleimann, D. 2011. *Taking Stock: EU Common Commercial Policy in the Lisbon Era*. CEPS Working Paper, No. 345 (April 2011), Brussels: CEPS.

Kono, D.Y. 2007. When do trade blocs block trade? *International Studies Quarterly*, 51(1), 165–181.

Koo, R. 2009. *The Holy Grail of Macro-Economics*. London: Wiley.

Koromenos, B., Lipson, C. and Snidal, D. 2001. The rational design of international institutions. *International Organization*, 55(4), 761–799.

Kubicki, W. 2014. *Freihandelsabkommen auf Eis legen* [Online: Liberale, 9 July]. Available at: http://www.liberale.de/content/freihandelsabkommen-auf-eis-legen [accessed: 28 August 2014].

Kupchan, C. 2013. *No One's World*. Oxford: Oxford University Press.

Laird, S. 2002. Market access issues and the WTO: an overview, in *Development, Trade and the WTO: A Handbook*, edited by B. Hoekman, A. Mattoo and P. English. Washington, DC: World Bank, 97–104.

Lapavistas, C. 2012. *Crisis in the Eurozone*. London: Verso.

Lehne, S. 2013. *Promoting a Comprehensive Approach to EU Foreign Policy*. Brussels: Carnegie Europe.

Li, C. 2013. Mei Ou Zi Mao Qu Yi Yu He Zai? [What's the intention of the transatlantic free trade area?]. *Shanghai Zhengquan Bao*, 2 April.

Löwy, T. 1964. American business, public policy, case-studies, and political theory. *World Politics*, 16(4), 677–715.

Ludlow, P. 2004. *The Making of the New Europe: The European Councils in Brussels and Copenhagen 2002*. Brussels: EuroComment, volume 1.

Mansfield, E.D. and Milner, H.V. 1999. The new wave of regionalism. *International Organization*, 53(3), 589–627.

Mansfield, E.D. and Solingen, E. 2010. Regionalism. *Annual Review of Political Science*, 13(1), 145–163.

Marangoni, A.-C. and Raube, K. 2014. Virtue or vice? The coherence of the EU's external policies. *Journal of European Integration*, 36(5), 473–489.

Marchetti, J. and Mavroidis, P.C. 2012. I now recognize you (and only you) as equal: an anatomy of (mutual) recognition agreements in the GATS, in *Regulating Trade in Services in the EU and the WTO: Trust, Distrust, and Economic Integration*, edited by I. Lianos and O. Odudu. Cambridge: Cambridge University Press, 415–443.

Martin, W. and Mattoo, A. 2010. The Doha development agenda: what's on the table? *Journal of International Trade and Economic Development*, 19(1), 81–107.

Martin, W. and Messerlin, P. 2007. Why is it so difficult? Trade liberalization under the Doha Agenda. *Oxford Review of Economic Policy*, 23(3), 347–366.

Mattoo, A. and Sauvé, P. 2011. Services, in *Preferential Trade Agreement Policies for Development: A Handbook*, edited by J.-P. Chauffour and J.-C. Maur. Washington, DC: The World Bank, 235–274.

Maurer, H. and Raik, K. 2014. *Pioneers of a European Diplomatic System: EU Delegations in Moscow and Washington*. FIIA Analysis, Helsinki: Finnish Institute of International Affairs.

May, C. 2010. Direct and indirect influence at the World Intellectual Property Organization, in *Business and Global Governance*, edited by M. Ougaard and A. Leander. London: Routledge, 39–56.

May, C. and Sell, S.K. 2006. *Intellectual Property Rights: A Critical History*. Boulder, CO: Lynne Rienner Publishers.

Mayer, H. 1997. Early at the beach and claiming territory? The evolution of German ideas on a new European Order. *International Affairs*, 73(4), 721–737.

——, H. 2013. The challenge of coherence in EU foreign policy, in *The EU's Foreign Policy: What Kind of Power and Diplomatic Action?*, edited by M. Telò and F. Ponjaert. Farnham: Ashgate, 105–117.

McCullough, D. 2011. *The Greater Journey: Americans in Paris*. New York, NY: Simon and Schuster.

Mei, X. 2013. Mei Ou Zi Mao Xie Ding Huo Fu Nan Ce [It is difficult to predict whether the TTIP is bane or boon]. *People's Daily (Overseas Edition)*, 16 February.

Merz, F. 2014. Ein hohes Maß an Mäkelei. *Handelsblatt*, 11 July, 10.

Messerlin, P. 2012. *The TPP and the EU Policy in East Asia (China Mainland Excluded)*, ECIPE Working Paper, May 15, Brussels: ECIPE.

Meunier, S. 2005a. *The European Union in International Commercial Negotiations*. Princeton, NJ: Princeton University Press.

——. 2005b. *Trading Voices: The European Union in International Commercial Negotiations*. Princeton, NJ: Princeton University Press.

Meunier, S. and Nicolaïdis, K. 1999. Who speaks for Europe? The delegation of trade authority in the EU. *Journal of European Public Policy*, 37(3), 477–501.

——. 2006. The European Union as a conflicted trade power. *Journal of European Public Policy*, 13(6), 906–925.

Mildner, S.-A. and Schmucker, C. 2013. *Trade Agreement with Side-Effects? European Union and United States to Negotiate Transatlantic Trade and Investment Partnership*. SWP Comments No. 18, Berlin: German Institute for International and Security Affairs.

Milner, H.V. 1997. *Interests Institutions Information*. Princeton, NJ: Princeton University Press.

Milner, H.V. and Tingley, D. 2011. Who supports global economic engagement? The sources of preferences in American foreign economic policy. *International Organization*, 65(1), 37–68.

Ministry of Foreign Affairs (MOFA). October 2002. *Japan's FTA Strategy*. Tokyo: Economic Affairs Bureau, MOFA (GoJ).

Morse, J.C. and Keohane, R.O. 2014. Contested multilateralism. *Review of International Organizations* [Online]. Available at: http://link.springer.com/art icle/10.1007%2Fs11558–014–9188–2 [accessed: 25 August 2014].

Munakata, N. 2004. Nihon no FTA senryaku [Japan's FTA Strategy], in *Nihon no higashi ajia kousou* [Japan's Vision for East Asia], edited by M. Tadokoro. Tokyo: Keio University Press.

Muraskin, W.A. 1998. *The Politics of International Health: The Children's Vaccine Initiative and the Struggle to Develop Vaccines for the Third World*. Albany, NY: SUNY Press.

——. 2002. The last years of the CVI and the birth of the GAVI, in *Public-Private Partnerships for Public Health*, edited by M.R. Reich. Cambridge, MA: Harvard Center for Population and Development Studies, 115–168.

Muzaka, V. and Bishop, M.L. 2015. Doha stalemate: the end of trade multilateralism? *Review of International Studies*, forthcoming. Available on CJO2014. doi:10.1017/S0260210514000266.

Naim, M. 2012. Minilateralism. *Foreign Policy*, 173, 135–136.

Nakamura, H. 2015. Japan as a 'proactive civilian power'? Domestic constraints and competing priorities, in *The European Union and Japan: A New Chapter in Civilian Power Cooperation?*, edited by P. Bacon, H. Mayer and H. Nakamura. Farnham: Ashgate.

North, D. 1991. Institutions. *Journal of Economic Perspectives*, 5, 97–112.

Novotná, T. 2012. *Negotiating the Accession: Transformation of the State during the German Unification and Eastern Enlargement of the EU*. Boston, MA: Boston University.

——. 2014. The EU's Voice in Third Countries: The Role of EU Delegations around the World. *Studia Diplomatica*, LXVII (1), 29–45.

——. 2015 (forthcoming). *Negotiating the Accession: How Germany Unified and the EU Enlarged. New Perspectives in German Political Studies*. Basingstoke: Palgrave Macmillan.

Nye, J. 1968. *International Regionalism*. Boston, MA: Little Brown.

O'Brien, R., Goetz, A., Scholte, J. and Williams, M. 2000. *Contesting Global Governance: Multilateral Economic Institutions and Global Social Movements*. Cambridge: Cambridge University Press.

O'Neill, J. 2001. *Building Better Global Economic BRICs*. Global Economics Paper No 66, London: Goldman Sachs.

——. 2013. *The Growth Map*. London: Penguin.

Oberthur, S. and Gehring, T. 2006. Institutional interaction in global environmental governance: the case of the Cartagena Protocol and the World Trade Organization. *Global Environmental Politics*, 6(2), 1–31.

OECD, WTO and UNCTAD. 2013. *Implications of Global Value Chains for Trade, Investment, Development and Jobs* [Online: United Nations Conference on Trade and Development, 6 August]. Available at: http://unctad.

org/en/PublicationsLibrary/unctad_oecd_wto_2013d1_en.pdf [accessed: 10 September 2014].

Oettli, J.-R. and Hovius, C. 2009. *The MFN Provision Contained in the CARIFORUM-EC Economic Partnership Agreement and its Consistency with WTO Law* [Online: Graduate Institute Geneva Trade Law Clinic]. Available at: http://graduateinstitute.ch/home/research/centresandprogrammes/ctei/projects-1/trade-law-clinic.html [accessed: 9 September 2014].

Olson, M. 1965. *The Logic of Collective Action: Public Goods and the Theory of Groups*. Cambridge, MA: Harvard University Press.

Orbie, J. and De Ville, F. 2014. A boost to our economies that doesn't cost a cent: EU trade policy discourse since the crisis, in *EU Foreign Policy through the Lens of Discourse Analysis: Making Sense of Diversity*, edited by C. Carta and J.-F. Morin. Farnham: Ashgate, 95–110.

Orsini, A., Morin, J.-F. and Young, O. 2013. Regime complexes: a buzz, a boom, or a boost for global governance? *Global Governance*, 19(1), 27–39.

Oyane, S. 2004. An East Asia FTA: Japan's Policy Change and Regional Initiatives. *Kokusai Mondai*, 528(March), 52–66.

Patrick, S. 2009. *The Best Laid Plans*. New York, NY: Rowman and Littlefield.

Pauwelyn, J. 2008. New trade politics for the 21st century. *Journal of International Economic Law*, 11(3), 559–573.

——. 2014. At the edge of chaos? Foreign investment law as a complex adaptive system, how it emerged and how it can be reformed. *ICSID Review*, 29(2), 372–418.

Pauwelyn, J. and Alschner, W. 2015. Forget about the WTO: the network of relations between PTAs and double PTAs, in *Trade Cooperation: The Purpose, Design and Effects of Preferential Trade Agreements*, edited by A. Dür and M. Elsig. Cambridge: Cambridge University Press, pp. 497–532.

Payne, A. 2010. How many Gs are there in 'global governance' after the crisis? The perspectives of the 'marginal majority' of the world's states. *International Affairs*, 86(3), 729–740.

Philip, A. 1927. *Le problème ouvrier aux Etats-Unis*. Paris: Alcan.

Piper, N. 1995. Das Spiel mit Tafta. *Die Zeit* [Online: 9 June]. Available at: http://www.zeit.de/1995/24/Das_Spiel_mit_Tafta [accessed: 28 August 2014].

Pollack, M. 1997. Representing diffuse interests in EC policy-making. *Journal of European Public Policy*, 4(4), 572–590.

Ponjaert, F. 2015. The political and institutional significance of an EU-Japan trade and partnership agreement, in *The European Union and Japan: A New Chapter in Civilian Power Cooperation?*, edited by P. Bacon, H. Mayer and H. Nakamura. Farnham: Ashgate.

Prusa, T. and Teh, R. 2010. *Protection Reduction and Diversion: PTAs and the Incidence of Antidumping Disputes*. NBER Working Paper No. 16276, Cambridge, MA: National Bureau of Economic Research.

Putnam, R.D. 1988. Diplomacy and domestic politics: the logic of two-level games. *International Organization*, 42(3), 427–460.

Reinecke, S. 2014. Kommentar: SPD und TTIP. Dafür und dagegen. *Die Tageszeitung (TAZ)* [Online: 21 May]. Available at: http://www.taz.de/!138941/ [accessed: 28 August 2014].

Renmin. 2013. Li Keqiang co-hosts a press conference with German Chancellor Merkel. *People* [Online: 27 May]. Available at: http://politics.people.com. cn/n/2013/0527/c70731–21626260.html [accessed: 9 September 2014].

Rexer, A. and Brühl, J. 2014. Freihandelsabkommen Ceta geleakt. 521 Seiten Stoff für Zoff. *Süddeutsche Zeitung* [Online: 14 August]. Available at: http:// www.sueddeutsche.de/wirtschaft/freihandelsabkommen-ceta-geleakt-seiten-stoff-fuer-zoff-1.2089966 [accessed: 14 August 2014].

Rifkin, J. 2005. *The European Dream: How Europe's Vision of the Future is Quietly Eclipsing the American Dream.* Cambridge: Polity.

Roderburg, E. 2013. Competitive liberalization and transatlantic market integration: the case for a transatlantic free trade agreement, in *EU Preferential Trade Agreements: Commerce, Foreign Policy, and Development Aspects*, edited by D. Kleimann. Florence: European University Institute, 81–97.

Rosamond, B. 2014. The EU's normative power and three modes of liberal communicative discourse, in *EU Foreign Policy through the Lens of Discourse Analysis: Making Sense of Diversity*, edited by C. Carta and J.-F. Morin. Farnham: Ashgate, 211–226.

Ruggie, J.G. 1993. *Multilateralism Matters: The Theory and Praxis of an Institutional Form.* New York, NY: Columbia University Press.

S2B. 2013. *A Brave New Transatlantic Partnership* [Online: October]. Available at: s2bnetwork.org [accessed: 25 August 2014].

Santoro, M. 1995. *Pfizer: Global Protection in Intellectual Property. Case study 9–392–073.* Boston, MA: Harvard Business School Publishing.

Sapir, A. 2007. *Fragmented Power: Europe and the Global Economy.* Brussels: Bruegel.

———. 2014. Le traité de libre-échange transatlantique a une ambition avant tout politique. *Les Echos*, 12 May.

Sapiro, M. 2014. *TTIP: Who Benefits More?* Jahresbericht 2013–2014, Berlin: Atlantik-Brücke, 6–7.

Sawatzki, A. 2014. *Merkel im TTIP-Wahlkampf: Lügen, die zum Himmel stinken* [Online: Campact Blog, 18 May]. Available at: blog.campact.de, http://blog. campact.de/2014/05/merkel-im-ttip-wahlkampf-luegen-die-zum-himmel-stinken [accessed: 17 July 2014].

Sbragia, A. 2007. European Union and NAFTA, in *European Union and New Regionalism: Regional Actors and Global Governance in a Post-Hegemonic Era*, edited by M. Telò. Second edition. Aldershot: Ashgate, 153–164.

———. 2009. *The EU, the US, and Trade Policy: Competitive Interdependence in the Management of Globalization.* European Union Studies Association 11th Biennal Conference, Marina Del Rey, California, USA, 23–25 April 2009.

———. 2010. The EU, the US, and trade policy: competitive interdependence in the management of globalization. *Journal of European Public Policy*, 17(3), 368–382.

Schattschneider, E.E. 1935. *Politics, Pressures, and the Tariff: A Study of Free Private Enterprise in Pressure Politics, as Shown in the 1929–1930 Revision of the Tariff.* New York, NY: Prentice Hall.

Scheurs, M. 2015. Environmental and energy policy: learning and cooperation between the European Union and Japan, in *The European Union and Japan: A New Chapter in Civilian Power Cooperation?*, edited by P. Bacon, H. Mayer and H. Nakamura. Farnham: Ashgate.

Schimmelfennig, F. 2001. The community trap: liberal norms, rhetorical action, and the Eastern enlargement of the EU. *International Organization*, 55(1), 47–80.

Schmidt, V. 2006. *Democracy in Europe: The EU and National Polities.* Oxford: Oxford University Press.

———. 2010. Taking ideas and discourse seriously: explaining change through discursive institutionalism as the fourth new institutionalism. *European Political Science Review*, 2(1), 1–25.

Schneider, C.J. 2008. *Conflict, Negotiation and European Union Enlargement.* Cambridge: Cambridge University Press.

Schott, J. 2004. Assessing US FTA policy, in *Free Trade Agreements: US Strategies and Priorities*, edited by J. Schott. Washington, DC: Institute for International Economics (IIE), 359–382.

Shinoda, T. 2004. *Kantei Gaiko: Seiji riidaashippu no yukue* [The Prime Minister's Office: The Future of Political Leadership]. Tokyo: Asahi Shinbunsha.

Shu, M. 2015. Three balancing acts: the EU's trade policy towards East Asia, in *The European Union and Japan: A New Chapter in Civilian Power Cooperation?*, edited by P. Bacon, H. Mayer and H. Nakamura. Farnham: Ashgate.

Steinberg, R.H. 2002. In the shadow of law or power? Consensus-based bargaining and outcomes in the GATT/WTO. *International Organization*, 56(2), 339–374.

Steingart, G. 2006. A NATO for the world economy: an argument for a trans-Atlantic free-trade zone. *Spiegel International* [Online: 20 October]. Available at: http://www.spiegel.de/international/a-nato-for-the-world-economy-an-argument-for-a-trans-atlantic-free-trade-zone-a-443306.html [accessed: 16 September 2014].

Stillerman, J. 2003. Transnational activist networks and the emergence of labor internationalism in the NAFTA countries. *Social Science History*, 27(4), 577–601.

Stockholm International Peace Research Institute. 2013. *SIPRI Yearbook 2013: Armaments, Disarmament and International Security.* Oxford: Oxford University Press.

Stone, R. 2011. *Controlling Institutions.* Cambridge: Cambridge University Press.

Stothard, M., Carnegy, H. and Arnold, M. 2014. France urges G20 to put issue of US bank fines on agenda. *Financial Times* [Online: 3 August]. Available at: http://ft.com/cms/s/0/da428604-1963-11e4-9745-00144feabdc0html [accessed: 4 August 2014].

Strange, M. 2011. 'Act now and sign our joint statement!' What role do online global group petitions play in transnational movement networks? *Media, Culture & Society*, 33(8), 1236–1253.

——. 2013. A European identity in global campaigning? Activist groups and the 'Seattle to Brussels' (S2B) Network. *Geopolitics*, 18(3), 612–632.

Sudo, S. 2005. *Evolution of ASEAN-Japan Relations*. Singapore: Institute of Southeast Asian Studies.

Sun, Z. 2013. Speech by Sun Zhenyu, Former Chinese Ambassador to the WTO at Bo'ao Forum. *Sina* [Online: 20 June]. Available at: http://finance.sina.com.cn/hy/20130620/160015859290.shtml [accessed: 9 September 2014].

Telička, P. and Barták, K. 2003. *Kterak jsme vstupovali*. Praha: Paseka.

Telò, M. 2006. *Europe a Civilian Power? European Union, Global Governance, World Order*. London: Palgrave Macmillan.

——. 2014a. *New Regionalism and the European Union*. Farnham: Ashgate.

——. 2014b. *Globalisation, Multilateralism, Europe. Towards a Better Global Governance?* Farnham: Ashgate.

Telò, M. and Ponjaert, F. 2013. *The EU's Foreign Policy: What Kind of Power and Diplomatic Action?* Farnham: Ashgate.

Terada, T. 2012. Trade winds: big power politics and Asia-Pacific economic integration. *Global Asia*, 7(1), 90–95.

Tsuruoka, M. 2008. Expectations deficit in EU-Japan relations: why the relationship cannot flourish. *Current Politics and Economics of Asia*, 17(1), 107–126.

US Department of Defense. 2012. *Sustaining U.S. Global Leadership: Priorities for 21st Century Defense* [Online: January]. Available at: http://www.defense.gov/news/defense_strategic_guidance.pdf [accessed: 23 September 2014].

USITC. 2013. *Interactive Tariff and Trade DataWeb* [Online: US International Trade Commission]. Available at: http://dataweb.usitc.gov/ [accessed: 5 April 2013].

USTR. 2013. *Notification Letter to the Congress on the TTIP* [Online: Office of the United States Trade Representative, 20 March]. Available at: http://www.ustr.gov/sites/default/files/03202013%20TTIP%20Notification%20Letter.PDF [accessed: 9 September 2014].

Vachudova, M.A. 2005. *Europe Undivided: Democracy, Leverage and Integration after Communism*. Oxford: Oxford University Press.

Van den Hoven, A. 2002. *Interest Group Influence on Trade Policy in a Multilevel Polity: Analysing the EU Position at the Doha WTO Ministerial Conference*. EUI Working Paper No. 2002/67, Florence: European University Institute.

Vasagar, J. 2014. Spy game snaps back at Berlin. *Financial Times*, 19 August, 6.

Vassiliou, G. 2007. *The Accession Story: The EU from 15 to 25 Countries*. Oxford: Oxford University Press.

ViEUws. 2014a. *TTIP: EU, US Clearly Divided on Tariff Liberalization* [Online: 14 March]. Available at: http://www.vieuws.eu/eutradeinsights/ttip-eu-us-clearly-divided-on-tariff-liberalisation/ [accessed: 26 April 2014].

———. 2014b. *Commission Continues push for ISDS* [Online: 1 April]. Available at: http://www.vieuws.eu/eutradeinsights/commission-continues-push-for-isds-2/ [accessed: 26 April 2014].

Wade, R. 2011. Emerging world order? From multipolarity to multilateralism in the G20, the World Bank, and the IMF. *Politics and Society*, 39(3), 347–378.

Wade, R. and Vestergaard, J. 2012. *The G20 Has Served its Purpose and Should Be Replaced with a Global Economic Council on a Firmer Constitutional Foundation* [Online: London School of Economics and Political Science British Politics and Policy Blog, 19 September]. Available at: http://blogs.lse.ac.uk/politicsandpolicy/g20-wade-vestergaard/ [accessed: 25 August 2014].

Wallach, L. and Woodall, P. 2004. *Whose Trade Organization? A Field Guide to the WTO*. New York, NY: The New Press.

Wang, W. 2013. Mei Ou Zi Mao Qu Qian Jing Zhan Wang [The forecast of the transatlantic free trade area]. *Wenweipo Hongkong*, 22 May.

Watal, J. 2001. *Intellectual Property Rights in the WTO and Developing Countries*. Boston, MA: Kluwer Academic Publishers.

White House. 2011. *Joint Statement: US-EU Summit* [Online: 28 November]. Available at: http://www.whitehouse.gov/the-press-office/2011/11/28/joint-statement-us-eu-summit [accessed: 23 September 2014].

Wilf, M. and Davis, C. 2011. *Joining the Club: Accession to the GATT/WTO*. APSA 2011 Annual Meeting Paper. Washington, DC: APSA.

Wilkinson, M. 1996. Lobbying for fair trade: northern NGDOs, the European Community and the GATT Uruguay Round. *Third World Quarterly*, 17(2), 251–267.

Wolfe, R. 2005. See you in Geneva? Legal (mis)representation of the trading system. *European Journal of International Relations*, 11(3), 339–365.

Woll, C. 2012. The brash and the soft-spoken: lobbying styles in a transatlantic comparison. *Interest Groups & Advocacy*, 1(2), 193–214.

Woolcock, S. 2005. European Union trade policy: domestic institutions and systemic factors, in *The Politics of International Trade in the Twenty-First Century: Actors, Issues and Regional Dynamics*, edited by K. Dominic and W. Grant. Basingstoke: Palgrave Macmillan, 234–251.

———. 2007. *European Union Policy towards Free Trade Agreements*. Working Paper No. 03/2007, Brussels: European Centre for International Political Economy.

———. 2012. *European Union Economic Diplomacy: The Role of the EU in External Economic Relations*. Farnham: Ashgate.

———. 2013. Policy diffusion in public procurement: the role of free trade agreements. *International Negotiation*, 18(1), 153–173.

WTI. 2014. *Potential Impacts of a EU-US Free Trade Agreement on the Swiss Economy and External Economic Relations*. Bern: World Trade Institute.

WTO. 1994. *Understanding on the Interpretation of Article XXIV of the General Agreement on Tariffs and Trade 1994* [Online: World Trade Organization]. Available at: http://www.wto.org/english/docs_e/legal_e/10-24_e.htm [accessed: 13 August 2014].

——. 1995. *Regionalism and the World Trading System.* Geneva: World Trade Organization.

——. 2001. *Ministerial Opening Statements by Pascal Lamy (EU) and Robert B. Zoellick (U.S.).* 4th Ministerial Conference, Doha, WT/MIN(01)/ST/4 and WT/MIN(01)/ST/3, World Trade Organization.

——. 2002. *Negotiating Group on Rules: Compendium of Issues Related to Regional Trade Agreements.* Background Note by the Secretariat, TN/RL/W/8/rev.1, World Trade Organization.

——. 2006. *Transparency Mechanism for Regional Trade Agreements, Decision of 14 December 2006* [Online: World Trade Organization]. Available at: http://www.wto.org/english/tratop_e/region_e/trans_mecha_e.htm [accessed: 13 August 2014].

——. 2010. *Lamy Stresses Importance of Concluding the Round to G20 Business Leaders* [Online: World Trade Organization, 26 June]. Available at: http://www.wto.org/english/news_e/sppl_e/sppl160_e.htm [accessed: 23 September 2014].

——. 2011a. *Negotiating Group on Rules: Summary Report of the Meeting Held on 17 March 2011* [Online: World Trade Organization]. Available at: http://www.wto.org/english/tratop_e/rulesneg_e/rulesneg_e.htm [accessed: 13 August 2014].

——. 2011b. *World Trade Report 2011. The WTO and Preferential Trade Agreements: From Co-Existence to Coherence.* Geneva: World Trade Organization.

——. 2013a. *Defining the Future of Trade: Report of the Panel on Defining the Future of Trade Convened by WTO Director-General Pascal Lamy* [Online: World Trade Organization, 24 April]. Available at: http://www.wto.org/english/thewto_e/dg_e/dft_panel_e/future_of_trade_report_e.pdf [accessed: 13 August 2014].

——. 2013b. *Ministerial Opening Statements by Karel De Gucht (EU) and Robert B. Zoellick (U.S.)* [Online: World Trade Organization, 3–6 December]. Available at: http://www.wto.org/english/thewto_e/minist_e/mc9_e/mc9_statements_e.htm [accessed: 25 May 2014].

——. 2013c. *Report of the Committee on Regional Trade Agreements to the General Council.* WT/REG/23, 22 October, World Trade Organization.

——. 2014a. *Dispute Settlement Gateway* [Online: World Trade Organization]. Available at: http://www.wto.org/english/tratop_e/dispu_e/dispu_e.htm [accessed: 29 May 2014].

——. 2014b. *Press Release: Azevêdo Welcomes Launch of Plurilateral Environmental Goods Negotiations* [Online: World Trade Organization, 7 July]. Available at: http://www.wto.org/english/news_e/news14_e/envir_08jul14_e.htm [accessed: 9 September 2014].

WTO, ITC and UNCTAD. 2012. *World Tariff Profiles 2012.* Geneva: World Trade Organization.

Wu, Z. 2013. Mei Ou Zi Mao Tan Pan Shuo Yi Xing Nan [The TTIP is easier said than done]. *Jie Fang Ri Bao* [Jiefang Daily], 27 February.

Xi, J. 2013. Remarks by Chinese President Xi Jinping at his meeting with US President Obama. *Sina* [Online: 9 June]. Available at: http://news.sina.com. cn/c/2013–06–09/050727357438.shtml [accessed: 9 September 2014].

Xinhua News Agency. 2012. *Foreign Minister Yang Jiechi Briefed about Premier Wen Jiabao's Visit in Brussels for the 15th EU-China Summit* [Online: 21 September]. Available at: http://www.gov.cn/jrzg/2012–09/21/ content_2230338.htm [accessed: 17 August 2013].

Young, A.R. 2002. *Extending European Cooperation: The European Union and the 'New' International Trade Agenda*. Manchester: Manchester University Press.

———. 2004. The Incidental Fortress: The Single European Market and World Trade. *Journal of Common Market Studies*, 42(2), 393–414.

———. 2007. Trade politics ain't what it used to be: the European Union in the Doha Round. *Journal of Common Market Studies*, 45(4), 789–811.

Yu, J. 2013a. Speech by Yu Jianhua, China's Deputy International Trade Representative at Bo'ao Forum. *Sina* [Online: 20 June]. Available at: http://finance.sina.com.cn/hy/20130620/092015853900.shtml [accessed: 9 September 2014].

———. 2013b. Zi Mao Qu Tan Pan Fang Ying Zun Zhong Ge Fang Hua Yu Quan [All parties' words should be listened to]. *Sina* [Online: 20 June]. Available at: http://finance.sina.com.cn/hy/20130620/092015853900.shtml [accessed: 9 September 2014].

Yu, P.K. 2005. Currents and crosscurrents in the international intellectual property regime. *Loyola of Los Angeles Law Review*, 38, 323–444.

Zeit Online. 2014a. *Bosbach fordert Aussetzung der TTIP-Verhandungen* [Online: 12 July]. Available at: http://www.zeit.de/politik/deutschland/2014–07/ bosbach-ttip-usa-spionage [accessed: 20 July 2014].

———. 2014b. *Merkel bezweifelt Einlenken der USA* [Online: 12 July]. Available at: http://www.zeit.de/politik/ausland/2014–07/us-spionage-bundesregierung-reaktionen [accessed: 20 July 2014].

———. 2014c. *Deutschland lehnt Freihandelsabkommen vorerst ab* [Online: 26 July]. Available at: http://www.zeit.de/wirtschaft/2014–07/ceta-ttip-deutschland [accessed: 29 July 2014].

———. 2014d. *TTIP-Blaupause schützt Klagerechte der Investoren* [Online: 15 August]. Available at: http://www.zeit.de/wirtschaft/2014–08/ceta-ttip-investitionsschutz-schiedsgerichte [accessed: 15 August 2014].

Zeitlin, J. and Sabel, C. 2011. *Experimentalist Governance*. Oxford: Oxford University Press.

Zhang, P. and Zhang, X. 2013. Mei Ou Gou Jian Kua Da Xi Yang Zi Mao Qu You Guan Qing Kuang Ji Ying Dui [The implications of the TTIP and China's responding strategy]. *Guo Ji Mao Yi* [InterTrade], June.

Zimmermann, H. 2007. *Drachenzähmung. Die EU und die USA in den Verhandlungen um die Integration Chinas in den Welthandel*. Frankfurt: Nomos.

Index

Page numbers in italic indicate figures, bold indicate tables. Notes have been referenced as 1n2 (page 1 note 2).

Other titles in the *Globalisation, Europe, Multilateralism* series:

The European Union and Japan
A New Chapter in Civilian Power Cooperation?
Edited by Paul Bacon, Hartmut Mayer and Hidetoshi Nakamura
ISBN 978-1-4724-5746-2 (hbk)
ISBN 978-1-4724-5749-3 (pbk)

The European External Action Service and National Foreign Ministries
Convergence or Divergence?
Edited by Rosa Balfour, Caterina Carta and Kristi Raik
ISBN 978-1-4724-4243-7 (hbk)
ISBN 978-1-4724-4644-2 (pbk)

The European Union with(in) International Organisations
Commitment, Consistency and Effects across Time
Edited by Amandine Orsini
ISBN 978-1-4724-2414-3 (hbk)
ISBN 978-1-4724-2415-0 (pbk)

The Eurozone Crisis and the Transformation of EU Governance
Internal and External Implications
Edited by Maria João Rodrigues and Eleni Xiarchogiannopoulou
ISBN 978-1-4724-3307-7 (hbk)
ISBN 978-1-4724-3310-7 (pbk)

EU Foreign Policy through the Lens of Discourse Analysis
Making Sense of Diversity
Edited by Caterina Carta and Jean-Frédéric Morin
ISBN 978-1-4094-6375-7 (hbk)
ISBN 978-1-4094-6376-4 (pbk)

Globalisation, Multilateralism, Europe
Towards a Better Global Governance?
Edited by Mario Telò
ISBN 978-1-4094-6448-8 (hbk)
ISBN 978-1-4094-6449-5 (pbk)

The EU's Foreign Policy
What Kind of Power and Diplomatic Action?
Edited by Mario Telò and Frederik Ponjaert
ISBN 978-1-4094-6451-8 (hbk)
ISBN 978-1-4094-6452-5 (pbk)

For Product Safety Concerns and Information please contact our EU
representative GPSR@taylorandfrancis.com
Taylor & Francis Verlag GmbH, Kaufingerstraße 24, 80331 München, Germany

www.ingramcontent.com/pod-product-compliance
Ingram Content Group UK Ltd.
Pitfield, Milton Keynes, MK11 3LW, UK
UKHW021006180425
457613UK00019B/829